ROYAL ARMOURED CORPS

This Corps was formed in April 1939 to
regiments of the Cavalry of the Line toge
Corps, thenceforth renamed the Royal Ta
armoured, the Household Cavalry are no

1 1st The Queen's Dragoon Guards*
2 The Royal Scots Dragoon Guards (Carabiniers and Greys)*
3 4th/7th Royal Dragoon Guards*
4 5th Royal Inniskilling Dragoon Guards*
5 The Queen's Own Hussars
6 The Queen's Royal Irish Hussars
7 9th/12th Royal Lancers (Prince of Wales's)
8 The Royal Hussars (Prince of Wales's Own)
9 13th/18th Royal Hussars (Queen Mary's Own)
10 14th/20th King's Hussars
11 15th/19th The King's Royal Hussars
12 16th/5th The Queen's Royal Lancers
13 17th/21st Lancers
14 Royal Tank Regiment

*Civilian laymen (and some foreign military) have sometimes been misled by the 'Guards' title, as implying Household troops status. The suffix originated when, in 1746 and 1788, the original Regiments of Horse were 'demoted' to Dragoons, and as some compensation for loss of prestige were granted the title 'Dragoon Guards'. This was, and is, a purely honorific distinction. At no time have these Regiments formed part of the Household Cavalry or enjoyed true Guards status.

REGIMENTS OF FOOT GUARDS

1 Grenadier Guards
2 Coldstream Guards
3 Scots Guards
4 Irish Guards
5 Welsh Guards

The above form The Guards Division (formerly Brigade of Guards), *see p. 17.*

REGIMENTS OF INFANTRY

1 The Royal Scots (The Royal Regiment)
2 The Queen's Regiment
3 The King's Own Royal Border Regiment
4 The Royal Regiment of Fusiliers
5 The King's Regiment
6 The Royal Anglian Regiment
7 The Devonshire and Dorset Regiment
8 The Light Infantry
9 The Prince of Wales's Own Regiment of Yorkshire
10 The Green Howards (Alexandra, Princess of Wales's Own Yorkshire Regiment)
11 The Royal Highland Fusiliers (Princess Margaret's Own Glasgow and Ayrshire Regiment)
12 The Cheshire Regiment
13 The Royal Welch Fusiliers
14 The Royal Regiment of Wales (24th/41st Foot)
15 The King's Own Scottish Borderers
16 The Cameronians (Scottish Rifles) (*disbanded* 1968)
17 The Royal Irish Rangers (27th (Inniskilling) 83rd and 87th)
18 The Gloucestershire Regiment
19 The Worcestershire and Sherwood Foresters Regiment (29th/45th Foot)
20 The Queen's Lancashire Regiment
21 The Duke of Wellington's Regiment (West Riding)
22 The Royal Hampshire Regiment
23 The Staffordshire Regiment (The Prince of Wales's)
24 The Black Watch (Royal Highland Regiment)
25 The Duke of Edinburgh's Royal Regiment (Berkshire and Wiltshire)
26 The York and Lancaster Regiment (*disbanded* 1968)
27 Queen's Own Highlanders (Seaforth and Camerons)
28 The Gordon Highlanders
29 The Argyll and Sutherland Highlanders (Princess Louise's)
30 The Parachute Regiment
31 The Brigade of Gurkhas
32 The Royal Green Jackets

Note. The Royal Marines when on parade with the Army take precedence immediately after The Duke of Edinburgh's Royal Regiment (Berkshire and Wiltshire).

INFANTRY DIVISIONS

These are administrative formations only, and do not correspond with operational Divisions formed for active service.

THE GUARDS DIVISION

Grenadier Guards
Coldstream Guards
Scots Guards
Irish Guards
Welsh Guards

Divisional Headquarters Wellington Barracks, Birdcage Walk, London SW1E 6HQ

THE SCOTTISH DIVISION

The Royal Scots (The Royal Regiment)
The Royal Highland Fusiliers (Princess Margaret's Own Glasgow and
   Ayrshire Regiment)
The King's Own Scottish Borderers
The Cameronians (Scottish Rifles)
The Black Watch (Royal Highland Regiment)
Queen's Own Highlanders (Seaforth and Camerons)
The Gordon Highlanders
The Argyll and Sutherland Highlanders (Princess Louise's)

Divisional Headquarters The Castle, Edinburgh EH1 2YT

THE QUEEN'S DIVISION

The Queen's Regiment
The Royal Regiment of Fusiliers
The Royal Anglian Regiment

Divisional Headquarters Bassingbourn Barracks, Royston, Hertfordshire

THE KING'S DIVISION

The King's Own Royal Border Regiment
The King's Regiment
The Prince of Wales's Own Regiment of Yorkshire
The Green Howards (Alexandra Princess of Wales's Own Yorkshire
  Regiment)
The Royal Irish Rangers (27th (Inniskilling) 83rd and 87th)
The Queen's Lancashire Regiment
The Duke of Wellington's Regiment (West Riding)
The York and Lancaster Regiment

Divisional Headquarters Imphal Barracks, York YO1 4HD

THE PRINCE OF WALES'S DIVISION

The Devonshire and Dorset Regiment
The Cheshire Regiment
The Royal Welch Fusiliers
The Royal Regiment of Wales (24th/41st Foot)
The Gloucestershire Regiment
The Worcestershire and Sherwood Foresters Regiment (29th/45th Foot)
The Royal Hampshire Regiment
The Staffordshire Regiment (The Prince of Wales's)
The Duke of Edinburgh's Royal Regiment (Berkshire and Wiltshire)

Divisional Headquarters Whittington Barracks, Lichfield,
Staffordshire WS14 9PY

THE LIGHT DIVISION

The Light Infantry
The Royal Green Jackets

Divisional Headquarters Peninsula Barracks, Winchester,
Hampshire SO23 8TS

THE LIFE GUARDS

The Regiment traces its origin to the noble friends of Charles II who accompanied their King during his exile on the continent, and who formed themselves into three Troops of Horse Guards. At the Restoration in 1660 these Troops returned with King Charles and escorted him to London, and in January 1661 were established in the new Standing Army.

Titles 1660 H.M. 1st, 2nd and 3rd Troops of Horse Guards
1661 Scottish (or 4th) Troop of Horse Guards raised in Edinburgh
1678 Three Troops of Horse Grenadier Guards formed and one Troop attached to each of the Troops of Horse Guards on English establishment
1686 4th (Scottish) Troop of Horse Grenadier Guards raised
1689 Dutch Troop of Horse Guards came on to English Establishment and designated 4th Troop of Horse Guards. This Troop was disbanded in 1699
1709 1st, 2nd, 3rd Troops of Horse Grenadier Guards redesignated as 1st Troop of Horse Grenadier Guards. Scottish (4th) Troop of Horse Grenadier Guards redesignated 2nd Troop of Horse Grenadier Guards
1746 3rd and 4th Troops of Horse Guards disbanded
1788 1st Troop of Horse Guards and 1st Troop of Horse Grenadier Guards reformed as 1st Regiment of Life Guards. 2nd Troop of Horse Guards and 2nd Troop of Horse Grenadier Guards reformed as 2nd Regiment of Life Guards
1922 1st and 2nd Regiments of Life Guards amalgamated to form The Life Guards (1st and 2nd)
1928 Regiment redesignated as The Life Guards

Battle honours Dettingen, Peninsula, Waterloo, Tel-el-Kebir, Egypt 1882, Relief of Kimberley, Paardeberg, South Africa 1899–1900.

The Great War—Mons, Le Cateau, Retreat from Mons, Marne 1914, Aisne 1914, Messines 1914, Armentieres 1914, Ypres 1914, 15, 17, Langemarck 1914, Gheluvelt, Nonne Bosschen, St. Julien, Frezenberg, Somme 1916, 18, Albert 1916, Arras 1917, 18, Scarpe 1917, 18,

Broodseinde, Poelcappelle, Passchendaele, Bapaume 1918, Hindenburg Line, Epehy, St. Quentin Canal, Beaurevoir, Cambrai 1918, Selle, France and Flanders 1914–18.

The Second World War—Mont Pincon, Souleuvre, Noireau Crossing, Amiens 1944, Brussels, Neerpelt, Nederrijn, Nijmegen, Lingen, Bentheim, North-West Europe 1944–45, Baghdad 1941, Iraq 1941, Palmyra, Syria 1941, El Alamein, North Africa 1942–43, Arezzo, Advance to Florence, Gothic Line, Italy 1944.

Motto *Honi Soit Qui Mal y Pense* (Evil to him who evil thinks)

Uniform Scarlet, facings blue

Regimental marches [Slow] Anonymous (Attributed to Duchess of Kent)
Men of Harlech (Traditional)

[Quick] *Milanollo* (Val Hamm)

Regimental journal *The Acorn*

Regimental headquarters c/o RHQ Household Cavalry, Horse Guards, Whitehall, London SW1A 2AX

Regimental museum Household Cavalry Museum, Combermere Barracks, Windsor

Nicknames The Bangers. The Gallopers. The Tins
(*The above have never been used within the Regiment.*)

THE BLUES AND ROYALS
(ROYAL HORSE GUARDS AND 1st DRAGOONS)

Formed 29th March 1969 by amalgamation of the Royal Horse Guards (The Blues) with The Royal Dragoons (1st Dragoons).

Battle honours Tangier 1662–80, Dettingen, Warburg, Beaumont, Willems, Fuentes d'Onor, Peninsula, Waterloo, Balaklava, Sevastopol, Tel-el-Kebir, Egypt 1882, Relief of Kimberley, Paardeberg, Relief of Ladysmith, South Africa 1899–1902.

The Great War—Mons, Le Cateau, Retreat from Mons, Marne 1914, Aisne 1914, Messines 1914, Armentieres 1914, Ypres 1914, 15, 17, Langemarck 1914, Gheluvelt, Nonne Bosschen, St. Julien, Frezenberg, Loos, Arras 1917, Scarpe 1917, Broodseinde, Poelcappelle, Passchendaele, Somme 1918, Amiens, Hindenburg Line, Cambrai 1918, Sambre, Pursuit to Mons, France and Flanders 1914–18.

The Second World War—Mont Pincon, Souleuvre, Noireau Crossing, Amiens 1944, Brussels, Neerpelt, Nederrijn, Nijmegen, Rhine, Lingen, Bentheim, North-West Europe 1944–45, Baghdad, Iraq 1941, Palmyra, Syria 1941, Knightsbridge, El Alamein, Advance on Tripoli, North Africa 1941–43, Sicily 1943, Arezzo, Advance to Florence, Gothic Line, Italy 1943–44.

Falkland Islands 1982.

Motto *Honi Soit Qui Mal y Pense* (Evil to him who evil thinks)

Uniform Blue, facings scarlet. The full dress tunic bears on the left shoulder the 'Waterloo Eagle' badge inherited from The Royal Dragoons.

Regimental marches [Slow] Anonymous (Attributed to Duchess of Kent)
[Quick] Grand March from *Aida* (Verdi)
Regimental March of The Royal Dragoons (Blankenburg)

Regimental journal *The Blue and Royal*

Regimental headquarters Horse Guards, Whitehall, London SW1A 2AX

Regimental museum Household Cavalry Museum, Combermere Barracks, Windsor

ROYAL HORSE GUARDS
(THE BLUES)

Raised by Charles II in January 1661, from Colonel Unton Crook's Regiment of Horse of the disbanded Parliamentary Army. Command given to Aubrey, Earl of Oxford, whose blue livery was adopted.

Titles 1661 The Royal Regiment of Horse (also known as Earl of Oxford's Regiment of Horse)
1685 Royal Regiment of Horse (Guards)
1714 Royal Regiment of Horse Guards

1875 Royal Horse Guards
1891 Royal Horse Guards (The Blues)
1969 Amalgamated with The Royal Dragoons (1st
     Dragoons) to form The Blues and Royals (Royal
     Horse Guards and 1st Dragoons)

Battle honours Dettingen, Warburg, Beaumont, Willems, Peninsula,
Waterloo, Tel-el-Kebir, Egypt 1882, Relief of Kimberley,
Paardeberg, South Africa 1899–1900.

The Great War—2 Regiments and Household Battalion
Mons, Le Cateau, Retreat from Mons, Marne 1914,
Aisne 1914, Messines 1914, Armentieres 1914, Ypres
1914, 15, 17, Langemarck 1914, Gheluvelt, Nonne
Bosschen, St. Julien, Frezenberg, Loos, Arras 1917,
Scarpe 1917, Broodseinde, Poelcappelle, Passchendaele,
Hindenburg Line, Cambrai 1918, Sambre, France and
Flanders 1914–18.

The Second World War—Mont Pincon, Souleuvre,
Noireau Crossing, Amiens 1944, Brussels, Neerpelt,
Nederrijn, Nijmegen, Lingen, Bentheim, North-West
Europe 1944–45, Baghdad 1941, Iraq 1941, Palmyra,
Syria 1941, El Alamein, North Africa 1942–43, Arezzo,
Advance to Florence, Gothic Line, Italy 1944.

Motto *Honi Soit Qui Mal y Pense*

Uniform Blue, facings scarlet

Regimental marches [Slow] Anonymous (Attributed to Duchess of Kent)
[Quick] Grand March from *Aida* (Verdi)

Regimental journal *The Blue*

Regimental headquarters Horse Guards, Whitehall, London SW1A 2AX

Regimental museum Household Cavalry Museum, Combermere Barracks,
Windsor

Nicknames Originally Oxford Blues. Latterly The Blues

THE ROYAL DRAGOONS
(1st DRAGOONS)

Raised in October 1661 as the Tangier Horse,
commanded by the Earl of Peterborough and forming the
cavalry element of the garrison of Tangier. In 1684 the
Tangier Horse returned to England, and with two freshly

raised Troops of Dragoons formed The King's Own Royal Regiment of Dragoons.

Titles 1661 The Tangier Horse
1684 The King's Own Royal Regiment of Dragoons
1690 The Royal Regiment of Dragoons
1751 1st (Royal) Dragoons
1920 1st The Royal Dragoons
1961 The Royal Dragoons (1st Dragoons)
1969 Amalgamated with the Royal Horse Guards (The Blues) to form The Blues and Royals (Royal Horse Guards and 1st Dragoons)

Battle honours Tangier 1662–80, Dettingen, Warburg, Beaumont, Willems, Fuentes d'Onor, Peninsula, Waterloo, Balaklava, Sevastopol, Relief of Ladysmith, South Africa 1899–1902.

The Great War—Ypres 1914, 15, Langemarck 1914, Gheluvelt, Nonne Bosschen, Frezenberg, Loos, Arras 1917, Scarpe 1917, Somme, 1918, St. Quentin, Avre, Amiens, Hindenburg Line, Beaurevoir, Cambrai 1918, Pursuit to Mons, France and Flanders 1914–18.

The Second World War—Nederrijn, Veghel, Rhine, North-West Europe 1944–45, Syria, 1941, Msus, Gazala, Knightsbridge, Defence of Alamein Line, El Alamein, El Agheila, Advance on Tripoli, North Africa 1941–43, Sicily 1943, Italy 1943.

Motto *Spectemur Agendo* (Let us be judged by our deeds)

Uniform Scarlet, facings blue

Regimental marches [Slow] *Regimental March of The Royal Dragoons* (Blankenburg)
[Quick] Quick version of above

Regimental journal *The Eagle*

Regimental museum Now incorporated in the Household Cavalry Museum, Combermere Barracks, Windsor

Nicknames The Royals. The Birdcatchers

Remarks The Eagle Badge, still worn on the full dress tunics of The Blues and Royals, commemorates the capture of Eagle Standard of the French 105th Regiment in the Charge of the Union Brigade at Waterloo.

1st THE QUEEN'S DRAGOON GUARDS

Formed 1st January 1959 by amalgamation of 1st King's Dragoon Guards with The Queen's Bays (2nd Dragoon Guards).

Battle honours Blenheim, Ramillies, Oudenarde, Malplaquet, Dettingen, Warburg, Beaumont, Willems, Waterloo, Sevastopol, Lucknow, Taku Forts, Pekin 1860, South Africa 1879, South Africa 1901–02.

The Great War—Mons, Le Cateau, Retreat from Mons, Marne 1914, Aisne 1914, Messines 1914, Armentieres 1914, Ypres 1914, 15, Frezenberg, Bellewaarde, Somme 1916, 18, Flers Courcelette, Morval, Arras 1917, Scarpe 1917, Cambrai 1917, 18, St. Quentin, Bapaume 1918, Rosieres, Amiens, Albert 1918, Hindenburg Line, St. Quentin Canal, Beaurevoir, Pursuit to Mons, France and Flanders 1914–18.

Afghanistan 1919.

The Second World War—Somme 1940, Withdrawal to Seine, North-West Europe 1940, Beda Fomm, Defence of Tobruk, Tobruk 1941, Tobruk Sortie, Relief of Tobruk, Msus, Gazala, Bir el Aslagh, Bir Hacheim, Cauldron, Knightsbridge, Via Balbia, Mersa Matruh, Defence of Alamein Line, Alam el Halfa, El Alamein, El Agheila, Advance on Tripoli, Tebaga Gap, Point 201 (Roman Wall), El Hamma, Akarit, El Kourzia, Djebel Kournine, Tunis, Creteville Pass, North Africa 1941–43, Capture of Naples, Scafati Bridge, Monte Camino, Garigliano Crossing, Capture of Perugia, Arezzo, Gothic Line, Coriano, Carpineta, Lamone Crossing, Defence of Lamone Bridgehead, Rimini Line, Ceriano Ridge, Cesena, Argenta Gap, Italy 1943–45, Athens, Greece 1944–45.

Motto *Pro Rege et Patria* (For King and Country)

Uniform Scarlet, facings blue

Regimental marches [Slow] *The Queen's Dragoon Guards*
[Quick] Arrangement of *Radesky March* (J. Strauss) and *Rusty Buckles*

Regimental journal *The Journal of the Queen's Dragoon Guards*

Home headquarters Maindy Barracks, Whitchurch Road, Cardiff CF4 3YE

Regimental museum Clive House, College Hill, Shrewsbury

1st KING'S DRAGOON GUARDS

Raised June 1685 by Sir John Lanier as The Queen's Regiment of Horse, and ranked as 2nd Horse.

Titles 1685 The Queen's Regiment of Horse (2nd Horse)
1714 The King's Own Regiment of Horse
1746 1st (or The King's) Regiment of Dragoon Guards
1856 1st (King's) Dragoon Guards
1920 1st King's Dragoon Guards
1959 Amalgamated with The Queen's Bays (2nd Dragoon Guards) to form 1st The Queen's Dragoon Guards

Battle honours Blenheim, Ramillies, Oudenarde, Malplaquet, Dettingen, Warburg, Beaumont, Waterloo, Sevastopol, Taku Forts, Pekin 1860, South Africa 1879, South Africa 1901–2.

The Great War—Somme 1916, Morval, France and Flanders 1914–17.

Afghanistan 1919.

The Second World War—Beda Fomm, Defence of Tobruk, Tobruk 1941, Tobruk Sortie, Relief of Tobruk, Gazala, Bir Hacheim, Defence of Alamein Line, Alam el Halfa, El Agheila, Advance on Tripoli, Tebaga Gap, Point 201 (Roman Wall), El Hamma, Akarit, Tunis, North Africa 1941–43, Capture of Naples, Scafati Bridge, Monte Camino, Garigliano Crossing, Capture of Perugia, Arezzo, Gothic Line, Italy 1943–44, Athens, Greece 1944–45.

Uniform Scarlet, facings blue

Regimental marches [Slow] *The King's Dragoon Guards* (Adapted from opera themes by Mercadente)

[Quick] *The Radetsky March* (J. Strauss)

Regimental journal *Regimental Journal of 1st King's Dragoon Guards*

Nicknames The Trades Union. Bland's Horse. The KDGs

Remarks On his appointment as Colonel-in-Chief in 1896, Franz Joseph, Emperor of Austria, granted the Regiment the right to wear the Austrian double-headed eagle as the Badge. This was discontinued in 1915, Austria having become an enemy, but was resumed in 1937, and has been inherited by the present Regiment. *The Radetsky March* is also owed to the Emperor Franz Joseph, who presented a set of Band parts.

THE QUEEN'S BAYS
(2nd DRAGOON GUARDS)

Raised June 1685 as The Earl of Peterborough's Regiment of Horse.

Titles 1685 The Earl of Peterborough's Regiment of Horse
Until 1715 designated by Colonels' names
1715 The Princess of Wales's Own Royal Regiment of Horse
1727 The Queen's Own Royal Regiment of Horse
1746 2nd or Queen's Regiment of Dragoon Guards
1870 2nd Dragoon Guards (Queen's Bays)
1921 The Queen's Bays (2nd Dragoon Guards)
1959 Amalgamated with 1st King's Dragoon Guards to form 1st The Queen's Dragoon Guards

Battle honours Warburg, Willems, Lucknow, South Africa 1901–02.

The Great War—Mons, Le Cateau, Retreat from Mons, Marne 1914, Aisne 1914, Messines 1914, Armentieres 1914, Ypres 1914, 15, Frezenberg, Bellewaarde, Somme 1916, 18, Flers-Courcelette, Arras 1917, Scarpe 1917, Cambrai 1917, 18, St. Quentin, Bapaume 1918, Rosieres, Amiens, Albert 1918, Hindenburg Line, St. Quentin Canal, Beaurevoir, Pursuit to Mons, France and Flanders 1914–18.

The Second World War—Somme 1940, Withdrawal to Seine, North-West Europe 1940, Msus, Gazala, Bir el Aslagh, Cauldron, Knightsbridge, Via Balbia, Mersa Matruh, El Alamein, Tebaga Gap, El Hamma, El Kourzia, Djebel Kournine, Tunis, Creteville Pass, North Africa 1941–43, Coriano, Carpineta, Lamone Crossing, Lamone Bridgehead, Rimini Line, Ceriano Ridge, Cesena, Argenta Gap, Italy 1944–45.

Motto *Pro Rege et Patria* (For King and Country)

Uniform   Scarlet, facings white

Regimental marches [Slow]   *The Queen's Bays*
               [Quick]   *Rusty Buckles*

Regimental journal   *Regimental Journal of The Queen's Bays (2nd Dragoon Guards)*

Nicknames   The Bays. Rusty Buckles

Remarks   In 1766 the Regiment was officially mounted on bay horses exclusively, this being the origin of the subsequent title, which was in popular use long before it became authorised in 1870.

THE ROYAL SCOTS DRAGOON GUARDS
(CARABINIERS AND GREYS)

Formed July 1971 by amalgamation of the 3rd Carabiniers (Prince of Wales's Dragoon Guards) with the Royal Scots Greys (2nd Dragoons).

Battle honours   Blenheim, Ramillies, Oudenarde, Malplaquet, Dettingen, Warburg, Beaumont, Willems, Waterloo, Talavera, Albuhera, Vittoria, Peninsula, Balaklava, Sevastopol, Delhi 1857, Abyssinia, Afghanistan 1879–80, Relief of Kimberley, Paardeberg, South Africa 1899–1902.

The Great War—Mons, Le Cateau, Retreat from Mons, Marne 1914, Aisne 1914, Messines 1914, Armentieres 1914, Ypres 1914, 15, Nonne Bosschen, Gheluvelt, Neuve Chapelle, St. Julien, Frezenberg, Bellewaarde, Loos, Arras 1917, Scarpe 1917, Cambrai 1917, 18, Lys, Hazebrouck, Somme 1918, St. Quentin, Avre, Amiens, Albert 1918, Bapaume, Hindenburg Line, Canal du Nord, St. Quentin Canal, Beaurevoir, Selle, Sambre, Pursuit to Mons, France and Flanders 1914–18.

The Second World War—Caen, Hill 112, Falaise, Venlo Pocket, Hochwald, Aller, Bremen, North-West Europe 1944–45, Merjayun, Syria 1941, Alam el Halfa, El Alamein, El Agheila, Nofilia, Advance on Tripoli, North

Africa 1942–43, Salerno, Battipaglia, Volturno Crossing, Italy 1943, Imphal, Tamu Road, Nunshigum, Bishenpur, Kanglatongbi, Kennedy Peak, Shwebo, Sagaing, Mandalay, Ava, Irrawaddy, Yenangyaung 1945, Burma 1944–45.

Motto	*Nemo Me Impune Lacessit* (No one provokes me with impunity)
Uniform	Scarlet, facings yellow. Distinctive bearskin cap of The Greys is retained, also the vandyke band round Number One Dress cap, but this is now yellow instead of white, as previously. Pipes and Drums wear Royal Stuart tartan (granted to Greys by King George VI), and feather bonnets.
Regimental marches [Slow]	*In the Garb of Old Gaul* (Reid)
[Quick]	*3 DG*
Regimental journal	*Eagle and Carbine*
Home headquarters	The Castle, Edinburgh EH1 2YT
Regimental museums	(3rd Carabiniers) The Castle, Chester (Royal Scots Greys) The Castle, Edinburgh

3rd CARABINIERS
(PRINCE OF WALES'S DRAGOON GUARDS)

Formed April 1922 by amalgamation of 3rd Dragoon Guards (Prince of Wales's) with The Carabiniers (6th Dragoon Guards).

Titles	1922 3rd/6th Dragoon Guards
	1928 3rd Carabiniers (Prince of Wales's Dragoon Guards)
Battle honours	Blenheim, Ramillies, Oudenarde, Malplaquet, Warburg, Beaumont, Willems, Talavera, Albuhera, Vittoria, Peninsula, Sevastopol, Delhi 1857, Abyssinia, Afghanistan 1879–80, Relief of Kimberley, Paardeberg, South Africa 1899–1902.

The Great War—Mons, Le Cateau, Retreat from Mons, Marne 1914, Aisne 1914, Messines 1914, Armentieres 1914, Ypres 1914, 15, Nonne Bosschen, St. Julien, Frezenberg, Bellewaarde, Loos, Arras 1917, Scarpe 1917, Cambrai 1917, 18, Somme 1918, St. Quentin, Avre,

Lys, Hazebrouck, Amiens, Bapaume 1918, Hindenburg Line, Canal du Nord, Beaurevoir, Selle, Sambre, France and Flanders 1914–18.

The Second World War—Imphal, Tamu Road, Nunshigum, Bishenpur, Kanglatongbi, Kennedy Peak, Shwebo, Sagaing, Mandalay, Ava, Irrawaddy, Yenangyaung 1945, Burma 1944–45.

Motto *Ich Dien* (I Serve)

Uniform Scarlet, facings yellow

Regimental marches [Slow] 6 DG
[Quick] 3 DG

Regimental journal *Feather and Carbine*

Nicknames The Carbs. The Old Canaries

3rd DRAGOON GUARDS
(PRINCE OF WALES'S)

Raised July 1685 by Thomas, 1st Earl of Plymouth and ranked as 4th Regiment of Horse.

Titles 1685 The Earl of Plymouth's Regiment of Horse *Title subsequently changed with Colonel's names*
1746 3rd Regiment of Dragoon Guards
1765 3rd (The Prince of Wales's) Dragoon Guards
1921 3rd Dragoon Guards (Prince of Wales's)
1922 Amalgamated with The Carabiniers (6th Dragoon Guards) to form 3rd/6th Dragoon Guards
1928 Title changed to 3rd Carabiniers (Prince of Wales's Dragoon Guards)

Battle honours Blenheim, Ramillies, Oudenarde, Malplaquet, Warburg, Beaumont, Willems, Talavera, Albuhera, Vittoria, Peninsula, Abyssinia, South Africa 1901–02.

The Great War—Ypres, 1914, 15, Nonne Bosschen, Frezenberg, Loos, Arras 1917, Scarpe 1917, Somme, 1918, St. Quentin, Avre, Amiens, Hindenburg Line, Beaurevoir, Cambrai 1918, Pursuit to Mons, France and Flanders, 1914–18.

Motto *Ich Dien* (I Serve)

Uniform Scarlet, facings yellow

Regimental marches [Slow] *March of the Men of Harlech* (Tradit.)
[Quick] *God Bless the Prince of Wales* (Richards)

Nickname The Old Canaries

THE CARABINIERS
(6th DRAGOON GUARDS)

Raised July 1685 by Richard, 1st Baron Lumley (later 1st Earl of Scarborough) and ranked as 9th Regiment of Horse.

Titles 1685 The Queen Dowager's Regiment of Horse (also Lumley's Horse)
1691 The Carabineers. Also 1st Carabineers, or The King's Carabineers (now ranked as 8th Horse)
1746 3rd Regiment of Horse (Irish Establishment)
1756 3rd Horse or Carabineers
1788 6th Dragoon Guards
1826 6th Dragoon Guards (Carabineers) *By 1855 spelling had been altered to 'Carabiniers'.*
1920 The Carabiniers (6th Dragoon Guards)
1922 Amalgamated with 3rd Dragoon Guards (Prince of Wales's) to form The 3rd Carabiniers (Prince of Wales's Dragoon Guards)

Battle honours Blenheim, Ramillies, Oudenarde, Malplaquet, Warburg, Willems, Sevastopol, Delhi 1857, Afghanistan 1879–80, Relief of Kimberley, Paardeberg, South Africa 1899–02.

The Great War—Mons, Le Cateau, Retreat from Mons, Marne 1914, Aisne 1914, Messines 1914, Armentieres 1914, Ypres 1915, St. Julien, Bellewaarde, Arras 1917, Scarpe 1917, Cambrai 1917, 18, Somme 1918, St. Quentin, Lys, Hazebrouck, Amiens, Bapaume 1918, Hindenburg Line, Canal du Nord, Selle, Sambre, France and Flanders 1914–18.

Uniform The Carabiniers were unique among all Dragoon Guards in wearing blue tunics instead of scarlet, resulting from their reclassification from Heavy to Light cavalry in 1851. Facings were white.

Regimental marches [Slow] *6th Dragoon Guards*
[Quick] *God Bless the Prince of Wales* (Richards)

Nicknames The Carbs. Tichborne's Own

Remarks The title 'Carabiniers' was conferred by King William III in recognition of the Regiment's distinguished services during his Irish campaign and at the Battle of the Boyne. The carbine (or 'carabine') was a shorter and lighter cavalry pattern of the regulation infantry musket.

THE ROYAL SCOTS GREYS
(2nd DRAGOONS)

Raised November 1681 by Lieut-General Thomas Dalyell of The Binns, from independent Troops of Scottish Dragoons.

Titles 1681 Royal Regiment of Scots Dragoons
(1688 Ranked as 2nd Dragoons)
1707 Royal Regiment of North British Dragoons *Also known as The Scots Regiment of White Horses*
1751 2nd (or Royal North British) Regiment of Dragoons
1866 2nd (Royal North British) Dragoons (Royal Scots Greys)
1877 2nd Dragoons (Royal Scots Greys)
1921 The Royal Scots Greys (2nd Dragoons)
1971 Amalgamated with 3rd Carabiniers (Prince of Wales's Dragoon Guards) to form The Royal Scots Dragoon Guards (Carabiniers and Greys)

Battle honours Blenheim, Ramillies, Oudenarde, Malplaquet, Dettingen, Warburg, Willems, Waterloo, Balaklava, Sevastopol, Relief of Kimberley, Paardeberg, South Africa 1899–1902.

The Great War—Mons, Retreat from Mons, Marne 1914, Aisne 1914, Messines 1914, Ypres 1914, 15, Gheluvelt, Neuve Chapelle, St. Julien, Bellewaarde, Arras 1917, Scarpe 1917, Cambrai 1917, 18, Lys, Hazebrouck, Amiens, Somme 1918, Albert 1918, Bapaume 1918, Hindenburg Line, St. Quentin Canal, Beaurevoir, Pursuit to Mons, France and Flanders 1914–18.

The Second World War—Caen, Hill 112, Falaise, Venlo Pocket, Hochwald, Aller, Bremen, North-West Europe 1944–45, Merjayun, Syria 1941, Alam El Halfa, El Alamein, El Agheila, Nofilia, Advance on Tripoli, North Africa 1942–43, Salerno, Battipaglia, Volturno Crossing, Italy 1943.

Motto *Nemo Me Impune Lacessit* (No one provokes me with impunity)

Uniform Scarlet, facings blue. The bearskin cap (unique among cavalry regiments) evolved from the Grenadier cap granted in 1706 in commemoration of the Regiment's defeat of the French *Régiment du Roi* at Ramillies.*

Regimental marches [Slow] *In the Garb of Old Gaul* (Reid)
[Quick] Quick version of above

Regimental journal *The Journal of the Royal Scots Greys*

Nicknames The Greys. The Birdcatchers

Remarks The French Eagle Badge of the Greys, inherited by the present Regiment, commemorates the capture of the Eagle Standard of the French 45th Regiment in the Charge of the Union Brigade at Waterloo.

The Greys and the 7th Hussars were the only two surviving cavalry regiments of the British Army to have been raised in Scotland.

4th/7th ROYAL DRAGOON GUARDS

Formed April 1922 by amalgamation of the 4th Royal Irish Dragoon Guards with the 7th Dragoon Guards (Princess Royal's).

Titles 1922 4th/7th Dragoon Guards
1936 4th/7th Royal Dragoon Guards

Battle honours Blenheim, Ramillies, Oudenarde, Malplaquet, Dettingen, Warburg, Peninsula, South Africa 1846–47, Balaklava, Sevastopol, Tel-el-Kebir, Egypt 1882, South Africa 1900–02.

---

* The 5th (Royal Irish) Dragoons fought in the same action and were granted the same dress distinction. But this Regiment was disbanded in 1799, and when re-raised as Lancers in 1858 the distinction was not resumed.

The Great War—Mons, Le Cateau, Retreat from Mons,
Marne 1914, Aisne 1914, La Bassee 1914, Messines
1914, Armentieres 1914, Ypres 1914, 15, Givenchy
1914, St. Julien, Frezenberg, Bellewaarde, Somme 1916,
18, Bazentin, Flers-Courcelette, Arras 1917, Scarpe
1917, Cambrai 1917, 18, St. Quentin, Rosieres, Avre,
Lys, Hazebrouck, Amiens, Albert 1918, Hindenburg
Line, St. Quentin Canal, Beaurevoir, Pursuit to Mons,
France and Flanders 1914–18.

The Second World War—Dyle, Dunkirk 1940,
Normandy Landing, Odon, Mont Pincon, Seine 1944,
Nederrijn, Geilenkirchen, Roer, Rhineland, Cleve,
Rhine, Bremen, North-West Europe 1940, 44–45.

Motto *Quis Separabit* (Who shall separate?)

Uniform Scarlet, facings royal blue

Regimental marches [Slow] *4th/7th Royal Dragoon Guards* (Anon.)
[Quick] *St. Patrick's Day* (Tradit.)

Regimental journal *4th/7th Royal Dragoon Guards Regimental Magazine*

Home headquarters 3 Tower Street, York YO1 1SB

Regimental museum As above

Nickname The First and the Last

4th ROYAL IRISH DRAGOON GUARDS

Raised July 1685 by James Hamilton (Douglas), Earl of
Arran, and ranked as 6th Horse.

Titles 1685 Arran's Horse (or Cuirassiers)
(1687 Re-ranked as 5th Horse) *Title subsequently changed
with Colonels' names*
1715 The Prince of Wales's Own Regiment of Horse
1746 1st Horse (Irish Establishment)
1788 4th (Royal Irish) Dragoon Guards
1921 4th Royal Irish Dragoon Guards
1922 Amalgamated with 7th Dragoon Guards (Princess
Royal's) to form 4th/7th Dragoon Guards ('Royal'
prefix granted 1936)

Battle honours Peninsula, Balaklava, Sevastopol, Tel-el-Kebir, Egypt
1882.

The Great War—Mons, Le Cateau, Retreat from Mons, Marne 1914, Aisne 1914, La Bassee 1914, Messines 1914, Armentieres 1914, Ypres 1914, 15, St. Julien, Frezenberg, Bellewaarde, Somme 1916, 18, Flers-Courcelette, Arras 1917, Scarpe 1917, Cambrai 1917, 18, St. Quentin, Rosieres, Amiens, Albert 1918, Hindenburg Line, Pursuit to Mons, France and Flanders 1914–18.

Motto *Quis Separabit* (Who shall separate?)

Uniform Scarlet, facings blue

Regimental marches [Slow] *4th Royal Irish Dragoon Guards* (Anon.)
[Quick] *St Patrick's Day* (Tradit.)

Regimental journal *4th Royal Irish Dragoon Guards Regimental Record*

Nicknames The Mounted Micks. The Blue Horse. The Buttermilks

Remarks On 22nd August 1914 a patrol of the Regiment under Captain C. W. Hornby made the first British contact with the German forces at Casteau in Belgium, and made the first killing of the War. A memorial now marks the spot.

7th DRAGOON GUARDS
(PRINCESS ROYAL'S)

Raised 31st December 1688 by William Cavendish, Earl of Devonshire, and ranked as 10th Horse.

Titles 1688 The Earl of Devonshire's Horse (Also known as Cavendish's Horse)
(1692 Re-ranked as 8th Horse) *Title subsequently changed with Colonels' names*
1746 4th Horse (Irish Establishment)
1788 7th (Princess Royal's) Dragoon Guards
1921 7th Dragoon Guards (Princess Royal's)
1922 Amalgamated with 4th Royal Irish Dragoon Guards to form 4th/7th Dragoon Guards ('Royal' prefix granted 1936)

Battle honours Blenheim, Ramillies, Oudenarde, Malplaquet, Dettingen, Warburg, South Africa 1846–47, Tel-el-Kebir, Egypt 1882, South Africa 1900–02.

The Great War—La Bassee 1914, Givenchy 1914, Somme 1916, 18, Bazentin, Flers-Courcelette, Cambrai

1917, 18, St. Quentin, Avre, Lys, Hazebrouck, Amiens, Hindenburg Line, St. Quentin Canal, Beaurevoir, Pursuit to Mons, France and Flanders 1914–18.

Motto	*Quo Fata Vocant* (Whither the Fates lead)
Uniform	Scarlet, facings black
Regimental march [Slow]	*7th (Princess Royal's) Dragoon Guards* (Anon.)
Regimental journal	*The Black Horse Gazette*
Nicknames	The Black Horse. Virgin Mary's Guards. Strawboots
Remarks	On 11th November 1918 a Squadron of the Regiment fought the last action of the British Army in the Great War, capturing the town of Lessines a few minutes before the 11 a.m. Armistice.

The oldest British cavalry Standard in existence was valiantly defended by Cornet Richardson of the Regiment (then Ligonier's Horse) at the Battle of Dettingen, 1743. It is now preserved in the National Army Museum, London.

5th ROYAL INNISKILLING DRAGOON GUARDS

Formed April 1922 by amalgamation of 5th Dragoon Guards (Princess Charlotte of Wales's) with The Inniskillings (6th Dragoons).

Titles	1922 5th/6th Dragoons
	1927 5th Inniskilling Dragoon Guards
	1935 5th Royal Inniskilling Dragoon Guards
Battle honours	Blenheim, Ramillies, Oudenarde, Malplaquet, Dettingen, Warburg, Beaumont, Willems, Salamanca, Vittoria, Toulouse, Peninsula, Waterloo, Balaklava, Sevastopol, Defence of Ladysmith, South Africa 1899–1902.

The Great War—Mons, Le Cateau, Retreat from Mons, Marne 1914, Aisne 1914, La Bassee 1914, Messines 1914, Armentieres 1914, Ypres 1914, 15, Frezenberg,

Bellewaarde, Somme 1916, 18, Flers-Courcelette, Morval, Arras 1917, Scarpe 1917, Cambrai 1917, 18, St. Quentin, Rosieres, Avre, Lys, Hazebrouck, Amiens, Albert 1918, Hindenburg Line, St. Quentin Canal, Beaurevoir, Pursuit to Mons, France and Flanders 1914–18.

The Second World War—Withdrawal to Escaut, St. Omer-La Bassee, Dunkirk 1940, Mont Pincon, St. Pierre La Vielle, Lisieux, Risle Crossing, Lower Maas, Roer, Ibbenburen, North-West Europe 1940, 44–45.

The Hook 1952, Korea 1951–52.

Motto	*Vestigia Nulla Retrorsum* (We do not retreat)
Uniform	Scarlet, overalls green with primrose stripe, facings royal blue
Regimental marches [Slow]	'Soldiers' Chorus' from *Faust* (Gounod)
[Quick]	*Fare thee Well Inniskilling* (Tradit.)
Regimental journal	*The Regimental Journal of the 5th Royal Inniskilling Dragoon Guards*
Home headquarters	The Castle, Chester CH1 2DN
Regimental museums	The Castle, Chester CH1 2DN
	Carrickfergus Castle, Co. Antrim, N. Ireland
Nickname	The Skins

5th DRAGOON GUARDS
(PRINCESS CHARLOTTE OF WALES'S)

Raised July 1685 by Charles, Earl of Shrewsbury, and ranked as 7th Horse.

Titles	1685 The Earl of Shrewsbury's Horse *Title subsequently changed with Colonels' names*
	(1698 Re-ranked as 6th Horse)
	1746 2nd Horse (Irish Establishment)
	1788 5th Dragoon Guards
	1804 5th (Princess Charlotte of Wales's) Dragoon Guards
	1920 5th Dragoon Guards (Princess Charlotte of Wales's)
	1922 Amalgamated with The Inniskillings (6th Dragoons) to form 5th/6th Dragoons

Battle honours Blenheim, Ramillies, Oudenarde, Malplaquet, Warburg, Willems, Sevastopol, Delhi 1857, Afghanistan 1879–80, Relief of Kimberley, Paardeberg, South Africa 1899–1902.

The Great War—Mons, Le Cateau, Retreat from Mons, Marne 1914, Aisne 1914, La Bassee 1914, Messines 1914, Armentieres 1914, Ypres, 1914, 15, Frezenberg, Bellewaarde, Somme 1916, 18, Flers-Courcelette, Arras 1917, Scarpe 1917, Cambrai 1917, 18, St. Quentin, Rosieres, Amiens, Albert 1918, Hindenburg Line, St. Quentin Canal, Beaurevoir, Pursuit to Mons, France and Flanders 1914–18.

Motto *Vestigia Nulla Retrorsum* (We do not retreat)

Uniform Scarlet, facings dark green

Regimental marches [Slow] 'Soldiers' Chorus' from *Faust* (Gounod)
[Quick] *The Gay Cavalier*

Regimental journal *The Green Horse*

Nicknames The Green Horse. The Old Farmers

THE INNISKILLINGS
(6th DRAGOONS)

Raised January 1690 from *ad hoc* Troops of Horse formed to defend the town of Enniskillen against ex-King James II's Catholic forces. Command given to Colonel Sir Albert Conyngham. Ranked as 6th Dragoons.

Titles 1690 Conyngham's Dragoons, or 6th Dragoons
Title subsequently changed with Colonels' names
1751 6th (Inniskilling) Dragoons
1921 The Inniskillings (6th Dragoons)
1922 Amalgamated with 5th Dragoon Guards (Princess Charlotte of Wales's) to form 5th/6th Dragoons

Battle honours Dettingen, Warburg, Willems, Waterloo, Balaklava, Sevastopol, South Africa 1899–1902.

The Great War—Somme 1916, 18, Morval, Cambrai 1917, 18, St. Quentin, Avre, Lys, Hazebrouck, Amiens, Hindenburg Line, St. Quentin Canal, Beaurevoir, Pursuit to Mons, France and Flanders 1914–18.

Uniform Scarlet, facings primrose

Regimental marches [Slow] *The Inniskilling Dragoons* (Anon.)
[Quick] *Fare thee Well Inniskilling* (Tradit.)

Regimental journal *The Inniskilliner*

Nicknames The Skins. The Old Inniskillings. The Skillingers

THE QUEEN'S OWN HUSSARS

Formed November 1958 by amalgamation of 3rd The King's Own Hussars with 7th Queen's Own Hussars.

Battle honours Dettingen, Warburg, Beaumont, Willems, Salamanca, Vittoria, Orthes, Toulouse, Peninsula, Waterloo, Cabool 1842, Moodkee, Ferozeshah, Sobraon, Chillianwallah, Goojerat, Punjab, Lucknow, South Africa 1901–02.

The Great War—Mons, Le Cateau, Retreat from Mons, Marne 1914, Aisne 1914, Messines 1914, Armentieres 1914, Ypres 1914, 15, Gheluvelt, St. Julien, Bellewaarde, Arras 1917, Scarpe 1917, Cambrai 1917, 18, Somme 1918, St. Quentin, Lys, Hazebrouck, Amiens, Bapaume 1918, Hindenburg Line, Canal du Nord, Selle, Sambre, France and Flanders 1914–18, Khan Baghdadi, Sharqat, Mesopotamia 1917–18.

The Second World War—Egyptian Frontier 1940, Sidi Barrani, Buq Buq, Beda Fomm, Sidi Suleiman, Sidi Rezegh 1941, El Alamein, North Africa 1940–42, Citta della Pieve, Ancona, Citta di Castello, Rimini Line, Italy 1944–45, Crete, Pegu, Paungde, Burma 1942.

Motto *Nec Aspera Terrent* (Neither do difficulties deter)

Uniform Blue, facings Garter blue

Regimental marches [Slow] *The Garb of Auld Gaul* (Reid)
[Quick] *Light Cavalry* (Suppé)

Regimental journal *The Journal of The Queen's Own Hussars*

Home headquarters 28 Jury Street, Warwick CV34 4EW

Regimental museum The Lord Leycester Hospital, High Street, Warwick

Remarks On ceremonial occasions the Band parades a mounted kettle-drummer, his horse carrying silver drums. These commemorate the capture of French kettledrums by the predecessors of the 3rd Hussars at the Battle of Dettingen (1743). All ranks of The Queen's Own Hussars wear on the left sleeve the Crest of the City of Warsaw. This distinction was conferred on the Regiment by the WWII Commander of the 2nd Polish Corps in recognition of their staunch support of the Polish forces during the Italian Campaign.

3rd THE KING'S OWN HUSSARS

Raised as regiment of Dragoons, August 1685, command being given to Charles Seymour, Duke of Somerset.

Titles 1685 The Queen Consort's Regiment of Dragoons *Also known by Colonels' names until 1751*
1714 3rd King's Own Regiment of Dragoons
1818 3rd King's Own Light Dragoons
1861 3rd King's Own Hussars
1921 3rd The King's Own Hussars
1958 Amalgamated with the 7th Queen's Own Hussars to form The Queen's Own Hussars

Battle honours Dettingen, Salamanca, Vittoria, Toulouse, Peninsula, Cabool 1842, Moodkee, Ferozeshah, Sobraon, Chillianwallah, Goojerat, Punjaub, South Africa 1902.

The Great War—Mons, Le Cateau, Retreat from Mons, Marne 1914, Aisne 1914, Messines 1914, Armentieres 1914, Ypres 1914, 15, Gheluvelt, St. Julien, Bellewaarde, Arras 1917, Scarpe 1917, Cambrai 1917, 18, Somme 1918, St. Quentin, Lys, Hazebrouck, Amiens, Bapaume 1918, Hindenburg Line, Canal du Nord, Selle, Sambre, France and Flanders 1914–18.

The Second World War—Sidi Barrani, Buq Buq, Beda Fomm, Sidi Suleiman, El Alamein, North Africa 1940–42, Citta della Pieve, Citta di Castello, Italy 1944, Crete.

Motto *Nec Aspera Terrent* (Neither do difficulties deter)

Uniform Blue, busby-bag Garter blue

Regimental marches [Slow] *The Third Hussars Slow March* (Anon.)
[Quick] *Robert the Devil* (from opera by Meyerbeer)

Regimental journal *3rd The King's Own Hussars Regimental Journal*

Nickname The Moodkee Wallahs

7th QUEEN'S OWN HUSSARS

Raised December 1690 from independent Troops of Scottish dragoons, command being given to Colonel Richard Cunningham.

Titles 1690 Cunningham's Dragoons *Title subsequently changed with Colonels' names*
1715 The Princess of Wales's Own Royal Regiment of Dragoons
1727 The Queen's Own Royal Regiment of Dragoons
1751 7th (or Queen's Own) Regiment of Dragoons
1783 7th (or Queen's Own) Light Dragoons
1807 7th (or The Queen's Own) Regiment of (Light) Dragoons (Hussars)
1861 7th (The Queen's Own) Regiment of Hussars
1880 7th (Queen's Own) Hussars
1921 7th Queen's Own Hussars
1958 Amalgamated with the 3rd The King's Own Hussars to form The Queen's Own Hussars

Battle honours Dettingen, Warburg, Beaumont, Willems, Orthes, Peninsula, Waterloo, Lucknow, South Africa 1901–02.

The Great War—Khan Baghdadi, Sharqat, Mesopotamia 1917–18.

The Second World War—Egyptian Frontier 1940, Beda Fomm, Sidi Rezegh 1941, North Africa 1940–41, Ancona, Rimini Line, Italy 1944–45, Pegu, Paungde, Burma 1942.

Uniform Blue, busby-bag scarlet

Regimental marches [Slow] *The Garb of Old Gaul* (Reid)
[Quick] *Bannocks o' Barley Meal* (also known as *The Kynegad Slashers*) (Tradit.)

Regimental journal *The Regimental Journal of the 7th (Queen's Own) Hussars*

Nicknames The Saucy Seventh. Strawboots

Remarks Until their amalgamation in 1958, the 7th Hussars were one of only two surviving cavalry regiments to have been raised in Scotland, the other being the Royal Scots Greys.

THE QUEEN'S ROYAL IRISH HUSSARS

Formed October 1958 by amalgamation of the 4th Queen's Own Hussars with the 8th King's Royal Irish Hussars.

Battle honours Dettingen, Leswarree, Hindoostan, Talavera, Albuhera, Salamanca, Vittoria, Toulouse, Peninsula, Ghuznee 1839, Afghanistan 1839, Alma, Balaklava, Inkerman, Sevastopol, Central India, Afghanistan 1879–80, South Africa 1900–02.

The Great War—Mons, Le Cateau, Retreat from Mons, Marne 1914, Aisne 1914, Messines 1914, Armentieres 1914, Ypres 1914, 15, Langemarck 1914, Gheluvelt, Givenchy 1914, St. Julien, Bellewaarde, Somme 1916, 18, Bazentin, Flers-Courcelette, Arras 1917, Scarpe 1917, Cambrai 1917, 18, St. Quentin, Bapaume 1918, Rosieres, Amiens, Albert 1918, Hindenburg Line, Canal du Nord, St. Quentin Canal, Beaurevoir, Pursuit to Mons, France and Flanders 1914–18.

The Second World War—Villers Bocage, Mont Pincon, Dives Crossing, Nederrijn, Best, Lower Maas, Roer, Rhine, North-West Europe 1944–45, Egyptian Frontier 1940, Sidi Barrani, Buq Buq, Sidi Rezegh 1941, Relief of Tobruk, Gazala, Bir el Igela, Mersa Matruh, Defence of Alamein Line, Ruweisat, Alam el Halfa, El Alamein, North Africa 1939–42, Coriano, San Clemente, Senio Pocket, Rimini Line, Conventello-Comacchio, Senio, Santerno Crossing, Argenta Gap, Italy 1944–45, Proasteion, Corinth Canal, Greece 1941.

Seoul, Hill 327, Imjin, Kowang-San, Korea 1950–51.

Motto *Mente et Manu* (With heart and hand)

Uniform Blue

Regimental marches [Slow] *Litany of Loretto* (Anon.)
[Quick] Arrangement of *Berkeley's Dragoons* and *St. Patrick's Day* (Tradit.)

Regimental journal *Cross-Belts*

Home headquarters Regents Park Barracks, Albany Street, London NW1.

Regimental museum Carrickfergus Castle, Carrickfergus, Co. Antrim, N. Ireland.

4th QUEEN'S OWN HUSSARS

Raised July 1685 by Colonel the Hon. John Berkeley from independent troops of dragoons.

Titles 1685 The Princess Anne of Denmark's Regiment of Dragoons *Also known as Berkeley's Dragoons*
1751 4th Dragoons
1788 4th (or Queen's Own) Regiment of Dragoons
1818 4th Regiment of Light Dragoons
1819 4th (or The Queen's Own) Light Dragoons
1861 4th (Queen's Own) Hussars
1921 4th Queen's Own Hussars
1958 Amalgamated with the 8th King's Royal Irish Hussars to form The Queen's Royal Irish Hussars

Battle honours Dettingen, Talavera, Albuhera, Salamanca, Vittoria, Toulouse, Peninsula, Ghuznee 1839, Affghanistan 1839, Alma, Balaklava, Inkerman, Sevastopol.

The Great War—Mons, Le Cateau, Retreat from Mons, Marne 1914, Aisne 1914, Messines 1914, Armentieres 1914, Ypres 1914, 15, Langemarck 1914, Gheluvelt, St. Julien, Bellewaarde, Arras 1917, Scarpe 1917, Cambrai 1917, Somme 1918, Amiens, Hindenburg Line, Canal du Nord, Pursuit to Mons, France and Flanders 1914–18.

The Second World War—Gazala, Defence of Alamein Line, Ruweisat, Alam el Halfa, El Alamein, North Africa 1942, Coriano, San Clemente, Senio Pocket, Rimini Line, Conventello-Comacchio, Senio, Santerno Crossing, Argenta Gap, Italy 1944–45, Proasteion, Corinth Canal, Greece 1941.

Motto *Mente et Manu* (With heart and hand)

Uniform Blue, busby-bag yellow

Regimental marches [Slow] *Litany of Loretto* (Anon.)
[Quick] *Berkeley's Dragoons* (Anon.)

Regimental journal *IV Hussars Journal*

Nickname Paget's Irregular Horse

8th KING'S ROYAL IRISH HUSSARS

Raised February 1693 from Irish Protestants. Command given to Lieut-Colonel Henry Conyngham of the Inniskilling Dragoons.

Titles 1693 Conyngham's (or Cunningham's) Regiment of Irish Dragoons *Title subsequently changed with Colonels' names*
1751 8th Regiment of Dragoons
1775 8th Regiment of Light Dragoons
1777 8th (or The King's Royal Irish) Regiment of Light Dragoons
1822 8th (or The King's Royal Irish) Regiment of Light Dragoons (Hussars)
1861 8th (King's Royal Irish) Hussars
1920 8th King's Royal Irish Hussars
1958 Amalgamated with the 4th Queen's Own Hussars to form The Queen's Royal Irish Hussars

Battle honours Leswaree, Hindoostan, Alma, Balaklava, Inkerman, Sevastopol, Central India, Afghanistan 1879–80, South Africa 1900–02.

The Great War—Givenchy 1914, Somme 1916, 18, Bazentin, Flers-Courcellette, Cambrai 1917, 18, St. Quentin, Bapaume 1918, Rosieres, Amiens, Albert 1918, Hindenburg Line, St. Quentin Canal, Beaurevoir, Pursuit to Mons, France and Flanders 1914–18.

The Second World War—Villers Bocage, Mont Pincon, Dives Crossing, Nederrijn, Best, Lower Maas, Roer, Rhine, North-West Europe 1944–45, Egyptian Frontier 1940, Sidi Barrani, Buq Buq, Sidi Rezegh 1941, Relief of Tobruk, Gazala, Bir el Igela, Mersa Matruh, Alam el Halfa, El Alamein, North Africa 1940–42.

Seoul, Hill 327, Imjin, Kowang-San, Korea 1950–51.

Motto *Pristinae Virtutis Memores* (Mindful of former valour)

Uniform Blue, busby-bag scarlet

Regimental marches [Slow] *Scottish Archers* (Anon.)
[Quick] *St. Patrick's Day* (tradit.)

Regimental journal *Cross-Belts*

Nicknames The Cross-Belts. St. George's. The Twenty-Fives

Remarks In 1710, at Saragossa, the 8th Dragoons captured an entire regiment of Spanish Horse and appropriated their sword-belts, worn over the right shoulder. They took to wearing these instead of the regulation Dragoon waistbelt, and thus with the existing pouch-belt, displayed two belts crossing diagonally over the chest—a fashion normally reserved to regiments of Horse. In recognition of their valour at Saragossa the wearing of the cross-belts was officially authorised. Hence the nickname.

9th/12th ROYAL LANCERS (PRINCE OF WALES'S)

Formed September 1960 by amalgamation of the 9th Queen's Royal Lancers with the 12th Royal Lancers (Prince of Wales's).

Battle honours Egypt (with the Sphinx), Salamanca, Peninsula, Waterloo, Punniar, Sobraon, Chillianwallah, Goojerat, Punjaub, South Africa 1851–53, Sevastopol, Delhi 1857, Central India, Lucknow, Charasiah, Kabul 1879, Kandahar 1880, Afghanistan 1878–80, Modder River, Relief of Kimberley, Paardeberg, South Africa 1899–1902.

The Great War—Mons, Le Cateau, Retreat from Mons, Marne 1914, Aisne 1914, La Bassée 1914, Messines 1914, Armentieres 1914, Ypres 1914, 15, Neuve Chapelle, Gravenstafel, St. Julien, Frezenberg, Bellewaarde, Somme 1916, 18, Pozieres, Flers-

Courcelette, Arras 1917, Scarpe 1917, Cambrai 1917, 18, St. Quentin, Rosieres, Avre, Lys, Hazebrouck, Amiens, Albert 1918, Hindenburg Line, St. Quentin Canal, Beaurevoir, Sambre, Pursuit to Mons, France and Flanders 1914–18.

The Second World War—Dyle, Defence of Arras, Arras Counter Attack, Dunkirk 1940, Somme 1940, Withdrawal to Seine, North-West Europe 1940, Chor es Sufan, Saunnu, Gazala, Bir el Aslagh, Sidi Rezegh 1942, Defence of Alamein Line, Ruweisat, Ruweisat Ridge, Alam el Halfa, El Alamein, Advance on Tripoli, Tebaga Gap, El Hamma, Akarit, El Kourzia, Djebel Kournine, Tunis, Creteville Pass, North Africa 1941–43, Citerna, Gothic Line, Coriano, Capture of Forli, Lamone Crossing, Pideura, Defence of Lamone Bridgehead, Conventello-Comacchio, Argenta Gap, Bologna, Sillaro Crossing, Idice Bridgehead, Italy 1944–45.

Uniform	Blue, facings scarlet
Regimental marches [Slow]	*March of the Men of Harlech* (Tradit.)
[Quick]	*God Bless the Prince of Wales* (Richards)
Regimental journal	*The Delhi Spearman. The Regimental Journal of The 9th/12th Royal Lancers*
Home headquarters	Glen Parva Barracks, Wigston, Leicester LE8 2UX
Regimental museum	Derby Museum & Art Gallery, The Strand, Derby

9th QUEEN'S ROYAL LANCERS

Raised by Maj-General Owen Wynn in July 1715, as regiment of Dragoons.

Titles	1715 Wynn's Dragoons *Title subsequently changed with Colonels' names*
	1751 9th Regiment of Dragoons
	1783 9th Regiment of (Light) Dragoons
	1816 9th Regiment of (Light) Dragoons (Lancers)
	1830 9th (The Queen's Royal) Lancers
	1878 9th (Queen's Royal) Lancers
	1921 9th Queen's Royal Lancers
	1960 Amalgamated with the 12th Royal Lancers (Prince of Wales's) to form 9th/12th Royal Lancers (Prince of Wales's)

Battle honours Peninsula, Punniar, Sobraon, Chillianwallah, Goojerat, Punjaub, Delhi 1857, Lucknow, Charasiah, Kabul 1879, Kandahar 1880, Afghanistan 1878–80, Modder River, Relief of Kimberley, Paardeberg, South Africa 1899–1902.

The Great War—Mons, Le Cateau, Retreat from Mons, Marne 1914, Aisne 1914, La Bassee 1914, Messines 1914, Armentieres 1914, Ypres 1914, 15, Gravenstafel, St. Julien Frezenberg, Bellewaarde, Somme 1916, 18, Pozieres, Flers-Courcelette, Arras 1917, Scarpe 1917, Cambrai 1917, 18, St. Quentin, Rosieres, Avre, Amiens, Albert 1918, Hindenburg Line, Pursuit to Mons, France and Flanders 1914–18.

The Second World War—Somme 1940, Withdrawal to Seine, North-West Europe 1940, Saunnu, Gazala, Bir el Aslagh, Sidi Rezegh 1942, Defence of Alamein Line, Ruweisat, Ruweisat Ridge, El Alamein, Tebaga Gap, El Hamma, El Kourzia, Tunis, Creteville Pass, North Africa 1942–43, Coriano, Capture of Forli, Lamone Crossing, Pideura, Lamone Bridgehead, Argenta Gap, Italy 1944–45.

Uniform Blue, facings scarlet

Regimental marches [Slow] 'Soldiers' Chorus' from *Faust* (Gounod)
[Quick] *March of the Men of Harlech* (Tradit.)

Regimental journal *The Delhi Spearman*

Nickname The Delhi Spearmen

Remarks The 9th Lancers were one of the first three British cavalry regiments to be converted to Lancers, in 1816.

12th ROYAL LANCERS
(PRINCE OF WALES'S)

Raised July 1715 by Colonel Phineas Bowles as a regiment of Dragoons.

Titles 1715 Bowles's Dragoons *Title subsequently changed with Colonels' names*
1751 12th Regiment of Dragoons
1768 12th (or The Prince of Wales's) Regiment of (Light) Dragoons

1816 12th (or The Prince of Wales's) Regiment of Lancers

1817 12th (or The Prince of Wales's) Royal Regiment of Lancers

1856 12th (Prince of Wales's Royal) Lancers

1921 12th Royal Lancers (Prince of Wales's)

1960 Amalgamated with the 9th Queen's Royal Lancers to form 9th/12th Royal Lancers (Prince of Wales's)

Battle honours Salamanca, Peninsula, Waterloo, South Africa 1851–2–3, Sevastopol, Central India, Relief of Kimberley, Paardeberg, South Africa 1899–1902.

The Great War—Mons, Retreat from Mons, Marne 1914, Aisne 1914, Messines 1914, Ypres 1914, 15, Neuve Chapelle, St. Julien, Bellewaarde, Arras 1917, Scarpe 1917, Cambrai 1917, 18, Somme 1918, St. Quentin, Lys, Hazebrouck, Amiens, Albert 1918, Hindenburg Line, St. Quentin Canal, Beaurevoir, Sambre, France and Flanders 1914–18.

The Second World War—Dyle, Defence of Arras, Arras counter attack, Dunkirk 1940, North-West Europe 1940, Chor es Sufan, Gazala, Alam el Halfa, El Alamein, Advance on Tripoli, Tebaga Gap, El Hamma, Akarit, El Kourzia, Djebel Kournine, Tunis, Creteville Pass, North Africa 1941–43, Citerna, Gothic Line, Capture of Forli, Conventello-Comacchio, Bologna, Sillaro Crossing, Idice Bridgehead, Italy 1944–45.

Motto *Ich Dien* (I Serve)

Uniform Blue, facings scarlet

Regimental marches [Slow] *Coburg* (Anon. Attd. to Michael Haydn)
[Quick] *God Bless the Prince of Wales* (Richards)

Regimental journal *The Twelfth Royal Lancers Journal*

Nickname The Supple Twelfth

Remarks The 12th Lancers were one of the first three British cavalry regiments to be converted to Lancers, in 1816. Together with the 11th Hussars they were also the first to be mechanised, converting to armoured cars in 1928.

THE ROYAL HUSSARS
(PRINCE OF WALES'S OWN)

Formed October 1969 by amalgamation of the 10th Royal Hussars (Prince of Wales's Own) with the 11th Hussars (Prince Albert's Own).

Battle honours Warburg, Beaumont, Willems, Egypt (with the Sphinx), Salamanca, Peninsula, Waterloo, Bhurtpore, Alma, Balaklava, Inkerman, Sevastopol, Ali Masjid, Afghanistan 1878–79, Egypt 1884, Relief of Kimberley, Paardeberg, South Africa 1899–1902.

The Great War—Mons, Le Cateau, Retreat from Mons, Marne 1914, Aisne 1914, Messines 1914, Armentieres 1914, Ypres 1914, 15, Langemark 1914, Gheluvelt, Nonne Bosschen, Frezenberg, Bellewaarde, Loos, Somme 1916, 18, Flers-Courcelette, Arras 1917, 18, Scarpe 1917, Cambrai 1917, 18, St. Quentin, Rosieres, Avre, Amiens, Albert 1918, Drocourt-Queant, Hindenburg Line, St. Quentin Canal, Beaurevoir, Cambrai 1918, Selle, Pursuit to Mons, France and Flanders 1914–18.

The Second World War—Somme 1940, Villers Bocage, Bourguebus Ridge, Mont Pincon, Jurques, Dives Crossing, La Vie Crossing, Lisieux, Le Touques Crossing, Risle Crossing, Roer, Rhine, Ibbenburen, Aller, North-West Europe 1940, 44–45, Egyptian Frontier 1940, Withdrawal to Matruh, Bir Enba, Sidi Barrani, Buq Buq, Bardia 1941, Capture of Tobruk, Beda Fomm, Halfaya 1941, Sidi Suleiman, Tobruk 1941, Gubi I, II, Gabr Saleh, Sidi Rezegh 1941, Taieb el Essem, Relief of Tobruk, Saunnu, Msus, Gazala, Bir el Aslagh, Defence of Alamein Line, Alam el Halfa, El Alamein, Advance on Tripoli, El Hamma, Enfidaville, El Kourzia, Djebel Kournine, Tunis, North Africa 1940–43, Capture of Naples, Volturno Crossing, Coriano, Santarcangelo, Cosina Canal Crossing, Senio Pocket, Cesena, Valli di Comacchio, Argenta Gap, Italy 1943–45.

Motto *Ich Dien* (I Serve)

Uniform Blue, trousers crimson, facings crimson

Regimental marches [Slow] *Coburg* (Anon. Attd. to Michael Haydn)
[Quick] *The Merry Month of May* (Tradit.)

Regimental journal *The Royal Hussars Journal*

Home headquarters Lower Barracks, Winchester, Hampshire

Regimental museum Southgate Street, Winchester, Hampshire

10th ROYAL HUSSARS
(PRINCE OF WALES'S OWN)

Raised July 1715 by Brigadier-General Humphrey Gore
as regiment of Dragoons.

Titles 1715 Gore's Regiment of Dragoons *Title subsequently*
changed with Colonels' names
1751 10th Dragoons
1783 10th (or The Prince of Wales's Own) Regiment of
(Light) Dragoons
1806 10th (or The Prince of Wales's Own) Regiment of
Light Dragoons (Hussars)
1811 10th (or The Prince of Wales's Own Royal)
Regiment of Light Dragoons (Hussars)
1860 10th (Prince of Wales's Own Royal) Hussars
1921 10th Royal Hussars (Prince of Wales's Own)
1969 Amalgamated with 11th Hussars (Prince Albert's
Own) to form The Royal Hussars (Prince of Wales's
Own)

Battle honours Warburg, Peninsula, Waterloo, Sevastopol, Ali Masjid,
Afghanistan 1878–79, Egypt 1884, Relief of Kimberley,
Paardeberg, South Africa 1899–1902.

The Great War—Ypres 1914, 15, Langemarck 1914,
Gheluvelt, Nonne Bosschen, Frezenberg, Loos, Arras
1917, 18, Scarpe 1917, Somme 1918, St. Quentin,
Avre, Amiens, Drocourt-Queant, Hindenburg Line,
Beaurevoir, Cambrai 1918, Pursuit to Mons, France and
Flanders 1914–18.

The Second World War—Somme 1940, North-West
Europe 1940, Saunnu, Gazala, Bir el Aslagh, Alam el
Halfa, El Alamein, El Hamma, El Kourzia, Djebel
Kournine, Tunis, North Africa 1942–43, Coriano,
Santarcangelo. Cosina Canal Crossing, Senio Pocket,

Cesena, Valli di Comacchio, Argenta Gap, Italy 1944–45.

Motto	*Ich Dien* (I Serve)
Uniform	Blue, busby-bag scarlet
Regimental marches [Slow]	*God Bless the Prince of Wales* (Richards)
[Quick]	*The Merry Month of May* (Tradit.)
Regimental journal	*The Tenth Royal Hussars Gazette*
Nicknames	The Shiny Tenth. The Chainy Tenth. Baker's Light Bobs
Remarks	The 10th were the first British cavalry regiment to be converted to Hussars, in 1806.

11th HUSSARS
(PRINCE ALBERT'S OWN)

Raised July 1715 by Brigadier-General Philip Honywood as regiment of Dragoons.

Titles 1715 Honywood's Regiment of Dragoons *Title subsequently changed with Colonels' names*
1751 11th Regiment of Dragoons
1783 11th Regiment of (Light) Dragoons
1840 11th (Prince Albert's Own) Hussars
1920 11th Hussars (Prince Albert's Own)
1969 Amalgamated with the 10th Royal Hussars (Prince Of Wales's Own) to form The Royal Hussars (Prince of Wales's Own)

Battle honours Warburg, Beaumont, Willems, Egypt (with the Sphinx), Salamanca, Peninsula, Waterloo, Bhurtpore, Alma, Balaklava, Inkerman, Sevastopol.

The Great War—Mons, Le Cateau, Retreat from Mons, Marne 1914, Aisne 1914, Messines 1914, Armentieres 1914, Ypres 1914, 15, Frezenberg, Bellewaarde, Somme 1916, 18, Flers-Courcelette, Arras 1917, Scarpe 1917, Cambrai 1917, 18, St. Quentin, Rosieres, Amiens, Albert 1918, Hindenburg Line, St. Quentin Canal, Beaurevoir, Selle, France and Flanders 1914–18.

The Second World War—Villers Bocage, Bourguebus Ridge, Mont Pincon, Jurques, Dives Crossing, La Vie Crossing, Lisieux, Le Touques Crossing, Risle Crossing,

Roer, Rhine, Ibbenburen, Aller, North-West Europe 1944–45, Egyptian Frontier 1940, Withdrawal to Matruh, Bir Enba, Sidi Barrani, Buq Buq, Bardia 1941, Capture of Tobruk, Beda Fomm, Halfaya 1941, Sidi Suleiman, Tobruk 1941, Gubi I, II, Gabr Saleh, Sidi Rezegh 1941, Taieb el Essem, Relief of Tobruk, Saunnu, Msus, Defence of Alamein Line, Alam el Halfa, El Alamein, Advance on Tripoli, Enfidaville, Tunis, North Africa, 1940–43, Capture of Naples, Volturno Crossing, Italy 1943.

Motto *Treu und Fest* (Staunch and steadfast).

Uniform Blue, overalls crimson, busby-bag crimson.

Regimental marches [Slow] *Coburg* (Anon. Attd. to Michael Haydn).
[Quick] *Moses in Egypt* (themes from opera by Rossini)

Regimental journal *The 11th Hussars Journal*

Nicknames The Cherrypickers. The Cherubims. Lord Cardigan's Bloodhounds

Remarks The 11th Hussars were unique among light cavalry regiments in wearing crimson overalls, a distinction authorised in 1840 by Queen Victoria, and inherited by the present Regiment. Together with the 12th Royal Lancers they were the first British cavalry to be mechanised, in 1928.

13th/18th ROYAL HUSSARS
(QUEEN MARY'S OWN)

Formed November 1922 by amalgamation of the 13th Hussars with the 18th Royal Hussars (Queen Mary's Own).

Titles 1922 13th/18th Hussars
1935 13th/18th Royal Hussars (Queen Mary's Own)

Battle honours Albuhera, Vittoria, Orthes, Toulouse, Peninsula, Waterloo, Alma, Balaklava, Inkerman, Sevastopol, Defence of Ladysmith, Relief of Ladysmith, South Africa 1899–1902.

The Great War—Mons, Le Cateau, Retreat from Mons, Marne 1914, Aisne 1914, La Bassee 1914, Messines 1914, Armentieres 1914, Ypres 1914, 15, Gravenstafel, St. Julien, Frezenberg, Bellewaarde, Somme 1916, 18, Flers-Courcelette, Arras 1917, Scarpe 1917, Cambrai 1917, 18, St. Quentin, Rosieres, Amiens, Albert 1918, Hindenburg Line, Pursuit to Mons, France and Flanders 1914–18, Kut al Amara 1917, Baghdad, Sharqat, Mesopotamia 1916–18.

The Second World War—Dyle, Withdrawal to Escaut, Ypres-Comines Canal, Normandy Landing, Bretteville, Caen, Bourguebus Ridge, Mont Pincon, St. Pierre la Vielle, Geilenkirchen, Roer, Rhineland, Waal Flats, Goch, Rhine, Bremen, North-West Europe 1940, 44–45.

Motto	*Viret in Aeternum. Pro Rege, Pro Lege, Pro Patria Conamur* (It flourishes for ever. For King, for laws, for country we strive)
Uniform	Blue, facings white
Regimental marches [Slow]	*13th and 18th Hussars*
[Quick]	*Balaklava*
Regimental journal	*13th/18th Journal*
Home headquarters	3/3A Tower Street, York YO1 1SB
Regimental museum	Cannon Hall Museum, Cawthorne, Barnsley, Yorkshire.

13th HUSSARS

Raised July 1715 by Brigadier-General Richard Munden as regiment of Dragoons.

Titles 1715 Munden's Dragoons *Title subsequently changed with Colonels' names*
1751 13th Regiment of Dragoons
1783 13th Regiment of (Light) Dragoons
1862 13th Hussars
1922 Amalgamated with the 18th Royal Hussars (Queen Mary's Own) to form 13th/18th Hussars

Battle honours Albuhera, Vittoria, Orthes, Toulouse, Peninsula, Waterloo, Alma, Balaklava, Inkerman, Sevastopol, Relief of Ladysmith, South Africa 1899–1902.
The Great War—France and Flanders 1914–16. Kut al Amara 1917, Baghdad, Sharqat, Mesopotamia 1916–18.

Motto	*Viret in Aeternum* (It flourishes for ever)
Uniform	Blue, collars buff
Regimental march [Slow]	*The 13th Hussars Slow March*
Nicknames	The Green Dragoons. The Evergreens. The Ragged Brigade. The Geraniums. The Lillywhites

18th ROYAL HUSSARS
(QUEEN MARY'S OWN)

Although the 18th Hussars was raised as such only as late as 1858, the Regiment traces its origins back to 1759 when a regiment of Light Dragoons was raised in Ireland by Charles Moor, 1st Marquess of Drogheda. It was popularly known as the Drogheda Light Horse, but was officially styled the 19th Light Dragoons. In 1766 it was renumbered 18th Light Dragoons, was converted to Hussars in 1807 and disbanded as the 18th Light Dragoons (Hussars) in 1821. The number 18 remained vacant until February 1858 when the 18th Hussars was raised at Leeds, inheriting the Battle Honours and traditions of the former Regiment.

Titles	1759 19th Light Dragoons, or Drogheda Light Horse
	1766 18th Light Dragoons
	1807 18th Light Dragoons (Hussars)
	1821 *Disbanded*
	1858 *Re-raised* as 18th Hussars
	1903 18th (Princess of Wales's) Hussars
	1910 18th (Queen Mary's Own) Hussars
	1919 18th Royal Hussars (Queen Mary's Own)
	1922 Amalgamated with the 13th Hussars to form 13th/18th Hussars

Battle honours Peninsula, Waterloo, Defence of Ladysmith, South Africa 1899–1902.

The Great War—Mons, Le Cateau, Retreat from Mons, Marne 1914, Aisne 1914, La Bassee 1914, Messines 1914, Armentieres 1914, Ypres 1914, 15, Gravenstafel, St. Julien, Frezenberg, Bellewaarde, Somme 1916, 18, Flers-Courcellette, Arras 1917, Scarpe 1917, Cambrai 1917, 18, St. Quentin, Rosieres, Amiens, Albert 1918, Hindenburg Line, Pursuit to Mons, France and Flanders 1914–18.

Motto   *Pro Rege, Pro Lege, Pro Patria Conamur* (For King, for laws, for country we strive)

Uniform   Blue, busby-bag blue

Regimental march [Slow]   *18th Hussars Slow March*

14th/20th KING'S HUSSARS

Formed April 1922 by amalgamation of the 14th King's Hussars with the 20th Hussars.

Titles   1922 14th/20th Hussars
       1936 14th/20th King's Hussars

Battle honours   Vimiera, Douro, Talavera, Fuentes d'Onor, Salamanca, Vittoria, Pyrenees, Orthes, Peninsula, Chillianwallah, Goojerat, Punjaub, Persia, Central India, Suakin 1885, Relief of Ladysmith, South Africa 1900–02.

The Great War—Mons, Retreat from Mons, Marne 1914, Aisne 1914, Messines 1914, Ypres 1914, 15, Neuve Chapelle, St. Julien, Bellewaarde, Arras 1917, Scarpe 1917, Cambrai 1917, 18, Somme 1918, St. Quentin, Lys, Hazebrouck, Amiens, Albert 1918, Bapaume 1918, Hindenburg Line, St. Quentin Canal, Beaurevoir, Sambre, France and Flanders 1914–18, Tigris 1916, Kut al Amara 1917, Baghdad, Mesopotamia 1915–18, Persia 1918.

The Second World War—Bologna, Medicina, Italy 1945.

Uniform   Blue, facings yellow

Regimental marches [Slow]   *The Eagle*
          [Quick]   *Royal Sussex*

Regimental journal   *The Hawk*

Home headquarters   Fulwood Barracks, Fulwood, Preston, Lancashire PR2 4AA

Regimental museum   Queen's Park Museum & Art Gallery, Queen's Park, Rochdale Road, Manchester.

Nickname   The Emperor's Chambermaids

Remarks The Regiment's Prussian Eagle Badge is inherited from
the 14th King's Hussars who were granted it in 1798
when they were given the subsidiary title 'Duchess of
York's Own'. The Duchess was Princess Frederica
Charlotte of Prussia who married the Duke of York, and
the Badge commemorated the connection with the
Prussian Royal House. Its use was dropped during the
1914–18 War but was resumed in 1931.

14th KING'S HUSSARS

Raised July 1715 by Brigadier-General James Dormer as
regiment of Dragoons.

Titles 1715 Dormer's Dragoons *Title subsequently changed with
Colonels' names*
1751 14th Regiment of Dragoons
1776 14th Regiment of (Light) Dragoons
1798 14th (or The Duchess of York's Own) Regiment of
(Light) Dragoons
1830 14th (The King's) Regiment of Light Dragoons
1861 14th (King's) Hussars
1921 14th King's Hussars
1922 Amalgamated with the 20th Hussars to form 14th/
20th Hussars

Battle honours Douro, Talavera, Fuentes d'Onor, Salamanca, Vittoria,
Pyrenees, Orthes, Peninsula, Chillianwallah, Goojerat,
Punjaub, Persia, Central India, Relief of Ladysmith,
South Africa 1900–02.

The Great War—Tigris 1916, Kut al Amara 1917,
Baghdad, Mesopotamia 1915–18, Persia 1918.

Uniform Blue, busby-bag yellow

Regimental march [Slow] *King of Prussia*

Nicknames The Emperor's Chambermaids. The Ramnuggur Boys

Remarks See above for the Prussian Eagle Badge. The singular
nickname 'Emperor's Chambermaids' was acquired after
the Battle of Vittoria (1813), when the 14th captured
King Joseph Buonaparte's coach and with it what was
described as 'a silver utensil', ie, His Majesty's chamber-
pot, which has ever since been preserved in the Mess and
does duty as a 'loving cup' on special occasions.

20th HUSSARS

Four cavalry regiments of the British Army have borne the number 20. The first was raised in Ireland in 1759, from the Light Troop of the 6th Inniskilling Dragoons, and was known as the 20th Light Inniskilling Dragoons. It was disbanded in 1763.

The second was the 20th Light Dragoons, raised in 1779 and disbanded in 1783.

The third was raised in 1791 for special service in Jamaica and titled 20th Jamaica Light Dragoons. The title 'Jamaica' was dropped in 1802 and the Regiment was disbanded as the 20th Light Dragoons in 1819.

The Regiment which finally emerged as the 20th Hussars originated as the Hon. East India Company's 2nd Bengal European Light Cavalry which had been raised in England in 1857 as reinforcements for the British forces during the Indian Mutiny. After the abolition of the Company and transfer of the Government of India to the Crown, the 2nd Bengal European Light Cavalry was transferred to the British service as the 20th Light Dragoons. It inherited the Battle Honours of the old Jamaica Light Dragoons.

Titles	1857 2nd Bengal European Light Cavalry (H.E.I.C.)
	1861 20th Light Dragoons
	1862 20th Hussars
	1922 Amalgamated with the 14th King's Hussars to form 14th/20th Hussars
Battle honours	Vimiera, Peninsula, Suakin 1885, South Africa 1901–2.
	The Great War—Mons, Retreat from Mons, Marne 1914, Aisne 1914, Messines 1914, Ypres 1914, 15, Neuve Chapelle, St. Julien, Bellewaarde, Arras 1917, Scarpe 1917, Cambrai 1917, 18, Somme 1918, St. Quentin, Lys, Hazebrouck, Amiens, Albert 1918, Bapaume 1918, Hindenburg Line, St. Quentin Canal, Beaurevoir, Sambre, France and Flanders 1914–18.
Uniform	Blue, busby-bag crimson
Regimental journal	*The Yellow Plume*
Nicknames	The Xs. Nobody's Own

15th/19th THE KING'S ROYAL HUSSARS

Formed April 1922 by amalgamation of the 15th The King's Hussars with the 19th Royal Hussars (Queen Alexandra's Own).

Titles
1922 15th/19th Hussars
1932 15th The King's Royal Hussars
1933 15th/19th The King's Royal Hussars

Battle honours
Emsdorff, Mysore, Villers-en-Cauchies, Willems, Seringapatam, Egmont-op-Zee, Assaye (with the Elephant), Sahagun, Vittoria, Niagara, Peninsula, Waterloo, Afghanistan 1870–80, Tel-el-Kebir, Egypt 1882–84, Nile 1884–85, Abu Klea, Defence of Ladysmith, South Africa 1899–1902.

The Great War—Mons, Le Cateau, Retreat from Mons, Marne 1914, Aisne 1914, Armentieres 1914, Ypres 1914, 15, Langemarck 1914, Gheluvelt, Nonne Bosschen, Frezenberg, Bellewaarde, Somme 1916, 18, Flers-Courcelette, Cambrai 1917, 18, St. Quentin, Rosieres, Amiens, Albert 1918, Bapaume 1918, Hindenburg Line, St. Quentin Canal, Beaurevoir, Pursuit to Mons, France and Flanders 1914–18.

The Second World War—Withdrawal to Escaut, Seine 1944, Hechtel, Nederrijn, Venraij, Rhineland, Hochwald, Rhine, Ibbenburen, Aller, North-West Europe 1940, 44–45.

Motto *Merebimur* (We shall be worthy)

Uniform Blue, facings scarlet

Regimental marches [Slow] Arrangement of *Eliott's Light Horse* and *Denmark*
[Quick] Arrangement of *The Bold King's Hussar* and *Haste to the Wedding*

Regimental journal *15th/19th The King's Royal Hussars*

Home headquarters Fenham Barracks, Barrack Road, Newcastle-upon-Tyne NE2 4NP

Regimental museum John George Joicey Museum, City Road, Newcastle-upon-Tyne

Remarks The 15th/19th are the only cavalry regiment to bear the Battle Honour *Assaye* gained by their predecessors the 19th Light Dragoons in India in 1803.

15th THE KING'S HUSSARS

Raised London, March 1759, by Colonel George Augustus Eliott (1st Lord Heathfield) as regiment of Light Dragoons.

Titles 1759 15th Light Dragoons *Also known as Eliott's Light Horse*
1766 1st* (or The King's Royal) Light Dragoons
1769 15th (or The King's) Light Dragoons
1807 15th (or The King's) Light Dragoons (Hussars)
1861 15th (King's) Hussars
1901 15th (The King's) Hussars
1921 15th The King's Hussars
1922 Amalgamated with 19th Royal Hussars (Queen Alexandra's Own) to form 15th/19th Hussars

Battle honours Emsdorff, Villers-en-Cauchies, Willems, Egmont-op-Zee, Sahagun, Vittoria, Peninsula, Waterloo, Afghanistan 1878–80.

The Great War—Mons, Retreat from Mons, Marne 1914, Aisne 1914, Ypres 1914, 15, Langemarck 1914, Gheluvelt, Nonne Bosschen, Frezenberg, Bellewaarde, Somme 1916, 18, Flers-Courcelette, Cambrai 1917, 18, St. Quentin, Rosieres, Amiens, Albert 1918, Bapaume 1918, Hindenburg Line, St. Quentin Canal, Beaurevoir, Pursuit to Mons, France and Flanders 1914–18.

Motto *Merebimur* (We shall be worthy)

Uniform Blue, busby-bag scarlet

Regimental marches [Slow] *Eliott's Light Horse*
[Quick] *The Bold King's Hussar*

Nicknames Eliott's Tailors. The Tabs. Fighting Fifteenth

Remarks The 15th was the first regiment of Light Cavalry to be raised in the British Army.

---

*The recently-formed regiments of Light Cavalry were then numbered separately from the rest of the cavalry.

19th ROYAL HUSSARS
(QUEEN ALEXANDRA'S OWN)

Four regiments of British cavalry have borne the number 19, as under.

1 19th Light Dragoons or Drogheda Light Horse, raised 1759, renumbered 18th in 1766 and disbanded, as Hussars in 1821 (*see* 13th/18th Hussars).

2 19th Light Dragoons raised 1779 and disbanded 1783.

3 23rd Light Dragoons raised 1781, renumbered 19th in 1786. Converted to Lancers in 1817 and disbanded 1821.

4 19th Royal Hussars (Queen Alexandra's Own). The Regiment was formed in 1861 from the 1st Bengal. European Light Cavalry of the defunct East India Company. It was permitted to inherit the Honours of the disbanded 19th Lancers.

Titles	1857 1st Bengal European Light Cavalry (H.E.I.C.)
	1861 19th Hussars
	1885 19th (Princess of Wales's Own) Hussars
	1902 19th (Alexandra Princess of Wales's Own) Hussars
	1908 19th (Queen Alexandra's Own Royal) Hussars
	1921 19th Royal Hussars (Queen Alexandra's Own)
	1922 Amalgamated with 15th The King's Hussars to form 15th/19th Hussars

Battle honours Seringapatam, Mysore, Assaye (with the Elephant), Niagara, Tel-el-Kebir, Egypt 1882–84, Abu Klea, Nile 1884–85, Defence of Ladysmith, South Africa 1899–1902.

The Great War—Le Cateau, Retreat from Mons, Marne 1914, Aisne 1914, Armentieres 1914, Ypres 1915, Frezenberg, Bellewaarde, Somme 1916, 18, Flers-Courcelette, Cambrai 1917, 18, St. Quentin, Rosieres, Amiens, Albert 1918, Bapaume 1918, Hindenburg Line, St. Quentin Canal, Beaurevoir, Pursuit to Mons, France and Flanders 1914–18.

Uniform Blue, busby-bag white

Regimental marches [Slow] *Denmark*
[Quick] *Haste to the Wedding*

Nickname The Dumpies

16th/5th THE QUEEN'S ROYAL LANCERS *

Formed April 1922 by amalgamation of 16th The Queen's Lancers with 5th Royal Irish Lancers.

Titles 1922 16th/5th Lancers
1954 16th/5th The Queen's Royal Lancers

Battle honours Blenheim, Ramillies, Oudenarde, Malplaquet, Beaumont, Willems, Talavera, Fuentes d'Onor, Salamanca, Vittoria, Nive, Peninsula, Waterloo, Bhurtpore, Ghuznee 1839, Affghanistan 1839, Maharajpore, Aliwal, Sobraon, Suakin 1885, Defence of Ladysmith, Relief of Kimberley, Paardeberg, South Africa 1899–1902.

The Great War—Mons, Le Cateau, Retreat from Mons, Marne 1914, Aisne 1914, Messines 1914, Armentieres 1914, Ypres 1914, 15, Gheluvelt, St. Julien, Bellewaarde, Arras 1917, Scarpe 1917, Cambrai 1917, Somme 1918, St. Quentin, Amiens, Hindenburg Line, Canal du Nord, Pursuit to Mons, France and Flanders 1914–18.

The Second World War—Kasserine, Fondouk, Kairouan, Bordj, Djebel Kournine, Tunis, Gromballa, Bou Ficha, North Africa 1942–43, Cassino II, Liri Valley, Monte Piccolo, Capture of Perugia, Arezzo, Advance to Florence, Argenta Gap, Traghetto, Italy 1944–45.

Motto *Aut Cursu, aut Cominus Armis* (Either in the charge or hand to hand)

Uniform Blue, facings blue

Regimental marches [Slow] *The Queen Charlotte* (arr. Noble)
[Quick] *Scarlet and Green* (arr. Noble)

Regimental journal *The Scarlet and Green*

---

*The exceptional reversed order of seniority in the numbering resulted from the fact that the 5th Lancers as such were raised only in 1858, whereas the 16th had an unbroken record of service from 1759.

Home headquarters Kitchener House, Lammascote Road, Stafford ST16 3TA

Regimental museum As above

Nickname The Scarlet Lancers

16th THE QUEEN'S LANCERS

Raised August 1759 by Colonel John Burgoyne as regiment of Light Dragoons.

Titles 1759 16th Regiment of (Light) Dragoons *Also known as Burgoyne's Light Horse*

1766 2nd* (or The Queen's) Regiment of (Light) Dragoons

1769 16th (or The Queen's) Regiment of Light Dragoons

1816 16th (or The Queen's) Regiment of Light Dragoons (Lancers)

1855 16th (Queen's) Lancers

1919 16th (The Queen's) Lancers

1921 16th The Queen's Lancers

1922 Amalgamated with 5th Royal Irish Lancers to form 16th/5th Lancers

Battle honours Beaumont, Willems, Talavera, Fuentes d'Onor, Salamanca, Vittoria, Nive, Peninsula, Waterloo, Bhurtpore, Ghuznee 1839, Affghanistan 1839, Maharajpore, Aliwal, Sobraon, Relief of Kimberley, Paardeberg, South Africa 1900–02.

The Great War—Mons, Le Cateau, Retreat from Mons, Marne 1914, Aisne 1914, Messines 1914, Armentieres 1914, Ypres 1914, 15, Gheluvelt, St. Julien, Bellewaarde, Arras 1917, Scarpe 1917, Cambrai 1917, Somme 1918, Amiens, Hindenburg Line, Canal du Nord, Pursuit to Mons, France and Flanders 1914–18.

Motto *Aut Cursu, aut Cominus Armis* (Either in the charge or hand to hand)

Uniform Scarlet, facings blue

Regimental marches [Slow] *The 16th Lancers Slow March*
[Quick] *The English Patrol*

---

*The newly-raised regiments of Light Dragoons were then numbered separately from the rest of the cavalry.

Nickname The Scarlet Lancers

Remarks In 1846 all Lancer regiments were ordered to change from scarlet to blue uniforms, but the 16th evaded the order and retained their distinctive scarlet down to amalgamation. Hence the nickname.

5th ROYAL IRISH LANCERS

This Regiment was raised in 1858, but it inherited the Number and the Honours (though not the seniority) of the 5th (Royal Irish) Dragoons which had been disbanded in 1799.

Titles 1689 Wynne's Regiment of Enniskillen Dragoons *Title subsequently changed with Colonels' names*
1704 The Royal Dragoons of Ireland
1751 5th (or Royal Irish) Regiment of Dragoons
1799 *Disbanded*
1858 *Re-raised* as 5th (Royal Irish) Dragoons
1861 5th (Royal Irish) Lancers
1921 5th Royal Irish Lancers
1922 Amalgamated with 16th The Queen's Lancers to form 16th/5th Lancers

Battle honours Blenheim, Ramillies, Oudenarde, Malplaquet, Suakin 1885, Defence of Ladysmith, South Africa 1899–1902.

The Great War—Mons, Le Cateau, Retreat from Mons, Marne 1914, Aisne 1914, Messines 1914, Ypres 1914, 15, Gheluvelt, St. Julien, Bellewaarde, Arras 1917, Scarpe 1917, Cambrai 1917, Somme 1918, St. Quentin, Amiens, Hindenburg Line, Canal du Nord, Pursuit to Mons, France and Flanders 1914–18.

Motto *Quis Separabit* (Who shall separate?)

Uniform Blue, facings scarlet

Regimental marches [Slow] *Let Erin Remember* and *The Harp that once through Tara's Halls*
[Quick] *St. Patrick's Day*

Nicknames The Irish Lancers. The Redbreasts

17th/21st LANCERS

Formed April 1922 by amalgamation of the 17th Lancers (Duke of Cambridge's Own) with the 21st Lancers (Empress of India's).

Battle honours Alma, Balaklava, Inkerman, Sevastopol, Central India, South Africa 1879, Khartoum, South Africa 1900–02.

The Great War—Festubert 1914, Somme 1916, 18, Morval, Cambrai 1917, 18, St. Quentin, Avre, Lys, Hazebrouck, Amiens, Hindenburg Line, St. Quentin Canal, Beaurevoir, Pursuit to Mons, France and Flanders 1914–18, N.W. Frontier India 1915, 16.

The Second World War—Tebourba Gap, Bou Arada, Kasserine, Thala, Fondouk, El Kourzia, Tunis, Hammam Lif, North Africa 1942–43, Cassino II, Monte Piccolo, Capture of Perugia, Advance to Florence, Argenta Gap, Fossa Cembalina, Italy 1944–45.

Motto Or Glory

Uniform Dark blue, facings white

Regimental marches [Slow] *Rienzi* (Wagner)
[Quick] *The White Lancer* (Richardson)

Regimental journal *The White Lancer and The Vedette*

Home headquarters Prince William of Gloucester Barracks, Grantham, Lincolnshire NG31 7TJ.

Regimental museum Belvoir Castle, Nr. Grantham, Lincolnshire.

Nicknames The Death or Glory Boys. The Tots

17th LANCERS
(DUKE OF CAMBRIDGE'S OWN)

The first cavalry regiment to bear the number 17 was the 17th (Edinburgh) Light Dragoons, raised in 1759. This was short-lived, being disbanded in 1763. The Regiment which became the 17th Lancers was raised as Light Dragoons in November 1759, by Lieut-Colonel John Hale, and bore the number 18.

Titles	1759 18th Regiment of (Light) Dragoons
	1763 17th Regiment of (Light) Dragoons
	1766 2nd Regiment of (Light) Dragoons
	1769 17th Regiment of (Light) Dragoons
	1823 17th Regiment of (Light) Dragoons (Lancers)
	1853 17th (Light) Dragoons (Lancers)
	1876 17th (Duke of Cambridge's Own) Lancers
	1921 17th Lancers (Duke of Cambridge's Own)
	1922 Amalgamated with 21st Lancers (Empress of India's) to form 17th/21st Lancers
Battle honours	Alma, Balaklava, Inkerman, Sevastopol, Central India, South Africa 1879, South Africa 1900–02.
	The Great War—Festubert 1914, Somme 1916, 18, Morval, Cambrai 1917, 18, St. Quentin, Avre, Lys, Hazebrouck, Amiens, Hindenburg Line, St. Quentin Canal, Beaurevoir, Pursuit to Mons, France and Flanders 1914–18.
Motto	Or Glory
Uniform	Dark blue, facings white
Regimental marches [Slow]	*Occasional Overture* (Handel)
[Quick]	*The White Lancer* (Richardson)
Regimental journal	*The White Lancer*
Nicknames	Death or Glory Boys. Bingham's Dandies. The Horse Marines. The Tots
Remarks	The Death's Head Badge (always termed 'Motto' in the Regiment) dates from 1759, having been devised by the founding Colonel, John Hale. It has always been unique in the British Army.

21st LANCERS
(EMPRESS OF INDIA'S)

Four British cavalry regiments have been numbered 21:

1 21st (Granby's) Light Dragoons, or Royal Foresters, raised by the Marquis of Granby in 1760 and disbanded 1763.
2 21st Light Dragoons, raised 1779 and disbanded 1783.
3 21st Light Dragoons, raised 1794 and disbanded 1819.
4 21st Lancers (Empress of India's). This Regiment was one of the three regiments of Light Cavalry formed from the Bengal European Light Cavalry of the East

India Company on the abolition of that Company in 1858. The Regiment was formed from the 3rd Bengal European Cavalry, and was the last to be converted to Lancers, in 1897.

Titles 1857 3rd Bengal European Light Cavalry (H.E.I.C)
1858 21st Light Dragoons
1863 21st Hussars
1897 21st Lancers
1899 21st (Empress of India's) Lancers
1921 21st Lancers (Empress of India's)
1922 Amalgamated with the 17th Lancers (Duke of Cambridge's Own) to form 17th/21st Lancers

Battle honours Khartoum, N.W. Frontier India 1915, 16.

Uniform Dark blue, facings French grey

Regimental marches [Slow] *Coburg* (Anon. Attd. to Michael Haydn)
[Quick] *The Merry Month of May* (Tradit.)

Regimental journal *The Vedette*

Nicknames The Grey Lancers. The Dumpies

Remarks The 21st were the only cavalry regiment to bear the Honour *Khartoum*. In their celebrated charge at the battle of Omdurman (1898) one of their Troops was commanded by the youthful Winston Churchill, attached from the 4th Hussars. The title 'Empress of India's' was personally awarded by Queen Victoria in recognition of the Regiment's valour at Omdurman.

ROYAL TANK REGIMENT

Formed 28th July 1917 from Heavy Branch, Machine Gun Corps.

Titles 1916 (Feb.) Heavy Section, Machine Gun Corps
(Nov.) Heavy Branch, Machine Gun Corps
1917 The Tank Corps
1923 Royal Tank Corps
1939 Royal Tank Regiment
(Renamed 'Regiment' on being deployed with the

mechanised cavalry in the newly-formed Royal
Armoured Corps.)

Battle honours *The Great War*—Somme 1916, 18, Arras 1917, 18,
Messines 1917, Ypres 1917, Cambrai 1917, St. Quentin
1918, Villers Bretonneux, Amiens, Bapaume 1918,
Hindenburg Line, Epehy, Selle, France and Flanders
1916–18, Gaza.

The Second World War—Arras counter attack, Calais
1940, St. Omer-La Bassee, Somme 1940, Odon, Caen,
Bourguebus Ridge, Mont Pincon, Falaise, Nederrijn,
Scheldt, Venlo Pocket, Rhineland, Rhine, Bremen,
North-West Europe 1940, 44–45. Abyssinia 1940. Sidi
Barrani, Beda Fomm, Sidi Suleiman, Tobruk 1941,
Sidi Rezegh 1941, Belhamed, Gazala, Cauldron,
Knightsbridge, Defence of Alamein Line, Alam el Halfa,
El Alamein, Mareth, Akarit, Fondouk, El Kourzia,
Medjez Plain, Tunis, North Africa 1940–43, Primosole
Bridge, Gerbini, Adrano, Sicily 1943, Sangro, Salerno,
Volturno Crossing, Garigliano Crossing, Anzio, Advance
to Florence, Gothic Line, Coriano, Lamone Crossing,
Rimini Line, Argenta Gap, Italy 1943–45, Greece 1941,
Burma 1942.

Korea 1951–53.

Motto Fear Naught

Uniform Blue, facings black. The service dress of black beret and
black tank overalls is the exclusive prerogative of the
Regiment.

Regimental marches [Quick] *My Boy Willie* (Tradit.)
[Slow] *Royal Tank Regiment*

Regimental journal *The Tank*

Regimental headquarters 1, Elverton Street, Horseferry Road, London SW1P 2QJ

Regimental museum The Tank Museum, Bovington Camp, Wareham, Dorset
BH20 6JG

Remarks The first great tank attack in history was mounted by the
Tank Corps on 20th November 1917, when 378 massed
tanks smashed through the Hindenburg Line at Cambrai,
contributing largely to the initial success of that offensive.
'Cambrai Day' is still celebrated annually by the
Regiment.

The Regimental colours of brown, red and green
originated with the makeshift flag flown by Maj-General
Elles on his command tank at Cambrai. He had the flag

made up from the only coloured silks he could find in a local draper's shop, and they were held to exemplify the early struggles of the Tank Corps: 'Through mud, through blood to the green fields beyond'.

ROYAL REGIMENT OF ARTILLERY

Prior to 1716 there was no permanent body of artillery in the British Army. When guns were required for a campaign it was necessary for a 'Train' of artillery to be authorised by Royal Warrant, and this was disbanded on the cessation of hostilities. Such *ad hoc* arrangements led to much confusion and delay when artillery was demanded at short notice. Matters came to a head during the Jacobite rebellion of 1715, when the formalities of authorising and organising a Train of Artillery were so protracted that the rebellion was over before the guns could take the field.

It was thus at last resolved that a permanent force of artillery should be raised on a regimental basis, and by Royal Warrant of George I dated 26th May 1716, two companies of field artillery were formed at Woolwich.

Although these were the true nucleus of the present Regiment, it was not until 1st April 1722 that they were grouped with other independent Trains at Gibraltar and Minorca to form a regiment with the title Royal Regiment of Artillery.

The Regiment was greatly expanded during the 18th century, and in February 1793 the first two Troops (later Batteries) of Royal Horse Artillery were raised, to give mobile fire-support to the cavalry. By the middle of the 19th century the Regiment could deploy 29 batteries of Horse Artillery, 73 field batteries and 88 garrison batteries.

Until 1855 the Royal Regiment of Artillery, like the Corps of Royal Engineers, was quite separate from the rest of the Army, being under the control of the Board of Ordnance, not the War Office. In May of that year however, the Board was abolished, and Royal Artillery and Royal Engineers conformed with cavalry and infantry, coming directly under the Commander-in-Chief and War Office.

In 1899 the Royal Artillery underwent a reorganisation when a Royal Warrant established two separate branches: Royal Horse and Royal Field Artillery, and Royal Garrison Artillery. The latter manned Coast Defence batteries, heavy and siege batteries and Mountain batteries. This organisation lasted until 1924, when the titles 'Royal Field' and 'Royal Garrison' were abolished, and the Regiment became a single corps—although the Royal Horse Artillery retained its title, and its separate cypher Badge.

In 1945 King George VI demanded the reforming of a mounted battery of Royal Horse Artillery at St. John's Wood, London, to perform the ceremonial duties carried out by such batteries stationed there before the War. This unit was formed early the following year and was titled The Riding Troop, RHA. In October 1947 the King visited the Troop and personally altered the title to 'The King's Troop', which has now become familiar to the public, at home and overseas. Among its other duties, The King's Troop is responsible for firing salutes on Royal birthdays and other State occasions.

Battle honours The Royal Regiment of Artillery has never carried Colours—its guns are regarded as its 'Colours'—and thus it does not display Battle Honours. Indeed it would be impractical for it to do so, for units of the Regiment have served in every campaign fought by the British Army. The Motto *Ubique* which signifies the single, all-embracing Battle Honour 'Everywhere', was authorised in 1833.

Mottoes *Ubique* (Everywhere)
Quo Fas et Gloria Ducunt (Whither Right and Glory lead)

Uniform Blue, facings scarlet

Regimental marches [Slow] *Royal Artillery Slow March* (Also known as *The Duchess of Kent's March*)

[Quick] Arrangement of *The British Grenadiers* (tradit.) and *Voice of the Guns* (Alford)

Regimental journals *The Journal of the Royal Artillery*
Gunner

Regimental headquarters Government House, New Road, Woolwich, London SE18 6XR

Regimental museums   Old Royal Military Academy, Woolwich, London SE18 4JJ
Museum of Artillery (The Rotunda), Repository Road, Woolwich, London SE18

Nicknames   (Royal Horse Artillery) Right of the Line. Four-wheeled Hussars. Galloping Gunners
(Royal Artillery) The Gunners

Remarks   When on parade with their guns, the Royal Horse Artillery take the right of the line and march at the head of all other regiments, including the Household Cavalry. This privilege was confirmed by Queen Victoria in 1869.

Since 1925 'Honour Titles' have been granted to certain RHA and RA Batteries to commemorate distinguished actions or celebrated commanders.

The impressive *Royal Artillery Slow March* is claimed to have been composed by Princess Victoria Mary Louisa, Duchess of Kent (mother of Queen Victoria).

CORPS OF ROYAL ENGINEERS

This Corps traces its origins to the early days of the Ordnance Office (later Board) in the 16th century, when military engineers were employed by the King for duty in the Royal arsenals and fortifications, and for the maintenance of warlike stores. When engineer tradesmen and specialists were required for a campaign they were impressed, and then disbanded on the cessation of hostilities.

In 1716 a permanent officer corps of engineers was established by the Board of Ordnance, with the title Corps of Engineers. The 'Royal' prefix was granted in 1787. A separate Corps of Royal Military Artificers was formed in 1787, consisting only of non-commissioned ranks, with officers attached from the other Corps. In 1813 the title of the Artificers Corps was changed to Royal Sappers and Miners, thus originating the nickname by which the Royal Engineers became familiarly known.

With the abolition of the Board of Ordnance in 1855, the two Corps came directly under the War Office, and finally the anomaly of maintaining one Engineer Corps of officers and another of soldiers was rectified when in 1856 the Corps of Royal Sappers and Miners was absorbed in the Corps of Royal Engineers, the latter title continuing unchanged.

Both the Royal Air Force and the Royal Corps of Signals (q.v.) had their origins in the Royal Engineers. From 1862 to 1912 the RE were responsible for military aviation, first with observation balloons, then aircraft. This role was relinquished on the formation of the Royal Flying Corps in 1912. Similarly, all army signalling and communications were handled by the RE until the formation of the Royal Corps of Signals in 1920.

Battle honours Like the Royal Artillery, whose Mottoes they share, the Royal Engineers have never carried Colours and do not display Battle Honours. The Motto *Ubique* signifies service in practically every campaign fought by the British Army.

Mottoes *Ubique* (Everywhere)
Quo Fas et Gloria Ducunt (Whither Right and Glory lead)

Uniform Blue, piping scarlet, facings blue

Regimental march [Quick] *Wings*

Regimental journals *The Royal Engineers Journal*
The Sapper

Regimental headquarters Brompton Barracks, Chatham, Kent ME4 4UG

Corps museum As above

Nicknames The Sappers. The Mudlarks

ROYAL CORPS OF SIGNALS

Formed as the Corps of Signals in June 1920, from the Royal Engineers Signal Service. Granted the 'Royal' prefix in August 1920.

The early history of Army signalling and

communications is largely that of the Royal Engineers. The electric telegraph was first used by the Army during the Crimean War, and in 1870 a Telegraph Troop RE was formed. After the invention of the Bell telephone in 1876, RE officers devised their own version, which was extensively used during the Afghan War of 1879–80. From 1908 all Army communications were co-ordinated under the Royal Engineers Signal Service, formed that year.

During the Great War this branch served in every theatre, employing every means of communication, from despatch riders, carrier pigeons and dogs, to the recently invented wireless. By 1920 it was realised that signals had become too specialised to remain the responsibility of the Royal Engineers with all their own multifarious duties, and the separate Royal Corps of Signals was established.

Motto	*Certa Cito* (Swift and sure)
Uniform	Blue, piping scarlet, facings black
Regimental marches [Quick]	*The Royal Signals March* (based on traditional airs *Begone Dull Care* and *Newcastle*)
[Slow]	*The Royal Signals Slow March, Her Royal Highness The Princess Royal* (R. R. Ricketts)
Regimental journals	*The Royal Signals Journal* *The Wire*
Corps headquarters	Cheltenham Terrace, Chelsea, London SW3 4RH
Corps museum	Royal Signals Museum, Blandford Camp, Dorset DT11 8RH

GRENADIER GUARDS

The First or Grenadier Regiment of Foot Guards originated in 1656, when the exiled King Charles II raised a regiment of Guards for his personal protection, giving the command to Colonel Lord Wentworth. Recruited from loyal men who had followed their King into exile, it was styled The Royal Regiment of Guards. After King Charles's restoration another regiment, The

King's Own Regiment of Foot Guards, was raised in November 1660 under Colonel John Russell. Following Lord Wentworth's death, in 1665, the two were combined to form The Royal Regiment of Foot Guards.

Titles 1656 Royal Regiment of Guards
1660 The King's Own Regiment of Foot Guards
1665 Royal Regiment of Foot Guards
1685 First Regiment of Foot Guards
1815 First or Grenadier Regiment of Foot Guards
1877 Grenadier Guards

Battle honours Tangier 1680, Namur 1695, Gibraltar 1704–5, Blenheim, Ramillies, Oudenarde, Malplaquet, Dettingen, Lincelles, Egmont-op-Zee, Corunna, Barrosa, Nive, Peninsula, Waterloo, Alma, Inkerman, Sevastopol, Tel-el-Kebir, Egypt 1882, Suakin 1885, Khartoum, Modder River, South Africa 1899–1902.

The Great War—Mons, Retreat from Mons, Marne 1914, Aisne 1914, Ypres 1914, 17, Langemarck 1914, Gheluvelt, Nonne Bosschen, Neuve Chapelle, Aubers, Festubert 1915, Loos, Somme 1916, 18, Ginchy, Flers-Courcelette, Morval, Pilckem, Menin Road, Poelcappelle, Passchendaele, Cambrai 1917, 18, St. Quentin, Bapaume 1918, Arras 1918, Lys, Hazebrouck, Albert 1918, Scarpe 1918, Hindenburg Line, Havrincourt, Canal du Nord, Selle, Sambre, France and Flanders 1914–18.

The Second World War—Dyle, Dunkirk 1940, Cagny, Mont Pincon, Nijmegen, Reichswald, Rhine, North-West Europe 1940, 44–45, Mareth, Medjez Plain, North Africa 1942–43, Salerno, Volturno Crossing, Monte Camino, Anzio, Gothic Line, Battaglia, Italy 1943–45.

Motto *Honi Soit Qui Mal y Pense* (Motto of the Garter) (Evil to him who evil thinks)

Uniform Scarlet, facings blue. Full dress tunic buttons evenly spaced. White plume on left of bearskin cap.

Regimental marches [Quick] *The British Grenadiers* (Tradit.)
[Slow] *Scipio* (Handel) and *The Grenadiers March* (Tradit.)

Regimental journal *The Grenadier Gazette*

Regimental headquarters Wellington Barracks, Birdcage Walk, London SW1E 6HQ

Regimental museum The Guards Museum, address as above

Nicknames No nicknames have ever been officially recognised by the Regiment.

Remarks In 1815, in commemoration of the Regiment's action in defeating Napoleon's Imperial Guard at the Battle of Waterloo, the Prince Regent decreed that henceforth the Regiment should be styled 'The First or Grenadier Regiment of Foot Guards'.

COLDSTREAM GUARDS

Although ranked as the Second Regiment of Foot Guards, the Coldstream are senior to the First Regiment in terms of continuous service. They originated in 1650 as Colonel Monck's Regiment of Foot in the Parliamentary Army. On the restoration of King Charles II in 1660 they were brought on the strength of the Royal Army, ranking next to the Regiment of Guards raised by the King in exile (later the Grenadiers). When Monck was created Duke of Albemarle they became known as 'The Duke of Albemarle's Regiment of Foot' or sometimes 'The Lord General's Regiment of Foot'. The title 'Guards' was added in 1661. After Monck's death in 1670, his Regiment was restyled 'The Coldstream Regiment of Foot Guards,' commemorating Monck's march from Coldstream to London in 1660. But ever since the Regiment's arrival in the capital they had been known by its citizens as 'the Coldstreamers'.

Titles 1650 Colonel Monck's Regiment of Foot
1660 Duke of Albemarle's Regiment of Foot (also The Lord General's Regiment of Foot)
1661 Duke of Albemarle's Regiment of Foot Guards
1670 Coldstream Regiment of Foot Guards
1855 Coldstream Guards

Battle honours Tangier 1680, Namur 1695, Gibraltar 1704–5, Oudenarde, Malplaquet, Dettingen, Lincelles, Talavera, Barrosa, Fuentes d'Onor, Salamanca, Nive, Peninsula, Waterloo, Alma, Inkerman, Sevastopol, Tel-el-Kebir,

Egypt 1882, Suakin 1885, Modder River, South Africa 1899–1902.

The Great War—Mons, Retreat from Mons, Marne 1914, Aisne 1914, Ypres 1914, 17, Langemarck 1914, Gheluvelt, Nonne Bosschen, Givenchy 1914, Neuve Chapelle, Aubers, Festubert 1915, Loos, Mount Sorrel, Somme 1916, 18, Flers-Courcelette, Morval, Pilckem, Menin Road, Poelcappelle, Passchendaele, Cambrai 1917, 18, St. Quentin, Bapaume 1918, Arras 1918, Lys, Hazebrouck, Albert 1918, Scarpe 1918, Drocourt-Queant, Hindenburg Line, Havrincourt, Canal du Nord, Selle, Sambre, France and Flanders 1914–18.

The Second World War—Dyle, Defence of Escaut, Dunkirk 1940, Cagny, Mont Pincon, Quarry Hill, Estry, Heppen, Nederrijn, Venraij, Meijel, Roer, Rhineland, Reichswald, Cleve, Goch, Moyland, Hochwald, Rhine, Lingen, Uelzen, North-West Europe 1940, 44–45, Egyptian Frontier 1940, Sidi Barrani, Halfaya 1941, Tobruk 1941, 1942, Msus, Knightsbridge, Defence of Alamein Line, Medenine, Mareth, Longstop Hill 1942, Sbiba, Steamroller Farm, Tunis, Hammam Lif, North Africa 1940–43, Salerno, Battipaglia, Cappezano, Volturno Crossing, Monte Camino, Calabritto, Garigliano Crossing, Monte Ornito, Monte Piccolo, Capture of Perugia, Arezzo, Advance to Florence Monte Domini, Catarelto Ridge, Argenta Gap, Italy 1943–45.

Motto	*Nulli Secundus* (Second to none)
Uniform	Scarlet, facings blue. Full dress tunic buttons in pairs. Scarlet plume on right of bearskin cap.
Regimental marches [Quick]	*Milanollo* (Van Ham)
[Slow]	*Figaro* (Mozart)
Regimental journal	*Coldstream Gazette*
Regimental headquarters	Wellington Barracks, Birdcage Walk, London SW1E 6HQ
Regimental museum	The Guards Museum, address as above.
Nickname	The Coldstreamers (but *never* 'Coldstreams')
Remarks	The Coldstream are the only direct descendants of Cromwell's infantry existing in today's British Army.

SCOTS GUARDS

The Third Regiment of Foot Guards was officially formed on 1st May 1662 when King Charles II warranted the establishment of 'a New Regiment of Foot Guards' consisting of Scottish soldiers. After numerous designations this Regiment eventually emerged as the Scots Guards, ranking as the Third Foot Guards.

But the Regiment claims that its true origins can be traced to March 1642 when King Charles I raised a 'Royal Regiment' of Scotsmen under command of the 1st Marquis of Argyll for service in the Irish Rebellion. The survivors of this Regiment returned to Scotland in 1649 and in July 1650 were reformed by King Charles II as 'The Footte Regiment of His Majesties Lyffe Guardes', Lord Lorne (Argyll's son) being appointed Colonel. As such they fought for the King in the Civil War, but after his defeat by Cromwell at Worcester in 1651 they were dispersed, together with the rest of the Royalist forces.

On King Charles's restoration in 1660 one of his first acts was to replace the English garrisons in Scotland by native Scottish troops. In October he ordered the raising of a company of Guards in Edinburgh, and shortly afterwards a second company was raised at Dumbarton. On 1st May 1662 a Royal Warrant directed that these companies should be augmented by four more and the whole regimented as the 'New Regiment of Foot Guards'. In September George Earl of Linlithgow was commissioned Lieutenant-Colonel commanding. In July 1666 he was appointed Colonel.

The new Regiment could claim links with the original Argyll's regiment of 1642, for certain of the officers (including Sir James Turner, author of *Pallas Armata*) had served in that regiment.

Titles   *From 1662 to 1686 numerous titles seem to have been current, within and without the Regiment, as under:*
Our Regiment of Guards
His Majesties Regiment of Guards
The King's Regiment
The King's Foot Guards
The King's Lyfe Guards of Foot

The Regiment of Guard of Foot
Linlithgow's Regiment
1686 Scotch Guards (or Scotts Guards)
1712 Third Regiment of Foot Guards
1831 Scots Fusilier Guards
1877 Scots Guards

Battle honours Namur 1695, Dettingen, Lincelles, Egypt (with the Sphinx), Talavera, Barrosa, Fuentes d'Onor, Salamanca, Nive, Peninsula, Waterloo, Alma, Inkerman, Sevastopol, Tel-el-Kebir, Egypt 1882, Suakin 1885, Modder River, South Africa 1899–1902.

The Great War—3 *Battalions*—Retreat from Mons, Marne 1914, Aisne 1914, Ypres 1914, 17, Langemarck 1914, Gheluvelt, Nonne Bosschen, Givenchy 1914, Neuve Chapelle, Aubers, Festubert 1915, Loos, Somme 1916, 18, Flers-Courcelette, Morval, Pilckem, Poelcappelle, Passchendaele, Cambrai 1917, 18, St. Quentin, Albert 1918, Bapaume 1918, Arras 1918, Drocourt-Queant, Hindenburg Line, Havrincourt, Canal du Nord, Selle, Sambre, France and Flanders 1914–18.

The Second World War—Stien, Norway 1940, Mont Pincon, Quarry Hill, Estry, Venlo Pocket, Rhineland, Reichswald, Cleve, Moyland, Hochwald, Rhine, Lingen, Uelzen, North-West Europe 1944–45, Halfaya 1941, Sidi Suleiman, Tobruk 1941, Gazala, Knightsbridge, Defence of Alamein Line, Medenine, Tadjera Khir, Medjez Plain, Grich el Oued, Djebel Bou Aoukaz 1943, I, North Africa 1941–43, Salerno, Battipaglia, Volturno Crossing, Rocchetta e Croce, Monte Camino, Anzio, Campoleone, Carroceto, Trasimene Line, Advance to Florence, Monte San Michele, Catarelto Ridge, Argenta Gap, Italy 1943–45.

Tumbledown Mountain, Falkland Islands 1982.

Motto *Nemo Me Impune Lacessit* (No one provokes me with impunity)

Uniform Scarlet, facings blue. Full dress tunic buttons grouped in threes. No plume. Regimental tartan: Royal Stuart.

Regimental marches [Quick] *Heilan' Laddie* (Tradit.)
[Slow] *The Garb of Old Gaul* (Reid)

Regimental journal *Scots Guards Magazine*

Regimental headquarters Wellington Barracks, Birdcage Walk, London SW1E 6HQ

Regimental museum The Guards Museum, address as above.

Remarks The Scots Guards is the only Regiment to have been officially designated 'Fusilier Guards', which title was bestowed by King William IV in 1831. He also restored the cherished 'Scots' title which had been dropped when the Regiment became simply 'Third Regiment of Foot Guards', in 1712. The bearskin cap was adopted in 1832, conforming to the other two Foot Guards, but unlike theirs, it has always been worn without any plume.

IRISH GUARDS

The Fourth Regiment of Foot Guards was raised by Queen Victoria under Army Order No. 77 of April 1900: 'Her Majesty the Queen, having deemed it desirable to commemorate the bravery shown by the Irish regiments in the recent operations in South Africa, has been graciously pleased to command that an Irish regiment of Foot Guards be formed. This regiment will be designated – "The Irish Guards".' The first Colonel of the Regiment was Field-Marshal Earl Roberts, VC.

Battle honours *The Great War*—Mons, Retreat from Mons, Marne 1914, Aisne 1914, Ypres 1914, 17, Langemarck 1914, Gheluvelt, Nonne Bosschen, Festubert 1915, Loos, Somme 1916, 18, Flers-Courcelette, Morval, Pilckem, Poelcappelle, Passchendaele, Cambrai 1917, 18, St. Quentin, Lys, Hazebrouck, Albert 1918, Bapaume 1918, Arras 1918, Scarpe 1918, Drocourt-Queant, Hindenburg Line, Canal du Nord, Selle, Sambre, France and Flanders 1914–18.

The Second World War—Pothus, Norway 1940, Boulogne 1940, Cagny, Mont Pincon, Neerpelt, Nijmegen, Aam, Rhineland, Hochwald, Rhine, Bentheim, North-West Europe 1944–45, Medjez Plain, Djebel Bou Aoukaz 1943, North Africa 1943, Anzio, Aprilia, Carroceto, Italy 1943–44.

Motto *Quis Separabit* (Who shall separate?)

Uniform Scarlet, facings blue. Full dress tunic buttons grouped in fours. Blue plume on right of bearskin.

Regimental marches [Quick] *St. Patrick's Day* (Tradit.)
[Slow] *Let Erin Remember* (Tradit.)

Regimental journal *Irish Guards Journal.*

Regimental headquarters Wellington Barracks, Birdcage Walk, London SW1E 6HQ

Regimental museum The Guards Museum, address as above

Nickname The Micks

WELSH GUARDS

Raised 26th February 1915 by King George V, with the present title.

Battle honours *The Great War*—Loos, Somme 1916, 18, Ginchy, Flers-Courcelette, Morval, Ypres 1917, Pilckem, Poelcappelle, Passchendaele, Cambrai, 1917, 18, Bapaume 1918, Arras 1918, Albert 1918, Drocourt-Queant, Hindenburg Line, Havrincourt, Canal du Nord, Selle, Sambre, France and Flanders 1915–18.

The Second World War—Defence of Arras, Boulogne 1940, St. Omer-La Bassee, Bourguebus Ridge, Cagny, Mont Pincon, Brussels, Hechtel, Nederrijn, Rhineland, Lingen, North-West Europe 1940, 44–45, Fondouk, Djebel el Rhorab, Tunis, Hammam Lif, North Africa 1943, Monte Ornito, Liri Valley, Monte Piccolo, Capture of Perugia, Arezzo, Advance to Florence, Gothic Line, Battaglia, Italy 1944–45.

Falklands Island 1982.

Motto *Cymru am Byth* (Wales for ever)

Uniform Scarlet, facings blue. Full dress tunic buttons grouped in fives. White-and-green plume on left of bearskin.

Regimental marches [Quick] *The Rising of the Lark* (Tradit.)
[Slow] *Men of Harlech* (Tradit.)

Regimental journal *Welsh Guards Regimental Magazine*

Regimental headquarters Wellington Barracks, Birdcage Walk, London SW1E 6HQ.

Regimental museum The Guards Museum, address as above.

Nickname Although referred to as 'The Taffs' by their sister Guards Regiments, the Welsh Guards do not recognise any nicknames.

THE ROYAL SCOTS
(THE ROYAL REGIMENT)
(1st)

The Royal Scots trace their origins to mercenary Scottish troops serving Continental monarchs during the Thirty Years War, and earlier. In 1633 King Charles I of England warranted Colonel Sir John Hepburn to raise a Scottish regiment for French service, and this was later augmented by those Scots who had earlier been serving under Gustavus Adolphus and Louis XIII. This Regiment was brought into British service in 1661, after the Restoration of Charles II, but did not finally return to England until 1678, when it was commanded by the 1st Earl of Dumbarton.

Titles 1633 Le Régiment d'Hébron (Hepburn)
1637 Le Régiment de Douglas
1678 Earl of Dumbarton's Regiment (1st Foot)
1684 The Royal Regiment of Foot
1751 1st (or the Royal) Regiment of Foot
1812 1st (or the Royal Scots) Regiment of Foot
1821 1st (or the Royal) Regiment of Foot
1871 1st (The Royal Scots) Regiment
1881 The Lothian Regiment (Royal Scots)
1882 The Royal Scots (Lothian Regiment)
1920 The Royal Scots (The Royal Regiment)

Battle honours Tangier 1680, Namur 1695, Blenheim, Ramillies, Oudenarde, Malplaquet, Louisburg, Havannah, Egmont-op-Zee, Egypt (with the Sphinx), St. Lucia 1803, Corunna, Busaco, Salamanca, Vittoria, St. Sebastian, Nive, Peninsula, Niagara, Waterloo, Nagpore, Maheidpoor, Ava, Alma, Inkerman, Sevastopol, Taku Forts, Pekin 1860, South Africa 1899–1902.

The Great War—Mons, Le Cateau, Retreat from Mons, Marne 1914, 18, Aisne 1914, La Bassee 1914, Neuve, Chapelle, Ypres 1915, 17, 18, Gravenstafel, St. Julien, Frezenburg, Bellewaarde, Aubers, Festubert 1915, Loos, Somme 1916, 18, Albert 1916, 18, Bazentin, Pozieres, Flers-Courcelette, Le Transloy, Ancre Heights, Ancre 1916, 18, Arras 1917, 18, Scarpe 1917, 18, Arleux, Pilckem, Langemarck 1917, Menin Road, Polygon Wood, Poelcappelle, Passchendaele, Cambrai, 1917, St. Quentin, Rosieres, Lys, Estaires, Messines 1918, Hazebrouck, Bailleul, Kemmel, Bethune, Soissonnais-Ourcq, Tardenois, Amiens, Bapaume 1918, Drocourt-Queant, Hindenburg Line, Canal du Nord, St. Quentin Canal, Beaurevoir, Courtrai, Selle, Sambre, France and Flanders 1914–18, Struma, Macedonia 1915–18, Helles, Landing at Helles, Krithia, Suvla, Scimitar Hill, Gallipoli 1915–16, Rumani, Egypt 1915–16, Gaza, El Mughar, Nebi Samwil, Jaffa, Palestine 1917–18, Archangel 1918–19.

The Second World War—Dyle, Defence of Escaut, St. Omer-La Bassee, Odon, Cheux, Defence of Rauray, Caen, Esquay, Mont Pincon, Aart, Nederrijn, Best, Scheldt, Flushing, Meijel, Venlo Pocket, Roer, Rhineland, Reichswald, Cleve, Goch, Rhine, Uelzen, Bremen, Artlenberg, North-West Europe 1940, 44–45, Gothic Line, Marradi, Monte Gamberaldi, Italy 1944–45, South East Asia 1941, Donbaik, Kohima, Relief of Kohima, Aradura, Shwebo, Mandalay, Burma 1943–45.

Motto *Nemo Me Impune Lacessit* (No one provokes me with impunity)

Uniform Doublet, archer green. Trews, Hunting Stuart tartan. Facings blue.

Regimental marches [Quick] *Dumbarton's Drums* (Tradit.) and *The Daughter of the Regiment* (Donizetti)
[Slow] *In the Garb of Old Gaul* (Reid)

Regimental journal *The Thistle*

Regimental headquarters The Castle, Edinburgh EH1 2YT

Regimental museum As above

Nickname Pontius Pilate's Bodyguard

Remarks With an unbroken record of service from 1633, the Royal Scots are indisputably the oldest Regiment still extant in the British Army.

Their Regimental March, *Dumbarton's Drums*, is also the oldest, its melody dating from the early 17th century.

THE QUEEN'S REGIMENT

(2nd, 3rd, 31st, 35th, 50th, 57th, 70th, 77th, 97th, 107th)

This Regiment was formed on 31st December 1966 by the amalgamation of

The Queen's Royal Surrey Regiment

The Queen's Own Buffs, The Royal Kent Regiment

The Royal Sussex Regiment

The Middlesex Regiment (Duke of Cambridge's Own)

These four were themselves the result of four previous amalgamations dating from 1959, while as can be seen from the ranking numbers quoted above, the present Regiment stems from a total of ten regiments of Foot existing before the Cardwell reforms of 1881. It is thus the largest amalgamation of any unit in the British Army; hence the extensive display of Battle Honours. It is also England's senior infantry Regiment of the Line.

Battle honours Tangier 1662–80, Namur 1695, Gibraltar 1704–5, Blenheim, Ramillies, Oudenarde, Malplaquet, Dettingen, Louisburg, Guadaloupe 1759, Quebec 1759, Belleisle, Martinique 1762, Havannah, St. Lucia 1778, Mysore, Martinique 1794, Seringapatam, Egypt (with the Sphinx), Maida, Vimiera, Corunna, Douro, Talavera, Guadaloupe 1810, Albuhera, Almaraz, Ciudad Rodrigo, Badajoz, Salamanca, Vittoria, Pyrenees, Nivelle, Nive, Orthes, Toulouse, Peninsula, Ghuznee 1839, Khelat, Affghanistan 1839, Cabool 1842, Punniar, Moodkee, Ferozeshah, Aliwal, Sobraon, South Africa 1851–53, Alma, Inkerman, Sevastopol, Lucknow, Taku Forts, Pekin 1860, New Zealand, Afghanistan 1878–79, South Africa 1879, Egypt 1882, Abu Klea, Nile 1884–85, Suakin 1885, Burma 1885–87, Chitral, Tirah, Relief of Ladysmith, Relief of Kimberley, Paardeberg, South Africa 1899–1902.

The Great War—Mons, Le Cateau, Retreat from Mons, Marne 1914, 18, Aisne 1914, La Bassee 1914, Messines 1914, 17, 18, Armentieres 1914, Ypres 1914, 15, 17, 18, Langemarck 1914, 17, Gheluvelt, Nonne Bosschen, Givenchy 1914, Neuve Chapelle, Hill 60, Gravenstafel, St. Julien, Frezenberg, Bellewaarde, Aubers, Festubert 1915, Hooge 1915, Loos, Somme 1916, 18, Albert 1916, 18, Bazentin, Delville Wood, Pozieres, Guillemont, Ginchy, Flers-Courcelette, Morval, Thiepval, Le Transloy, Ancre Heights, Ancre 1916, 18, Bapaume 1917, 18, Arras 1917, 18, Vimy 1917, Scarpe 1917, 18, Arleux, Oppy, Bullecourt, Pilckem, Menin Road, Polygon Wood, Broodseinde, Poelcappelle, Passchendaele, Cambrai 1917, 18, St. Quentin, Rosieres, Avre, Villers Bretonneux, Lys, Estaires, Hazebrouck, Bailleul, Kemmel, Scherpenberg, Soissonnais-Ourcq, Amiens, Drocourt-Queant, Hindenburg Line, Epehy, Canal du Nord, St. Quentin Canal, Beaurevoir, Courtrai, Selle, Valenciennes, Sambre, France and Flanders 1914–18, Piave, Vittorio Veneto, Italy 1917–18, Struma, Doiran 1917, 18, Macedonia 1915–18, Suvla, Landing at Suvla, Scimitar Hill, Gallipoli 1915, Rumani, Egypt 1915–17, Gaza, El Mughar, Nebi Samwil, Jerusalem, Jericho, Jordan, Tell' Asur, Megiddo, Sharon, Palestine 1917–18, Aden, Defence of Kut al Amara, Tigris 1916, Kut al Amara 1917, Baghdad, Khan Baghdadi, Sharqat, Mesopotamia 1915–18, N.W. Frontier India 1915, 1916–17, Murman 1918–19, Dukhovskaya, Siberia 1918–19.

Afghanistan 1919.

The Second World War—Dyle, Defence of Escaut, Amiens 1940, St. Omer-La Bassee, Foret de Nieppe, Ypres-Comines Canal, Dunkirk 1940, Withdrawal to Seine, Normandy Landing, Cambes, Breville, Villers Bocage, Odon, Caen, Orne, Hill 112, Bourguebus Ridge, Troarn, Mont Pincon, Falaise, Seine 1944, Nederrijn, Le Havre, Lower Maas, Venraij, Meijel, Geilenkirchen, Venlo Pocket, Roer, Rhineland, Reichswald, Goch, Rhine, Lingen, Brinkum, Bremen, North West-Europe 1940, 44–45, Karora-Marsa Taclai, Cubcub, Mescelit Pass, Keren, Mt. Englahat, Massawa, Abyssinia 1941, Syria 1941, Sidi Barrani, Sidi Suleiman, Tobruk 1941, Tobruk Sortie, Omars, Alem Hamza, Benghazi, Alam el Halfa, Deir el Munassib, El Alamein, El Agheila, Advance on Tripoli, Medenine, Mareth,

Tebaga Gap, El Hamma, Akarit, Djebel el Meida, Djebel Roumana, Djebel Abiod, Tebourba, Djebel Azzag 1942, 43, Robaa Valley, Fort McGregor, Oued Zarga, Djebel Bech Chekaoui, Djebel Ang, Heidous, Djebel Djaffa Pass, Medjez Plain, Longstop Hill 1943, Si Abdallah, Tunis, Montarnaud, North Africa 1940–43, Francofonte, Sferro, Adrano, Sferro Hills, Centuripe, Monte Rivoglia, Sicily 1943, Termoli, Trigno, San Salvo, Sangro, Romagnoli, Impossible Bridge, Villa Grande, Salerno, Monte Stella, Scafati Bridge, Volturno Crossing, Monte Camino, Garigliano Crossing, Damiano, Anzio, Carroceto, Cassino, Monastery Hill, Castle Hill, Liri Valley, Aquino, Piedimonte Hill, Rome, Trasimene Line, Arezzo, Advance to Florence, Monte Scalari, Gothic Line, Coriano, Pian di Castello, Gemmano Ridge, Monte Reggiano, Capture of Forli, Casa Fortis, Senio Pocket, Senio Floodbank, Rimini Line, Casa Fabbri Ridge, Savio Bridgehead, Monte Pianoereno, Monte Spaduro, Monte Grande, Senio, Menate, Filo, Argenta Gap, Italy 1943–45, Greece 1944–45, Leros, Middle East 1943, Malta 1940–42, Kampar, Malaya 1941–42, Hong Kong, South East Asia 1941, North Arakan, Razabil, Mayu Tunnels, Kohima, Defence of Kohima, Pinwe, Shweli, Myitson, Taungtha, Yenangyaung 1945, Sittang 1945, Chindits 1944, Burma 1943–45.

Naktong Bridgehead, Chongju, Chongchon II, Chaum-Ni, Kapyong-chon, Kapyong, Korea 1950–51.

Motto	Unconquered I Serve
Uniform	Scarlet, facings blue
Regimental marches [Quick]	*Soldiers of the Queen* (Stuart)
[Slow]	*The Caledonian*
Regimental journal	*The Journal of The Queen's Regiment*
Regimental headquarters	Howe Barracks, Canterbury, Kent CT1 1JY
Regimental museum	As above

THE QUEEN'S ROYAL SURREY REGIMENT
(2nd, 31st, 70th)

Formed 14th October 1959 by amalgamation of The Queen's Royal Regiment (West Surrey) with The East Surrey Regiment.

Note Since this Regiment existed for only seven years under the above title, further details are omitted.

THE QUEEN'S ROYAL REGIMENT
(WEST SURREY)
(2nd)

Raised September 1661 by Henry Mordaunt, Earl of Peterborough, as part of garrison of Tangier, and styled The Tangier Regiment.

Titles 1661 The Tangier Regiment of Foot *Also known by Colonel's name*
1684 The Queen's Regiment of Foot
1686 The Queen Dowager's Regiment of Foot
1703 The Queen's Royal Regiment
1714 H.R.H. The Princess of Wales's Own Regiment of Foot
1727 The Queen's Own Royal Regiment of Foot
1751 The Queen's (Second) Royal Regiment of Foot
1855 2nd (Queen's Royal) Regiment
1881 The Queen's (Royal West Surrey Regiment)
1921 The Queen's Royal Regiment (West Surrey)
1959 Amalgamated with The East Surrey Regiment to form The Queen's Royal Surrey Regiment

Battle honours Tangier 1662–80, Namur 1695, Egypt (with the Sphinx), Vimiera, Corunna, Salamanca, Vittoria, Pyrenees, Nivelle, Toulouse, Peninsula, Ghuznee 1839, Khelat, Affghanistan 1839, South Africa 1851–2–3, Taku Forts, Pekin 1860, Burma 1885–87, Tirah, Relief of Ladysmith, South Africa 1899–1902.

The Great War—31 *Battalions*—Mons, Retreat from
Mons, Marne 1914, 18, Aisne 1914, Ypres 1914, 17, 18,
Langemarck 1914, Gheluvelt, Aubers, Festubert 1915,
Loos, Somme 1916, 18, Albert 1916, 18, Bazentin,
Delville Wood, Pozieres, Guillemont, Flers-Courcelette,
Morval, Thiepval, Le Transloy, Ancre Heights, Ancre
1916, 18, Arras 1917, 18, Scarpe 1917, Bullecourt,
Messines 1917, Pilckem, Menin Road, Polygon Wood,
Broodseinde, Passchendaele, Cambrai 1917, 18, St.
Quentin, Bapaume 1918, Rosieres, Avre, Villers
Bretonneux, Lys, Hazebrouck, Bailleul, Kemmel,
Soissonnais-Ourcq, Amiens, Hindenburg Line, Epehy,
St. Quentin Canal, Courtrai, Selle, Sambre, France and
Flanders 1914–18, Piave, Vittoria Veneto, Italy 1917–18,
Doiran 1917, Macedonia 1916–17, Suvla, Landing at
Suvla, Scimitar Hill, Gallipoli 1915, Rumani, Egypt
1915–16, Gaza, El Mughar, Nebi Samwil, Jerusalem,
Jericho, Jordan, Tell' Asur, Megiddo, Sharon, Palestine
1917–18, Khan Baghdadi, Mesopotamia 1915–18, N.W.
Frontier India 1916–17.

Afghanistan 1919.

The Second World War—Defence of Escaut, Villers
Bocage, Mont Pincon, Lower Maas, Roer, North-West
Europe 1940, 44–45, Syria 1941, Sidi Barrani, Tobruk
1941, Tobruk Sortie, Deir el Munasib, El Alamein,
Advance on Tripoli, Medenine, Tunis, North Africa
1940–43, Salerno, Monte Stella, Scafati Bridge, Volturno
Crossing, Monte Camino, Garigliano Crossing,
Damiano, Anzio, Gothic Line, Gemmano Ridge, Senio
Pocket, Senio Floodbank, Casa Fabbri Ridge, Menate,
Filo, Argenta Gap, Italy 1943–45, North Arakan,
Kohima, Yenangyaung 1945, Sittang 1945, Chindits
1944, Burma 1943–45.

Mottoes *Pristinae Virtutis Memor* (Mindful of former virtues)*
Vel Exuviae Triumphant (Even in defeat triumphant)*

Uniform Scarlet, facings blue

Regimental marches [Quick] *Old Queens/Braganza/We'll gang nae mair to Yon Town*
[Slow] *Scipio* (Handel)

Regimental journal *The Journal of The Queen's Royal Regiment*

Nicknames The Tangerines. Kirke's Lambs. The Mutton Lancers

*The Regimental versions are 'Mindful of the gallant actions of the past' and 'Even in
defeat there can be triumph'.

THE EAST SURREY REGIMENT

(31st & 70th)

Formed 1881 by amalgamation of the 31st (Huntingdonshire) Regiment with the 70th (Surrey) Regiment, which became 1st and 2nd Battalions respectively of the new Regiment.

Battle honours Gibraltar 1704–5, Dettingen, Martinique 1794, Talavera, Guadaloupe 1810, Albuhera, Vittoria, Pyrenees, Nivelle, Nive, Orthes, Peninsula, Cabool 1842, Moodkee, Ferozeshah, Aliwal, Sobraon, Sevastopol, Taku Forts, New Zealand, Afghanistan 1878–79, Suakin 1885, Relief of Ladysmith, South Africa 1899–1902.

The Great War—18 *Battalions*—Mons, Le Cateau, Retreat from Mons, Marne 1914, Aisne 1914, La Bassee 1914, Armentieres 1914, Hill 60, Ypres 1915, 17, 18, Gravenstafel, St. Julien, Frezenberg, Bellewaarde, Loos, Somme 1916, 18, Albert 1916, 18, Bazentin, Delville Wood, Pozieres, Guillemont, Flers-Courcelette, Morval, Thiepval, Le Transloy, Ancre Heights, Ancre 1916, Arras 1917, 18, Vimy, 1917, Scarpe 1917, Messines 1917, Pilckem, Langemarck 1917, Menin Road, Polygon Wood, Broodseinde, Poelcappelle, Passchendaele, Cambrai 1917, 18, St. Quentin, Bapaume 1918, Rosieres, Avre, Lys, Estaires, Hazebrouck, Amiens, Hindenburg Line, Epehy, Canal du Nord, St. Quentin Canal, Courtrai, Selle, Sambre, France and Flanders 1914–18, Italy 1917–18, Struma, Doiran 1918, Macedonia 1915–18, Egypt 1915, Aden, Mesopotamia 1917–18, Murman 1919.

The Second World War—Defence of Escaut, Dunkirk 1940, North-West Europe 1940, Tebourba, Fort McGregor, Oued Zarga, Djebel Ang, Djebel Djaffa Pass, Medjez Plain, Longstop Hill 1943, Tunis, Montarnaud, North Africa 1942–43, Adrano, Centuripe, Sicily 1943, Trigno, Sangro, Cassino, Capture of Forli, Argenta Gap, Italy 1943–45, Greece 1944–45, Kampar, Malaya 1941–42.

Uniform Scarlet, facings white

Regimental marches [Quick] A *Southerly Wind and a Cloudy Sky* and *The Lass o' Gowrie**

[Slow] *Lord Charles Montague's Huntingdonshire March*

Regimental journal *The Journal of The East Surrey Regiment*

Nicknames The Young Buffs (1st Battalion). The Glasgow Greys (2nd Battalion)

31st (HUNTINGDONSHIRE) REGIMENT

Raised February 1702 by Colonel George Villiers, as a regiment of Marines.

Titles 1702 Colonel Villiers's Regiment of Marines *Title subsequently changed with Colonels' names*
1713 31st Regiment of Foot
1782 31st (or Huntingdonshire) Regiment of Foot
1855 31st (Huntingdonshire) Regiment
1881 Amalgamated with the 70th (Surrey) Regiment to form The East Surrey Regiment

Battle honours Gibraltar 1704–5, Dettingen, Martinique 1794, Talavera, Albuhera, Vittoria, Pyrenees, Nivelle, Nive, Orthes, Peninsula, Cabool 1842, Moodkee, Ferozeshah, Aliwal, Sobraon, Sevastopol, Taku Forts.

Uniform Scarlet, facings buff

Nickname The Young Buffs

Remarks The nickname is unique in having been bestowed by a monarch. At the Battle of Dettingen (1743) King George II mistook the Regiment for the Buffs (East Kent Regiment) as they wore similar facings, and cried 'Well done the Buffs!' When informed of his error he added 'Well done then, Young Buffs!'

---

*In 1942, on the initiative of the Royal Marines, The East Surrey Regiment was permitted to play A *Life on the Ocean Wave* on all Regimental occasions.

70th (SURREY) REGIMENT

Raised 1756, at Glasgow, as 2nd Battalion of the above 31st Regiment, but reconstituted as separate unit in 1758.

Titles 1756 31st Regiment of Foot (2nd Battalion) *Known as '2nd/31st Regiment of Foot'*
1758 70th Regiment of Foot
1782 70th (or The Surrey) Regiment of Foot
1813 70th (or Glasgow Lowland) Regiment of Foot
1825 70th (or Surrey) Regiment of Foot
1855 70th (Surrey) Regiment
1881 Amalgamated with 31st (Huntingdonshire) Regiment to form The East Surrey Regiment

Battle honours Guadaloupe 1810, New Zealand, Afghanistan 1878–79.

Uniform Scarlet, facings black

Nickname The Glasgow Greys

THE QUEEN'S OWN BUFFS, THE ROYAL KENT REGIMENT

(3rd, 50th, 97th)

Formed March 1961 by amalgamation of The Buffs (Royal East Kent Regiment) with The Queen's Own Royal West Kent Regiment.

Note Since this Regiment existed for only five years under the above title, further details are omitted.

THE BUFFS

(ROYAL EAST KENT REGIMENT)
(3rd)

The Buffs traced their ancestry to a body of London Train-Bands sent over to Holland to aid the Protestant cause in 1572. This unit was disbanded by the Dutch in 1665, when some of the officers and men returned to

England to be formed by Charles II into a new 'Holland Regiment'. Command was given to Colonel Robert Sydney.

Titles 1665 The Holland Regiment
1689 Prince George of Denmark's Regiment of Foot (3rd Foot) *By 1702 the Regiment had become popularly known as 'The Buffs'*
1751 3rd (or The Buffs) Regiment of Foot
1782 3rd (or the East Kent) Regiment of Foot, or The Buffs
1855 3rd (East Kent, The Buffs) Regiment
1881 The Buffs (East Kent Regiment)
1935 The Buffs (Royal East Kent Regiment)
1961 Amalgamated with The Queen's Own Royal West Kent Regiment to form The Queen's Own Buffs, The Royal Kent Regiment

Battle honours Blenheim, Ramillies, Oudenarde, Malplaquet, Dettingen, Guadaloupe 1759, Belleisle, Douro, Talavera, Albuhera, Vittoria, Pyrenees, Nivelle, Nive, Orthes, Toulouse, Peninsula, Punniar, Sevastopol, Taku Forts, South Africa 1879, Chitral, Relief of Kimberley, Paardeberg, South Africa 1900–02.

The Great War—16 *Battalions*—Aisne 1914, Armentieres 1914, Ypres 1915, 17, Gravenstafel, St. Julien, Frezenberg, Bellewaarde, Hooge 1915, Loos, Somme 1916, 18, Albert 1916, 18, Bazentin, Delville Wood, Pozieres, Flers-Courcelette, Morval, Thiepval, Le Transloy, Ancre Heights, Ancre 1916, 18, Arras 1917, Scarpe 1917, Messines 1917, Pilckem, Passchendaele, Cambrai 1917, 18, St. Quentin, Avre, Amiens, Bapaume 1918, Hindenburg Line, Epehy, St. Quentin Canal, Selle, Sambre, France and Flanders 1914–18, Struma, Doiran 1918, Macedonia 1915–18, Gaza, Jerusalem, Tell' Asur, Palestine 1917–18, Aden, Tigris 1916, Kut al Amara 1917, Baghdad, Mesopotamia 1915–18.

The Second World War—Defence of Escaut, St. Omer–La Bassee, Withdrawal to Seine, North-West Europe 1940, Sidi Suleiman, Alem Hamza, Alam el Halfa, El Alamein, El Agheila, Advance on Tripoli, Tebaga Gap, El Hamma, Akarit, Djebel Azzag 1943, Robaa Valley, Djebel Bech Chekaoui, Heidous, Medjez Plain, Longstop Hill 1943, North Africa 1941–43, Centuripe, Monte Rivoglia, Sicily 1943, Termoli, Trigno, Sangro, Anzio, Cassino I, Liri Valley, Aquino, Rome, Trasimene Line,

Coriano, Monte Spaduro, Senio, Argenta Gap, Italy 1943–45, Leros, Middle East 1943, Malta 1940–42, Shweli, Myitson, Burma 1945.

Motto *Veteri Frondescit Honore* (Ever green with ancient honour)

Uniform Scarlet, facings buff

Regimental marches [Quick] *The Buffs*
[Slow] *The Men of Kent*

Regimental journal *The Dragon*

Nicknames The Old Buffs. The Buff Howards. The Nutcrackers. The Resurrectionists

THE QUEEN'S OWN ROYAL WEST KENT REGIMENT
(50th, 97th)

Formed 1881 by amalgamation of the 50th (Queen's Own) Regiment with the 97th (Earl of Ulster's) Regiment, which formed 1st and 2nd Battalions respectively of the new Regiment.

Titles 1881 The Queen's Own (Royal West Kent Regiment)
1921 The Royal West Kent Regiment (Queen's Own)
1922 The Queen's Own Royal West Kent Regiment

Battle honours Egypt (with the Sphinx), Vimiera, Corunna, Almaraz, Vittoria, Pyrenees, Nive, Orthes, Peninsula, Punniar, Moodkee, Ferozeshah, Aliwal, Sobraon, Alma, Inkerman, Sevastopol, Lucknow, New Zealand, Egypt 1882, Nile 1884–85, South Africa 1900–02.

The Great War—18 Battalions—Mons, Le Cateau, Retreat from Mons, Marne 1914, Aisne 1914, La Bassee 1914, Messines 1914, 17, Ypres 1914, 15, 17, 18, Hill 60, Gravenstafel, St. Julien, Frezenberg, Loos, Somme 1916, 18, Albert 1916, 18, Bazentin, Delville Wood, Pozieres, Guillemont, Flers-Courcelette, Morval, Thiepval, Le Transloy, Ancre Heights, Ancre 1916, 18, Arras 1917, 18, Vimy 1917, Scarpe 1917, Oppy, Pilckem, Langemarck 1917, Menin Road, Polygon Wood, Broodseinde, Passchendaele, Cambrai 1917, 18, St. Quentin, Rosieres, Avre, Villers Bretonneux, Lys, Hazebrouck, Kemmel, Amiens, Bapaume 1918,

Hindenburg Line, Epehy, Canal du Nord, St. Quentin Canal, Courtrai, Selle, Sambre, France and Flanders 1914–18, Italy 1917–18, Suvla, Landing at Suvla, Scimitar Hill, Gallipoli 1915, Rumani, Egypt 1915–16, Gaza, El Mughar, Jerusalem, Jericho, Tell'Asur, Palestine 1917–18, Defence of Kut al Amara, Sharqat, Mesopotamia 1915–18.

Afghanistan 1919.

The Second World War—Defence of Escaut, Foret de Nieppe, North-West Europe 1940, Alam el Halfa, El Alamein, Djebel Abiod, Djebel Azzag 1942, Oued Zarga, Djebel Ang, Medjez Plain, Longstop Hill 1943, Si Abdallah, North Africa 1942–43, Centuripe, Monte Rivoglia, Sicily 1943, Termoli, San Salvo, Sangro, Romagnoli, Impossible Bridge, Villa Grande, Cassino, Castle Hill, Liri Valley, Piedimonte Hill, Trasimene Line, Arezzo, Advance to Florence, Monte Scalari, Casa Fortis, Rimini Line, Savio Bridgehead, Monte Pianoereno, Monte Spaduro, Senio, Argenta Gap, Italy 1943–45, Greece 1944–45, Leros, Malta 1940–42, North Arakan, Razabil, Mayu Tunnels, Defence of Kohima, Taungtha, Sittang 1945, Burma 1943–45.

Motto *Quo Fas et Gloria Ducunt* (Whither right and glory lead)

Uniform Scarlet, facings blue

Regimental marches [Quick] A *Hundred Pipers*
[Slow] *The Men of Kent*

Nicknames The Dirty Half-Hundred. The Celestials

50th (QUEEN'S OWN) REGIMENT

Raised January 1756 as 52nd Regiment of Foot, with Colonel James Abercromby commanding. Renumbered 50th in December 1756.

Titles 1756 (January) 52nd Regiment of Foot
(December) 50th Regiment of Foot
1782 50th or West Kent Regiment of Foot
1827 50th (or the Duke of Clarence's) Regiment of Foot
1831 50th or The Queen's Own Regiment of Foot
1855 50th (Queen's Own) Regiment

1881 Amalgamated with 97th (Earl of Ulster's) Regiment to form The Queen's Own (Royal West Kent Regiment)

Battle honours Egypt (with the Sphinx), Vimiera, Corunna, Almaraz, Vittoria, Pyrenees, Nive, Orthes, Peninsula, Punniar, Moodkee, Ferozeshah, Aliwal, Sobraon, Alma, Inkerman, Sevastopol, New Zealand.

Motto *Invicta* (Invincible—Motto of County of Kent)

Uniform Scarlet, facings blue

Regimental march [Quick] *A Hundred Pipers*

Nicknames The Dirty Half-Hundred. The Blind Half-Hundred

97th (EARL OF ULSTER'S) REGIMENT OF FOOT

Raised March 1824 as the 97th (Earl of Ulster's) Regiment of Foot. The Earldom of Ulster was the Irish honour of the Duke of Cambridge. The Regiment's title remained unchanged until amalgamation with the 50th (Queen's Own) Regiment in 1881.

Battle honours Sevastopol, Lucknow.

Motto *Quo Fas et Gloria Ducunt* (Whither right and glory lead)

Uniform Scarlet, facings sky blue

Regimental march [Quick] *Paddy's Resource*

Nickname The Celestials (from unique sky-blue facings)

THE ROYAL SUSSEX REGIMENT
(35th and 107th)

Formed 1881 by amalgamation of the 35th (Royal Sussex) Regiment with the 107th (Bengal Infantry) Regiment, which became 1st and 2nd Battalions, respectively, of the new Regiment.

Battle honours Gibraltar 1704–5, Louisburg, Quebec 1759, Martinique 1762, Havannah, St. Lucia 1778, Maida, Egypt 1882,

Abu Klea, Nile 1884–85, South Africa 1900–02.

The Great War—23 *Battalions*—Mons, Retreat from Mons, Marne 1914, 18, Aisne 1914, Ypres 1914, 17, 18, Gheluvelt, Nonne Bosschen, Givenchy 1914, Aubers, Loos, Somme 1916, 18, Albert 1916, 18, Bazentin, Delville Wood, Pozieres, Flers-Courcelette, Morval, Thiepval, Le Transloy, Ancre Heights, Ancre 1916, 18, Arras 1917, 18, Vimy 1917, Scarpe 1917, Arleux, Messines 1917, Pilckem, Langemarck 1917, Menin Road, Polygon Wood, Broodseinde, Poelcappelle, Passchendaele, Cambrai 1917, 18, St. Quentin, Bapaume 1918, Rosieres, Avre, Lys, Kemmel, Scherpenberg, Soissonnais-Ourcq, Amiens, Drocourt-Queant, Hindenburg Line, Epehy, St. Quentin Canal, Beaurevoir, Courtrai, Selle, Sambre, France and Flanders 1914–18, Piave, Vittorio Veneto, Italy 1917–18, Suvla, Landing at Suvla, Scimitar Hill, Gallipoli 1915, Rumani, Egypt 1915–17, Gaza, El Mughar, Jerusalem, Jericho, Tell' Asur, Palestine 1917–18, N.W. Frontier, India 1915, 1916–17, Murman 1918–19.

Afghanistan 1919.

The Second World War—Defence of Escaut, Amiens 1940, St. Omer-La Bassee, Foret de Nieppe, North-West Europe 1940, Karora-Marsa Taclai, Cub cub, Mescelit Pass, Keren, Mt. Engiahat, Massawa, Abyssinia 1941, Omars, Benghazi, Alam el Halfa, El Alamein, Akarit, Djebel el Meida, Tunis, North Africa 1940–43, Cassino, Monastery Hill, Gothic Line, Pian di Castello, Monte Reggiano, Italy 1944–45, North Arakan, Pinwe, Shweli, Burma 1943–45.

Uniform	Scarlet, facings blue
Regimental marches [Quick]	*The Royal Sussex*
[Slow]	*Roussillon*
Regimental journal	*Roussillon Gazette*
Nickname	The Orange Lillies

35th (ROYAL SUSSEX) REGIMENT

Raised June 1701, at Belfast, by Colonel Arthur Chichester, 3rd Earl of Donegal.

Titles 1701 The Earl of Donegal's Regiment of Foot (Also known as The Belfast Regiment) *Title subsequently changed with Colonels' names*
1751 35th Regiment of Foot
1782 35th (or the Dorsetshire) Regiment of Foot
1805 35th (or the Sussex) Regiment of Foot
1832 35th (Royal Sussex) Regiment
1881 Amalgamated with 107th (Bengal Infantry) Regiment to form The Royal Sussex Regiment

Battle honours Quebec 1759, Louisburg, Maida.

Uniform Scarlet, facings blue

Regimental marches *Royal Sussex* and *Roussillon*

Nickname The Orange Lillies

107th (BENGAL INFANTRY) REGIMENT

Raised 1854 as 3rd Bengal European Infantry in the Hon. East India Company's forces. Transferred to the British Establishment in 1861.

Titles 1854 3rd Bengal European Infantry (*H.E.I.C*)
1861 107th (Bengal Infantry) Regiment (*British Army*)
1881 Amalgamated with 35th (Royal Sussex) Regiment to form The Royal Sussex Regiment

Uniform Scarlet, facings white

Regimental march [Quick] *The Lass of Richmond Hill*

94

THE MIDDLESEX REGIMENT (DUKE OF CAMBRIDGE'S OWN)

(57th and 77th)

Formed 1881 by amalgamation of 57th (West Middlesex) Regiment with 77th (East Middlesex) Regiment (Duke of Cambridge's Own).

Titles 1881 The Duke of Cambridge's Own (Middlesex Regiment)
1921 The Middlesex Regiment (Duke of Cambridge's Own)

Battle honours Mysore, Seringapatam, Albuhera, Ciudad Rodrigo, Badajoz, Vittoria, Pyrenees, Nivelle, Nive, Peninsula, Alma, Inkerman, Sevastopol, New Zealand, South Africa 1879, Relief of Ladysmith, South Africa 1900–02.

The Great War—46 Battalions—Mons, Le Cateau, Retreat from Mons, Marne 1914, Aisne 1914, 18, La Bassee 1914, Messines 1914, 17, 18, Armentieres 1914, Neuve Chapelle, Ypres 1915, 17, 18, Gravestafel, St. Julien, Frezenberg, Bellewaarde, Aubers, Hooge 1915, Loos, Somme 1916, 18, Albert 1916, 18, Bazentin, Delville Wood, Pozieres, Ginchy, Flers-Courcelette, Morval, Thiepval, Le Transloy, Ancre Heights, Ancre 1916, 18, Bapaume 1917, 18, Arras 1917, 18, Vimy 1917, Scarpe 1917, 18, Arleux, Pilckem, Langemarck 1917, Menin Road, Polygon Wood, Broodseinde, Poelcappelle, Passchendaele, Cambrai 1917, 18, St. Quentin, Rosieres, Avre, Villers Bretonneux, Lys, Estaires, Hazebrouck, Bailleul, Kemmel, Scherpenberg, Hindenburg Line, Canal du Nord, St. Quentin Canal, Courtrai, Selle, Valenciennes, Sambre, France and Flanders 1914–18, Italy 1917–18, Struma, Doiran 1918, Macedonia 1915–18, Suvla, Landing at Suvla, Scimitar Hill, Gallipoli 1915, Rumani, Egypt 1915–17, Gaza, El Mughar, Jerusalem, Jericho, Jordan, Tell'Asur,' Palestine 1917–18, Mesopotamia 1917–18, Murman 1919, Dukhovskaya, Siberia 1918–19.

The Second World War—Dyle, Defence of Escaut, Ypres-Comines Canal, Dunkirk 1940, Normandy Landing, Cambes, Breville, Odon, Caen, Orne, Hill 122, Bourguebus Ridge, Troarn, Mont Pincon, Falaise, Seine 1944, Nederrijn, Le Havre, Lower Maas, Venraij, Meijel, Geilenkirchen, Venlo Pocket, Rhineland, Reichswald, Goch, Rhine, Lingen, Brinkum, Bremen, North-West Europe 1940, 44–45, El Alamein, Advance on Tripoli, Mareth, Akarit, Djebel Roumana, North Africa 1942–43, Francofonte, Sferro, Sferro Hills, Sicily 1943, Anzio, Carroceto, Gothic Line, Monte Grande, Italy 1944–45, Hong Kong, South-East Asia 1941.

Naktong Bridgehead, Chongju, Chongchon II, Chaum-Ni, Kapyong-chon, Kapyong, Korea 1950–51.

Motto	*Ich Dien* (I Serve)
Uniform	Scarlet, facings lemon yellow
Regimental marches [Quick] [Slow]	*Sir Manley Power* and *Paddy's Resource* *Caledonian* and *In the Garb of Old Gaul* (Reid)
Regimental journal	*The Die Hards*
Nicknames	The Die Hards. The Steel Backs

57th (WEST MIDDLESEX) REGIMENT

Raised December 1755 as 59th Regiment of Foot. Command given to Colonel John Arabin.

Titles	1755 59th Regiment of Foot 1757 *Renumbered* 57th Regiment of Foot 1782 57th (or the West Middlesex) Regiment of Foot 1881 Amalgamated with 77th (East Middlesex) Regiment of Foot to form The Duke of Cambridge's Own (Middlesex Regiment)
Battle honours	Albuhera, Vittoria, Pyrenees, Nivelle, Nive, Peninsula, Inkerman, Sevastopol, New Zealand, South Africa 1879.
Uniform	Scarlet, facings yellow
Regimental marches [Quick] [Slow]	*Sir Manley Power* *Caledonian*
Nicknames	The Die Hards. The Steel Backs

Remarks In 1816 the Regiment was authorised to adopt 'the Albuhera Badge'—a laurel wreath with a scroll inscribed *Albuhera*. This was in recognition of the 57th's heroic stand at the Battle of Albuhera (1811) when they lost 422 all ranks out of a total of 570, and earned their nickname 'The Die Hards'.

77th (EAST MIDDLESEX) REGIMENT
(DUKE OF CAMBRIDGE'S OWN)

Raised October 1787 as the 77th Regiment of Foot, commanded by Colonel James Marsh.

Titles 1787 77th Regiment of Foot
1807 77th (The East Middlesex) Regiment of Foot
1876 77th (East Middlesex) Regiment (Duke of Cambridge's Own)
1881 Amalgamated with 57th (West Middlesex) Regiment to form The Duke of Cambridge's Own (Middlesex Regiment)

Battle honours Mysore, Seringapatam, Ciudad Rodrigo, Badajoz, Peninsula, Alma, Inkerman, Sevastopol.

Uniform Scarlet, facings yellow

Regimental march [Quick] *Paddy's Resource*

Nickname The Pot-Hooks

THE KING'S OWN ROYAL BORDER REGIMENT

(4th, 34th, 55th)

Formed October 1959 by amalgamation of The King's Own Royal Regiment (Lancaster) with The Border Regiment.

Battle honours Namur 1695, Gibraltar 1704–5, Guadaloupe 1759, Havannah, St. Lucia 1778, Corunna, Albuhera, Arroyo dos Molinos, Badajoz, Salamanca, Vittoria, St. Sebastian, Pyrenees, Nivelle, Nive, Orthes, Peninsula, Bladensburg, Waterloo, China (with the Dragon), Alma, Inkerman, Sevastapol, Lucknow, Abyssinia, South Africa 1879, Relief of Ladysmith, South Africa 1899–1902.

*The Great War—32 Battalions—*Le Cateau, Retreat from Mons, Marne 1914, Aisne 1914, Armentieres 1914, Ypres 1914, 15, 17, 18, Langemarck 1914, 17, Gheluvelt, Neuve Chapelle, Gravenstafel, St. Julien, Frezenberg, Bellewaarde, Aubers, Festubert 1915, Loos, Somme 1916, 18, Albert 1916, 18, Bazentin, Delville Wood, Pozieres, Guillemont, Ginchy, Flers-Courcelette, Morval, Thiepval, Le Transloy, Ancre Heights, Ancre 1916, Arras 1917, 18, Scarpe 1917, 18, Arleux, Bullecourt, Messines 1917, 18, Pilckem, Menin Road, Polygon Wood, Broodseinde, Poelcappelle, Passchendaele, Cambrai 1917, 18, St. Quentin, Rosieres, Lys, Estaires, Hazebrouck, Bailleul, Kemmel, Bethune, Scherpenberg, Aisne 1918, Amiens, Bapaume 1918, Drocourt-Queant, Hindenburg Line, Epehy, Canal du Nord, St. Quentin Canal, Beaurevoir, Courtrai, Selle, Valenciennes, Sambre, France and Flanders 1914–18, Piave, Vittorio Veneto, Italy 1917–18, Struma, Doiran 1917, 18, Macedonia 1915–18, Helles, Landing at Helles, Krithia, Suvla, Sari Bair, Landing at Suvla, Scimitar Hill, Gallipoli 1915–16, Egypt 1916, Tigris 1916, Kut al Amara 1917, Baghdad, Mesopotamia 1916–18, N. W. Frontier India 1916–17.

Afghanistan 1919.

The Second World War—Defence of Escaut, St. Omer-La Bassee, Dunkirk 1940, Somme 1940, Arnhem 1944, N.W. Europe 1940, 44, Defence of Habbaniya, Falluja, Iraq 1941, Merjayun, Jebel Mazar, Syria 1941, Tobruk 1941, Tobruk Sortie, North Africa 1940–42, Landing in Sicily, Montone, Citta di Castello, San Martino Sogliano, Lamone Bridgehead, Italy 1944–45, Malta 1941–42, Imphal, Sakawng, Tamu Road, Shenam Pass, Kohima, Ukhrul, Mandalay, Myinmu Bridgehead, Meiktila, Rangoon Road, Pyawbew, Sittang 1945, Chindits 1944, Burma 1943–45.

Uniform Blue, piping scarlet, facings blue

Regimental marches [Quick] Arrangement of *D'ye Ken John Peel*, *Lass o' Gowrie* and *Corn Rigs are Bonny*

[Slow] *And Shall Trelawney Die*

Regimental journal *The Lion and The Dragon*

Regimental headquarters The Castle, Carlisle, Cumbria CA3 8UR

Regimental museums (The King's Own Royal Regiment) City Museum, Market Square, Lancaster LA1 1HT

(The Border Regiment and The King's Own Royal Border Regiment)
The Castle, Carlisle, Cumbria CA3 8UR

THE KING'S OWN ROYAL REGIMENT
(LANCASTER)

Raised July 1680 by Colonel Charles Fitzcharles, 1st Earl of Plymouth, for the garrison of Tangier, and ranked as 4th Regiment of Foot.

Titles 1680 The Earl of Plymouth's Regiment of Foot for Tangier
1684 The Duchess of York and Albany's Regiment
1685 The Queen's Own Regiment of Foot
1703 The Royal Regiment of Marines (1710–1715, *known by Colonels' names*)
1715 The King's Own Regiment of Foot
1747 4th (or the King's Own) Regiment of Foot
1759 4th (The King's Own) Regiment of Foot
1881 The King's Own (Royal Lancaster Regiment)

1921 The King's Own Royal Regiment (Lancaster)
1959 Amalgamated with The Border Regiment to form
The King's Own Royal Border Regiment

Battle honours Namur 1695, Gibraltar 1704–5, Guadaloupe, 1759, St. Lucia 1778, Corunna, Badajoz, Salamanca, Vittoria, St. Sebastian, Nive, Peninsula, Bladensburg, Waterloo, Alma, Inkerman, Sevastopol, Abyssinia, South Africa 1879, Relief of Ladysmith, South Africa 1899–1902.

*The Great War—16 Battalions—*Le Cateau, Retreat from Mons, Marne 1914, Aisne 1914, Armentieres 1914, Ypres 1915, 17, Gravenstafel, St. Julien, Frezenberg, Bellewaarde, Festubert 1915, Loos, Somme 1916, 18, Albert 1916, 18, Bazentin, Delville Wood, Pozieres, Guillemont, Ginchy, Flers-Courcelette, Morval, Le Transloy, Ancre Heights, Ancre 1916, Arras 1917, 18, Scarpe 1917, 18, Arleux, Messines 1917, Pilckem, Menin Road, Polygon Wood, Broodseinde, Poelcappelle, Passchendaele, Cambrai 1917, 18, St. Quentin, Lys, Estaires, Hazebrouck, Bethune, Bapaume, 1918, Drocourt-Queant, Hindenburg Line, Canal du Nord, Selle, Valenciennes, Sambre, France and Flanders, 1914–18, Struma, Doiran 1917, 18, Macedonia 1915–18, Suvla, Sari Bair, Gallipoli 1915, Egypt 1916, Tigris 1916, Kut al Amara 1917, Baghdad, Mesopotamia 1916–18.

*The Second World War—*St. Omer-La Bassee, Dunkirk 1940, North-West Europe 1940, Defence of Habbaniya, Falluja, Iraq 1941, Merjayun, Jebel Mazar, Syria, 1941, Tobruk 1941, Tobruk Sortie, North Africa 1940–42, Montone, Citta di Castello, San Martino Sogliano, Lamone Bridgehead, Italy 1944–45, Malta 1941–42, Chindits 1944, Burma 1944.

Uniform Blue, piping scarlet, facings blue

Regimental marches [Quick] *Corn Rigs are Bonny*
[Slow] *And Shall Trelawney Die*

Regimental journal *The Lion & the Rose*

Regimental museum City Museum, Market Square, Lancaster

Nicknames The Lions. Barrell's Blues

Remarks The Regiment has always claimed that its ancient Badge, the Lion of England, was bestowed on it by King William III because it had been the first English unit to join his Standard when he landed as Prince William of Orange at Torbay in 1688. The first nickname is derived from the Badge.

THE BORDER REGIMENT

Formed 1881 by amalgamation of 34th (Cumberland) Regiment with 55th (Westmoreland) Regiment.

Battle honours Havannah, St. Lucia 1778, Albuhera, Arroyo dos Molinos, Vittoria, Pyrenees, Nivelle, Nive, Orthes, Peninsula, Alma, Inkerman, Sevastopol, Lucknow, Relief of Ladysmith, South Africa 1899–1902.

The Great War—16 *Battalions*—Ypres 1914, 15, 17, 18, Langemarck 1914, 17, Gheluvelt, Neuve Chapelle, Frezenberg, Bellewaarde, Aubers, Festubert 1915, Loos, Somme 1916, 18, Albert 1916, 18, Bazentin, Delville Wood, Pozieres, Guillemont, Flers-Courcelette, Morval, Thiepval, Le Transloy, Ancre Heights, Ancre 1916, Arras 1917, 18, Scarpe 1917, Bullecourt, Messines 1917, 18, Pilckem, Polygon Wood, Broodseinde, Poelcappelle, Passchendaele, Cambrai, 1917, 18, St. Quentin, Rosieres, Lys, Estaires, Hazebrouck, Bailleul, Kemmel, Scherpenberg, Aisne 1918, Amiens, Bapaume 1918, Hindenburg Line, Epehy, St. Quentin Canal, Beaurevoir, Courtrai, Selle, Sambre, France and Flanders 1914–18, Piave, Vittorio Veneto, Italy 1917–18, Doiran 1917, 18, Macedonia 1915–18, Helles, Landing at Helles, Krithia, Suvla, Landing at Suvla, Scimitar Hill, Gallipoli 1915–16, Egypt 1916, N.W. Frontier, India 1916–17.

Afghanistan, 1919.

The Second World War—Defence of Escaut, Dunkirk 1940, Somme 1940, Arnhem 1944, North-West Europe 1940, 44, Tobruk 1941, Landing in Sicily, Imphal, Sakawng, Tamu Road, Shenam Pass, Kohima, Ukhrul, Mandalay, Myinmu Bridgehead, Meiktila, Rangoon Road, Pyawbwe, Sittang 1945, Chindits 1944, Burma 1943–45.

Uniform Scarlet, piping yellow, facings yellow

Regimental marches [Quick] Arrangement of *D'Ye Ken John Peel, 34me Régiment March* and *Lass o' Gowrie*

[Slow] The Regiment had no Slow March until 1950 when it adopted an arrangement of *Chinese Airs*, *The Horn of the Hunter* and *Soldier Will You Marry Me*. This was never officially approved. *Chinese Airs* was a selection of melodies arranged by BM (later Lieut-Colonel) O.M. Geary when both 1st and 2nd Bns The Border Regiment were serving together at Shanghai in 1927. The score has never been published.

Regimental journal *The Border Magazine*

Regimental museum The Castle, Carlisle, Cumbria CA3 8UR

Nicknames The Cattle Reeves. The Two Fives

Remarks At the Battle of Arroyo dos Molinos (Peninsula) in 1811, the 34th (Cumberland) Regiment captured the entire *34me Régiment* of France, together with drums and Drum-Major's staff. On the anniversary of the Battle a ceremonial parade is held by the present Regiment, on which the captured drums are 'trooped' by the Drummer-boys of the Regiment dressed in the uniform of the *34me Régiment*.

34th (CUMBERLAND) REGIMENT

Raised February 1702 by Colonel Robert, 3rd Lord Lucas, and ranked as 34th Regiment of Foot.

Titles 1702 Lord Lucas's Regiment of Foot *Title subsequently changed with Colonels' names*
1747 34th Regiment of Foot
1782 34th (or the Cumberland) Regiment of Foot
1881 Amalgamated with 55th (Westmoreland) Regiment to form The Border Regiment

Battle honours Albuhera, Arroyo dos Molinos, Vittoria, Pyrenees, Nivelle, Nive, Orthes, Peninsula, Sevastopol, Lucknow.

Uniform Scarlet, facings yellow.

Regimental march [Quick] *D'Ye Ken John Peel*

Nickname The Cattle Reeves

55th (WESTMORELAND) REGIMENT

Raised at Stirling, December 1755, by Colonel George Perry and ranked as 57th Regiment of Foot.

Titles 1755 57th Regiment of Foot
1757 55th Regiment of Foot
1782 55th (or the Westmoreland) Regiment of Foot
1881 Amalgamated with 34th (Cumberland) Regiment to form The Border Regiment

Battle honours China (with the Dragon), Alma, Inkerman, Sevastopol.

Uniform Scarlet, facings Kendal green

Regimental march [Quick] *The Lass o' Gowrie*

Nickname The Two Fives

THE ROYAL REGIMENT OF FUSILIERS
(5th, 6th, 7th, 20th)

Formed 23rd April 1968 by amalgamation of The Royal Northumberland Fusiliers, The Royal Warwickshire Fusiliers, The Royal Fusiliers (City of London Regiment) and the Lancashire Fusiliers.

Battle honours Namur 1695, Dettingen, Minden, Wilhelmstahl, St. Lucia 1778, Martinique 1794, 1809, Egmont-op-Zee, Egypt (with the Sphinx), Maida, Rolica, Vimiera, Corunna, Talavera, Busaco, Ciudad Rodrigo, Badajoz, Albuhera, Salamanca, Vittoria, Pyrenees, Nivelle, Orthes, Toulouse, Peninsula, Niagara, South Africa 1846–47, 1851, 52, 53, Alma, Inkerman, Sevastopol, Lucknow, Kandahar 1880, Afghanistan 1878–80, Atbara, Khartoum, Modder River, Relief of Ladysmith, South Africa 1899–1902.

The Great War—Mons, Le Cateau, Retreat from Mons, Marne 1914, 18, Aisne 1914, 18, La Bassee 1914, Messines 1914, 17, 18, Armentieres 1914, Ypres 1914, 15, 17, 18, Langemarck 1914, 17, Gheluvelt, Nonne Bosschen, Neuve Chapelle, Gravenstafel, St. Julien, Frezenburg, Bellewaarde, Hooge 1915, Aubers, Festubert 1915, Loos, Somme 1916, 18, Albert 1916, 18, Bazentin, Delville Wood, Pozieres, Guillemont, Ginchy, Flers-Courcelette, Morval, Thiepval, Le Transloy, Ancre Heights, Ancre 1916, 18, Arras 1917, 18, Vimy 1917, Scarpe 1917, 18, Arleux, Bullecourt, Oppy,Pilckem, Menin Road, Polygon Wood, Broodseinde, Poelcappelle, Passchendaele, Cambrai 1917, 18, St. Quentin, Bapaume 1918, Rosieres, Avre, Villers Bretonneux, Lys, Estaires, Hazebrouck, Bailleul, Kemmel, Bethune, Scherpenberg, Amiens, Drocourt-Queant, Hindenburg Line, Havrincourt, Epehy, Canal du Nord, St. Quentin Canal, Beaurevoir, Courtrai, Selle, Valenciennes, Sambre, France and Flanders 1914–18, Piave, Vittorio Veneto, Italy 1917–18, Struma, Doiran 1917, Macedonia 1915–18, Helles, Landing at Helles, Krithia, Suvla, Sari Bair, Landing at Suvla, Scimitar Hill, Gallipoli 1915–16, Rumani, Egypt 1915–17, Megiddo, Nablus, Palestine 1918, Tigris 1916, Kut al Amara 1917, Baghdad, Mesopotamia 1916–18, Baku, Persia 1918, Troitsa, Archangel 1919, Kilimanjaro, Behobeho, Nyangao, East Africa 1915–17.

The Second World War—Defence of Escaut, Arras counter attack, St. Omer-La Bassee, Wormhoudt, Ypres-Comines Canal, Dunkirk 1940, Normandy Landing, Odon, Caen, Bourguebus Ridge, Cagny, Mont Pincon, Falaise, Nederrijn, Venraij, Rhineland, Lingen, Brinkum, Bremen, North-West Europe 1940, 44–45, Agordat, Keren, Syria 1941, Sidi Barrani, Defence of Tobruk, Tobruk 1941, Belhamed, Cauldron, Ruweisat Ridge, El Alamein, Advance on Tripoli, Medenine, Djebel Tebaga, Medjez el Bab, Oued Zarga, Peter's Corner, North Africa 1940–43, Adrano, Sicily 1943, Termoli, Trigno, Sangro, Mozzagrogna, Caldari, Salerno, St. Lucia, Battipaglia, Teano, Volturno Crossing, Monte Camino, Garigliano Crossing, Damiano, Anzio, Cassino II, Ripa Ridge, Trasimene Line, Gabbiano, Advance to Florence, Monte Scalari, Gothic Line, Coriano, Croce, Monte Ceco, Casa Fortis, Monte Spaduro, Savio Bridgehead, Vali di Comacchio, Senio, Argenta Gap, Italy 1943–45, Athens, Greece

1944–45, Malta 1941–42, Singapore Island, Rathedaung, Htizwe, Kohima, Naga Village, Chindits 1944, Burma 1943–45.

Seoul, Imjin, Kowang-San, Korea 1950–53.

Motto *Honi Soit Qui Mal y Pense* (Motto of the Garter) (Evil to him who evil thinks)

Uniform Scarlet, piping scarlet, facings blue

Regimental marches [Quick] *The British Grenadiers* (Tradit.)
[Slow] *Rule Britannia* (Arne)

Regimental journal *The Fusilier*

Regimental headquarters H.M. Tower of London, London EC3N 4AB

Regimental museums (Royal Northumberland Fusiliers)
The Abbot's Tower, Alnwick Castle, Alnwick, Northumberland NE66 1NG

(The Royal Warwickshire Fusiliers)
St. John's House, Warwick CV34 4NF

(The Royal Fusiliers)
H.M. Tower of London, London EC3N 4AB

(The Lancashire Fusiliers)
Wellington Barracks, Bury, Lancashire BL8 2PL

THE ROYAL NORTHUMBERLAND FUSILIERS

(5th)

The Regiment traces its origins to a British regiment of Foot raised in August 1674 for service in the Netherlands with Prince William of Orange, its Colonel being Daniel O'Brien, 3rd Viscount Clare. The Regiment was recalled to England by James II in 1685, but returned to Holland in 1686. In 1688 the Regiment came to England with Prince William, and on his accession as King was placed on the establishment of the Standing Army, ranking as the 5th Regiment of Foot, with Colonel Thomas Tollemache in command.

Titles 1674 Lord O'Brien's Regiment (or The Irish Regiment)
1688 Colonel Tollemache's Regiment of Foot *Title
subsequently changed with Colonels' names*
1751 5th Regiment of Foot
1782 5th (or the Northumberland) Regiment of Foot
1836 5th Regiment of Foot (Northumberland Fusiliers)
1881 The Northumberland Fusiliers
1935 The Royal Northumberland Fusiliers
1968 Amalgamated with The Royal Warwickshire
Fusiliers, The Royal Fusiliers and The Lancashire
Fusiliers to form The Royal Regiment of Fusiliers

Battle honours Wilhelmstahl, St. Lucia 1778, Rolica, Vimiera,
Corunna, Busaco, Ciudad Rodrigo, Badajoz, Salamanca,
Vittoria, Nivelle, Orthes, Toulouse, Peninsula,
Lucknow, Afghanistan 1878–80, Khartoum, Modder
River, South Africa 1899–1902.

The Great War—52 *Battalions*—Mons, Le Cateau,
Retreat from Mons, Marne 1914, Aisne 1914, 18, La
Bassee 1914, Messines 1914, 17, 18, Armentieres, 1914,
Ypres 1914, 15, 17, 18, Nonne Bosschen, Gravenstafel,
St. Julien, Frezenberg, Bellewaarde, Loos, Somme 1916,
18, Albert 1916, 18, Bazentin, Delville Wood, Pozieres,
Flers-Courcelette, Morval, Thiepval, Le Transloy, Ancre
Heights, Ancre 1916, Arras 1917, 18, Scarpe 1917, 18,
Arleux, Pilckem, Langemarck 1917, Menin Road,
Polygon Wood, Broodseinde, Passchendaele, Cambrai,
1917, 18, St. Quentin, Bapaume, 1918, Rosieres, Lys,
Estaires, Hazebrouck, Bailleul, Kemmel, Bethune,
Scherpenberg, Drocourt-Queant, Hindenburg Line,
Epehy, Canal du Nord, St. Quentin Canal, Beaurevoir,
Courtrai, Selle, Valenciennes, Sambre, France and
Flanders 1914–18, Piave, Vittorio Veneto, Italy 1917–18,
Struma, Macedonia 1915–18, Suvla, Landing at Suvla,
Scimitar Hill, Gallipoli 1915, Egypt 1916–17.

The Second World War—Defence of Escaut, Arras
counter attack, St. Omer-La Bassee, Dunkirk 1940,
Odon, Caen, Cagny, Falaise, Nederrijn, Rhineland,
North-West Europe 1940, 44–45, Sidi Barrani, Defence
of Tobruk, Tobruk 1941, Belhamed, Cauldron, Ruweisat
Ridge, El Alamein, Advance on Tripoli, Medenine,
North Africa 1940–43, Salerno, Volturno Crossing,
Monte Camino, Garigliano Crossing, Cassino II, Italy
1943–45, Singapore Island

Seoul, Imjin, Kowang-San, Korea, 1950–51.

Motto *Quo Fata Vocant* (Whither the Fates summon)

Uniform Scarlet, piping and facings Gosling green

Regimental marches [Quick] *The British Grenadiers* and *Blaydon Races* (Tradit.)
[Slow] *St. George*

Regimental journal *St. George's Gazette*

Nicknames The Fighting Fifth. The Old and Bold. The Shiners. Wellington's Bodyguard

Remarks In recognition of their defeat of the Royal Grenadiers of France and another Royal regiment at the battle of Wilhelmstahl (1792), the 5th Foot were authorised to wear the Grenadier (or Fusilier) cap in place of the regulation tricorne. The Regiment was the only British Army unit to be awarded the Battle Honour *Wilhelmstahl*.

THE ROYAL WARWICKSHIRE FUSILIERS

(6th)

Raised 1674 from British companies fighting in the Dutch service under command of Sir Walter Vane, the first Colonel being Luke Lillingston. The Regiment accompanied William of Orange to England in 1688 and was taken on the English establishment with Colonel Philip Babington as Colonel.

Titles 1674 Colonel Lillingston's Regiment of Foot
1688 Colonel Babington's Regiment of Foot *Title subsequently changed with Colonels' names*
1751 6th Regiment of Foot
1782 6th (or the 1st Warwickshire) Regiment of Foot
1832 6th (The Royal 1st Warwickshire) Regiment of Foot
1881 The Royal Warwickshire Regiment
1963 The Royal Warwickshire Fusiliers
1968 Amalgamated with The Royal Northumberland Fusiliers, The Royal Fusiliers and The Lancashire Fusiliers to form The Royal Regiment of Fusiliers

Battle honours Namur 1695, Martinique 1794, Rolica, Vimiera, Corunna, Vittoria, Pyrenees, Nivelle, Orthes, Peninsula, Niagara, South Africa 1846–47, 1851–52–53, Atbara, Khartoum, South Africa 1899–1902.

The Great War— 30 *Battalions*—Le Cateau, Retreat from Mons, Marne 1914, Aisne 1914, 18, Armentieres 1914, Ypres 1914, 15, 17, Langemarck 1914, 17, Gheluvelt, Neuve Chapelle, St. Julien, Frezenberg, Bellewaarde, Aubers, Festubert 1915, Loos, Somme 1916, 18, Albert 1916, 18, Bazentin, Delville Wood, Pozieres, Guillemont, Flers-Courcelette, Morval, Le Transloy, Ancre Heights, Ancre 1916, Arras 1917, 18, Vimy 1917, Scarpe 1917, 18, Arleux, Oppy, Bullecourt, Messines 1917, 18, Pilckem, Menin Road, Polygon Wood, Broodseinde, Poelcappelle, Passchendaele, Cambrai 1917, 18, St. Quentin, Bapaume 1918, Rosieres, Lys, Estaires, Hazebrouck, Bailleul, Kemmel, Bethune, Drocourt-Queant, Hindenburg Line, Epehy, Canal du Nord, Beaurevoir, Selle, Valenciennes, Sambre, France and Flanders 1914–18, Piave, Vittorio Veneto, Italy 1917–18, Suvla, Sari Bair, Gallipoli 1915–16, Tigris 1916, Kut al Amara 1917, Baghdad, Mesopotamia 1916–18, Baku, Persia 1918.

The Second World War—Defence of Escaut, Wormhoudt, Ypres-Comines Canal, Normandy Landing, Caen, Bourguebus Ridge, Mont Pincon, Falaise, Venraij, Rhineland, Lingen, Brinkum, Bremen, North-West Europe 1940, 44–45, Burma 1945.

Motto *Honi Soit Qui Mal y Pense* (Motto of the Garter)

Uniform Scarlet, piping scarlet, facings blue

Regimental marches [Quick] *The British Grenadiers* and *Warwickshire Lads*
[Slow] *MacBean's Slow March*

Regimental journal *The Antelope.*

Nicknames Dutch Guards. Guise's Geese. Saucy Sixth

Remarks Tradition has it that the Warwickshires' Antelope Badge was authorised for the 6th Foot in 1743, to commemorate the capture, at Saragossa in 1710, of several Moorish Standards, one bearing an Antelope device. For many years an Indian Blackbuck was the Regimental Mascot of the 6th, and is today the Mascot of The Royal Regiment of Fusiliers.

THE ROYAL FUSILIERS
(CITY OF LONDON REGIMENT)
(7th)

Raised in the Tower of London by James II, June 1685.
Armed with the fusil, its primary role was an escort to the
Train of Artillery, also quartered in the Tower. The first
Colonel was George Legge, 1st Lord Dartmouth, Master-
General of the Ordnance.

Titles 1685 Royal Regiment of Fuzilieers (or Ordnance
Regiment)
1688 7th Regiment of Foot (or the Royal Fuzileers)
Spelling later altered to 'Fusiliers'
1881 The Royal Fusiliers (City of London Regiment)
1968 Amalgamated with Royal Northumberland
Fusiliers, The Royal Warwickshire Fusiliers and
The Lancashire Fusiliers to form The Royal
Regiment of Fusiliers

Battle honours Namur 1695, Martinique 1809, Talavera, Busaco,
Albuhera, Badajoz, Salamanca, Vittoria, Pyrenees,
Orthes, Toulouse, Peninsula, Alma, Inkerman,
Sevastopol, Kandahar 1880, Afghanistan 1879–80, Relief
of Ladysmith, South Africa 1899–1902.

The Great War—51 *Battalions*—Mons, Le Cateau,
Retreat from Mons, Marne 1914, Aisne 1914, La Bassee
1944, Messines 1914, 17, Armentieres 1914, Ypres 1914,
15, 17, 18, Nonne Bosschen, Gravenstafel, St. Julien,
Frezenberg, Bellewaarde, Hooge 1915, Loos, Aubers,
Somme 1916, 18, Albert 1916, 18, Bazentin, Delville
Wood, Pozieres, Flers-Courcelette, Thiepval, Le
Transloy, Ancre Heights, Ancre 1916, 18, Arras 1917,
18, Vimy 1917, Scarpe, 1917, Arleux, Pilckem,
Langemarck 1917, Bullecourt, Menin Road, Polygon
Wood, Broodseinde, Poelcappelle, Passchendaele,
Cambrai 1917, 18, St. Quentin, Bapaume 1918,
Rosieres, Avre, Villers Bretonneux, Lys, Estaires,
Hazebrouck, Bethune, Amiens, Drocourt-Queant,
Hindenburg Line, Havrincourt, Epehy, Canal du Nord,
St. Quentin Canal, Beaurevoir, Courtrai, Selle, Sambre,
France and Flanders 1914–18, Italy 1917–18, Struma,
Macedonia 1915–18, Helles, Landing at Helles, Krithia,
Suvla, Scimitar Hill, Gallipoli 1915–16, Egypt 1916,

Megiddo, Nablus, Palestine 1918, Troitsa, Archangel 1919, Kilimanjaro, Behobeho, Nyangao, E. Africa 1915–17.

The Second World War—Dunkirk 1940, North-West Europe 1940, Agordat, Keren, Syria 1941, Sidi Barrani, Djebel Tebaga, Peters Corner, North Africa 1940, 43, Sangro, Mozzagrogna, Caldari, Salerno, St. Lucia, Battipaglia, Teano, Monte Camino, Garigliano Crossing, Damiano, Anzio, Cassino II, Ripa Ridge, Gabbiano, Advance to Florence, Monte Scalari, Gothic Line, Coriano, Croce, Casa Fortis, Savio Bridgehead, Valli di Comacchio, Senio, Argenta Gap, Italy 1943–45, Athens, Greece 1944–45.

Korea 1952–53.

Motto	*Honi Soit Qui Mal y Pense* (Motto of the Garter)
Uniform	Scarlet, piping scarlet, facings blue
Regimental marches [Quick]	*The British Grenadiers*
[Slow]	*De Normandie*
Regimental journal	*The Royal Fusiliers Chronicle*
Nickname	The Elegant Extracts
Remarks	Raised in London, The Royal Fusiliers always recruited exclusively in that City and were truly a 'London Regiment' throughout their separate existence.

In 1903–04 four companies of the 1st Battalion fought in Tibet and entered Lhasa with the Younghusband Mission. They and a section of Mountain Gunners and a small detachment of the Norfolk Regiment were the only European troops to see 'the Forbidden City'.

THE LANCASHIRE FUSILIERS
(20th)

The Regiment's origins are traced to independent companies of Foot raised at Exeter by Colonel Sir Robert Peyton in November 1688, for service with the newly-landed Prince William of Orange's forces. Peyton's command was augmented as a regiment and taken on the English Establishment in February 1689.

Titles 1688 Colonel Sir Robert Peyton's Companies of Foot
1689 Colonel Sir Robert Peyton's Regiment of Foot *Title
subsequently changed with Colonels' names*
1751 20th Regiment of Foot
1782 20th (or the East Devonshire) Regiment of Foot
1881 The Lancashire Fusiliers
1968 Amalgamated with The Royal Northumberland
Fusiliers, The Royal Warwickshire Fusiliers and
The Royal Fusiliers to form The Royal Regiment of
Fusiliers

Battle honours Dettingen, Minden, Egmont-op-Zee, Egypt (with the
Sphinx), Maida, Vimiera, Corunna, Vittoria, Pyrenees,
Orthes, Toulouse, Peninsula, Alma, Inkerman,
Sevastopol, Lucknow, Khartoum, Relief of Ladysmith,
South Africa 1889–1902.

The Great War— 30 *Battalions*—Le Cateau, Retreat
from Mons, Marne 1914, Aisne 1914, 18, Armentieres
1914, Ypres 1915, 17, 18, St. Julien, Bellewaarde,
Somme 1916, 18, Albert 1916, 18, Bazentin, Delville
Wood, Pozieres, Ginchy, Flers-Courcelette, Morval,
Thiepval, Le Transloy, Ancre Heights, Ancre 1916, 18,
Arras 1917, 18, Scarpe 1917, 18, Arleux, Messines 1917,
Pilckem, Langemarck 1917, Menin Road, Polygon
Wood, Broodseinde, Poelcappelle, Passchendaele,
Cambrai 1917, 18, St. Quentin, Bapaume 1918,
Rosieres, Lys, Estaires, Hazebrouck, Bailleul, Kemmel,
Bethune, Scherpenberg, Amiens, Drocourt-Queant,
Hindenburg Line, Epehy, Canal du Nord, St. Quentin
Canal, Courtrai, Selle, Sambre, France and Flanders
1914–18, Doiran 1917, Macedonia 1915–18, Helles,
Landing at Helles, Krithia, Suvla, Landing at Suvla,
Scimitar Hill, Gallipoli 1915, Rumani, Egypt 1915–17.

The Second World War—Defence of Escaut, St. Omer-
La Bassee, Caen, North-West Europe 1940, 44, Medjez
el Bab, Oued Zarga, North Africa 1942–43, Adrano,
Sicily 1943, Termoli, Trigno, Sangro, Cassino II,
Trasimene Line, Monte Ceco, Monte Spaduro, Senio,
Argenta Gap, Italy 1943–45, Malta 1941–42,
Rathedaung, Htizwe, Kohima, Naga Village, Chindits
1944, Burma 1943–45.

Motto *Omnia Audax* (In all things daring)

Uniform Scarlet, piping scarlet, facings white

Regimental marches [Quick] *The British Grenadiers* (Tradit.) and *The Minden March* (Based on old hymn tune *Lammas Day*)

[Slow] *The Lancashire Fusiliers Slow March*

Regimental journal *The Gallipoli Gazette*

Remarks The 20th Foot (or Kingsley's Regiment) were one of the six British infantry regiments who defeated the French cavalry at Minden (1759), and thereafter donned their 'Minden Roses' on every anniversary of the battle, as does the present Regiment.

In 1820–21 the Regiment provided the guard for the captive Napoleon Bonaparte on the island of St. Helena, and on the Emperor's death, men of the Regiment carried the coffin to the grave.

In Gallipoli (1915) the 1st Battalion won six VCs 'before breakfast' at what became known as the 'Lancashire Landing'.

THE KING'S REGIMENT
(8th, 63rd, 96th)

Formed September 1958 by amalgamation of The King's Regiment (Liverpool) with The Manchester Regiment to form The King's Regiment (Manchester and Liverpool). In December 1968 the title was changed to The King's Regiment.

Battle honours Blenheim, Ramillies, Oudenarde, Malplaquet, Dettingen, Guadaloupe 1759, Egmont-op-Zee, Egypt (with the Sphinx), Peninsula, Martinique 1809, Guadaloupe 1810, Niagara, New Zealand, Alma, Inkerman, Sevastopol, Delhi 1857, Lucknow, Peiwar Kotal, Afghanistan 1878–80, Egypt 1882, Burma 1885–87, Defence of Ladysmith, South Africa 1899–1902.

The Great War—Mons, Le Cateau, Retreat from Mons, Marne 1914, Aisne 1914, La Bassee 1914, Armentieres 1914, Ypres 1914, 15, 17, 18, Langemarck 1914, 17, Gheluvelt, Nonne Bosschen, Givenchy 1914. Neuve Chapelle, Gravenstafel, St. Julien, Frenzenberg Bellewaarde, Aubers, Festubert 1915, Loos, Somme

1916, 18, Albert 1916, 18, Bazentin, Delville Wood,
Giullemont, Ginchy, Flers-Courcelette, Morval,
Thiepval, Le Transloy, Ancre Heights, Ancre 1916, 18,
Bapaume 1917, 18, Arras 1917, 18, Scarpe 1917, 18,
Arleux, Bullecourt, Messines 1917, 18, Pilckem, Menin
Road, Polygon Wood, Broodseinde, Poelcappelle,
Passchendaele, Cambrai 1917, 18, St. Quentin, Rosieres,
Avre, Lys, Estaires, Bailleul, Kemmel, Bethune, Amiens,
Scherpenberg, Drocourt-Queant, Hindenburg Line,
Epehy, Canal du Nord, St. Quentin Canal, Beaurevoir,
Courtrai, Selle, Sambre, France and Flanders 1914–18,
Piave, Vittorio Veneto, Italy 1917–18, Doiran 1917,
Macedonia 1915–18, Helles, Krithia, Suvla, Landing at
Suvla, Scimitar Hill, Gallipoli 1915, Rumani, Egypt
1915–17, Megiddo, Sharon, Palestine 1918, Tigris 1916,
Kut al Amara 1917, Baghdad, Mesopotamia 1916–18,
N.W. Frontier India 1915, Archangel 1918–19.

Afghanistan 1919.

The Second World War—Dyle, Withdrawal to Escaut,
Defence of Escaut, Defence of Arras, St. Omer-La
Bassee, Ypres-Comines Canal, Normandy Landing,
Caen, Esquay, Falaise, Nederrijn, Scheldt, Walcharen
Causeway, Flushing, Lower Maas, Venlo Pocket, Roer,
Ourthe, Rhineland, Reichswald, Goch, Weeze, Rhine,
Ibbenburen, Dreirwalde, Aller, Bremen, North-West
Europe 1940, 44–45, Cassino II, Trasimene Line, Tuori,
Gothic Line, Monte Gridolfo, Coriano, San Clemente,
Gemmano Ridge, Montilgallo, Capture of Forli, Lamone
Crossing, Defence of Lamone Bridgehead, Rimini Line,
Montescudo, Cesena, Italy 1944–45, Malta 1940,
Athens, Greece 1944–45, Singapore Island, Malaya
1941–42, North Arakan, Kohima, Pinwe, Schwebo,
Myinmu Bridgehead, Irrawaddy, Chindits 1943, Chindits
1944, Burma 1943–45.

The Hook 1953, Korea 1952–53.

Motto	*Nec Aspera Terrent* (Nor do difficulties deter)
Uniform	Scarlet, piping and facings deep green
Regimental marches [Quick]	*The Kingsman*
[Slow]	*The English Rose*
Regimental journal	*The Kingsman*
Regimental headquarters	TA Centre, Townsend Avenue, Liverpool L11 5AF

Regimental museums (The King's Regiment (Liverpool))
Merseyside County Museums, William Brown Street,
Liverpool L3 8EN

(The Manchester Regiment)
Queen's Park Museum and Art Gallery, Queen's Park,
Rochdale Road, Manchester M9 1SH

THE KING'S REGIMENT
(LIVERPOOL)
(8th)

Raised June 1685 by Colonel Robert Shirley, 1st Earl
Ferrers, as The Princess Anne of Denmark's Regiment of
Foot.

Titles 1685 The Princess Anne of Denmark's Regiment of Foot
1702 The Queen's Regiment of Foot
1716 The King's Regiment of Foot
1751 8th (or the King's) Regiment of Foot
1881 The King's (Liverpool Regiment)
1921 The King's Regiment (Liverpool)
1958 Amalgamated with The Manchester Regiment to
form The King's Regiment (Manchester and
Liverpool)

Battle honours Blenheim, Ramillies, Oudenarde, Malplaquet,
Dettingen, Egypt (with the Sphinx), Martinique 1809,
Niagara, Delhi 1857, Lucknow, Peiwar Kotal,
Afghanistan 1878–80, Burma 1885–87, Defence of
Ladysmith, South Africa 1899–1902.

The Great War—45 *Battalions*—Mons, Retreat from
Mons, Marne 1914, Aisne 1914, Ypres 1914, 15, 17,
Langemarck 1914, 17, Gheluvelt, Nonne Bosschen,
Neuve Chapelle, Gravenstafel, St. Julien, Frezenberg,
Bellewaarde, Aubers, Festubert 1915, Loos, Somme
1916, 18, Albert 1916, 18, Bazentin, Delville Wood,
Guillemont, Ginchy, Flers-Courcelette, Morval, Le
Transloy, Ancre 1916, Bapaume 1917, 18, Arras 1917,
18, Scarpe 1917, 18, Arleux, Pilckem, Menin Road,
Polygon Wood, Poelcappelle, Passchendaele, Cambrai
1917, 18, St. Quentin, Rosieres, Avre, Lys, Estaires,
Messines 1918, Bailleul, Kemmel, Bethune,
Scherpenberg, Drocourt-Queant, Hindenburg Line,
Epehy, Canal du Nord, St. Quentin Canal, Selle,

Sambre, France and Flanders 1914–18, Doiran 1917, Macedonia 1915–18, N.W. Frontier India 1915, Archangel 1918–19.

Afghanistan 1919.

The Second World War—Normandy Landing, North-West Europe 1944, Cassino II, Trasimene Line, Tuori, Capture of Forli, Rimini Line, Italy 1944–45, Athens, Greece 1944–45, Chindits 1943, Chindits 1944, Burma 1943–44.

The Hook 1953, Korea 1952–53.

Motto	*Nec Aspera Terrent* (Nor do difficulties deter)
Uniform	Scarlet, piping and facings blue
Regimental marches [Quick]	*Zakhmi Dil* (Tradit. Pathan)* and *Here's to the Maiden of Bashful Fifteen* (Tradit.)
[Slow]	*The English Rose*
Regimental journal	*The Kingsman*
Nickname	The Leather Hats

THE MANCHESTER REGIMENT
(63rd, 96th)

Formed 1881 by amalgamation of the 63rd (West Suffolk) Regiment of Foot with the 96th Regiment of Foot.

Battle honours Guadaloupe 1759, Egmont-op-Zee, Egypt (with the Sphinx), Peninsula, Martinique 1809, Guadaloupe 1810, New Zealand, Alma, Inkerman, Sevastopol, Afghanistan 1879–80, Egypt 1882, Defence of Ladysmith, South Africa 1899–1902.

Zakhmi Dil (Wounded Heart) was well known on the North-West Frontier of India as a folk song of the Pathan tribesmen (with risqué words). Its lilting melody made it a splendid marching tune and it was adopted by several (British) Indian Army units as a regimental march. How it came to be adopted by The King's Regiment is not stated, but it was probably acquired when one of the Battalions was serving on the North-West Frontier. It is unique in the British Army.

The Great War—42 *Battalions*—Mons, Le Cateau,
Retreat from Mons, Marne 1914, Aisne 1914, La Bassee
1914, Armentieres 1914, Givenchy 1914, Neuve
Chapelle, Ypres 1915, 17, 18, Gravenstafel, St. Julien,
Frezenberg, Bellewaarde, Aubers, Somme 1916, 18,
Albert 1916, 18, Bazentin, Delville Wood, Guillemont,
Flers-Courcelette, Thiepval, Le Transloy, Ancre Heights,
Ancre 1916, 18, Arras 1917, 18, Scarpe 1917,
Bullecourt, Messines 1917, Pilckem, Langemarck 1917,
Menin Road, Polygon Wood, Broodseinde, Poelcappelle,
Passchendaele, St. Quentin, Bapaume 1918, Rosieres,
Lys, Kemmel, Amiens, Hindenburg Line, Epehy, Canal
du Nord, St. Quentin Canal, Beaurevoir, Cambrai 1918,
Courtrai, Selle, Sambre, France and Flanders, 1914–18,
Piave, Vittorio Veneto, Italy 1917–18, Doiran 1917,
Macedonia 1915–18, Helles, Krithia, Suvla, Landing at
Suvla, Scimitar Hill, Gallipoli 1915, Rumani, Egypt
1915–17, Megiddo, Sharon, Palestine 1918, Tigris, 1916,
Kut al Amara 1917, Baghdad, Mesopotamia 1916–18.

The Second World War—Dyle, Withdrawal to Escaut,
Defence of Escaut, Defence of Arras, St. Omer-La
Bassee, Ypres-Comines Canal, Caen, Esquay, Falaise,
Nederrijn, Scheldt, Walcheren Causeway, Flushing,
Lower Maas, Venlo Pocket, Roer, Ourthe, Rhineland
Reichswald, Goch, Weeze, Rhine, Ibbenburen,
Dreirwalde, Aller, Bremen, North-West Europe 1940,
44–45, Gothic Line, Monte Gridolfo, Coriano, San
Clemente, Gemmano Ridge, Montilgallo, Capture of
Forli, Lamone Crossing, Lamone Bridgehead, Rimini
Line, Montescudo, Cesena, Italy 1944, Malta 1940,
Singapore Island, Malaya 1941–42, North Arakan,
Kohima, Pinwe, Shwebo, Myinmu Bridgehead,
Irrawaddy, Burma 1944–45.

Uniform	Scarlet, facings white
Regimental marches [Quick]	*The Young May Moon* (Tradit.)
[Slow]	Slow version of above
Regimental journal	*The Manchester Regiment Gazette*
Nickname	The Bloodsuckers

63rd (WEST SUFFOLK) REGIMENT OF FOOT

Raised 1756 as 2nd Battalion of the 8th (The King's) Regiment of Foot. Became separate corps in 1758 as the 63rd Regiment of Foot under Colonel Robert Armiger.

Titles 1756 8th (The King's) Regiment of Foot (2nd Battalion)
1758 63rd Regiment of Foot
1782 63rd (or the West Suffolk) Regiment of Foot
1881 Amalgamated with the 96th Regiment of Foot to form The Manchester Regiment

Battle honours Egmont-op-Zee, Martinique, Guadaloupe, Alma, Inkerman, Sevastopol, Afghanistan 1878–80.

Uniform Scarlet, facings Lincoln green

Nickname The Bloodsuckers

96th REGIMENT OF FOOT

Raised January 1824, with Colonel Sir Joseph Fuller as Colonel. It inherited the traditions and Honours of a previous 96th (or Queen's Own) Regiment of Foot which had been raised in 1798 and disbanded in 1818.

Battle honours Egypt (with the Sphinx), Peninsula, New Zealand.

Uniform Scarlet, facings yellow

Nickname The Ups and Downs

THE ROYAL ANGLIAN REGIMENT

(9th, 10th, 12th, 16th, 17th, 44th, 48th, 56th, 58th)

As can be seen from the 'roll call' of numbers above, The Royal Anglian Regiment is the present-day representative of nine previous Regiments, and as such is second only to The Queen's Regiment in being one of the largest amalgams in the British Army.

The Regiment was formed 1st September 1964 by the amalgamation of

> 1st East Anglian Regiment (Royal Norfolk and Suffolk)
> 2nd East Anglian Regiment (Duchess of Gloucester's Own Royal Lincolnshire and Northamptonshire)
> 3rd East Anglian Regiment (16th/44th Foot)
> The Royal Leicestershire Regiment (17th).

Battle honours Namur 1695, Blenheim, Ramillies, Oudenarde, Malplaquet, Dettingen, Louisburg, Minden, Quebec 1759, Belleisle, Martinique 1762, Moro, Havannah, Gibraltar 1779–83, Martinique 1794, India, Seringapatam, Surinam, Maida, Rolica, Vimiera, Peninsula, Corunna, Douro, Talavera, Busaco, Albuhera, Badajoz, Salamanca, Vittoria, Pyrenees, St. Sebastian, Nivelle, Nive, Orthes, Tolouse, Bladensburg, Waterloo, Ava, Affghanistan 1839, Ghuznee 1839, Khelat, Cabool 1842, Moodkee, Ferozeshah, Sobraon, New Zealand, Mooltan, Goojerat, Punjaub, South Africa 1851–53, Alma, Inkerman, Sevastopol, Lucknow, Taku Forts, South Africa 1879, Afghanistan 1878–80, Ali Masjid, Kabul 1879, Nile 1884–85, Chitral, Tirah, Atbara, Khartoum, South Africa 1899–1902, Modder River, Relief of Kimberley, Paardeburg, Defence of Ladysmith.

The Great War—Mons, Le Cateau, Retreat from Mons, Marne 1914, Aisne 1914, 18, La Bassee 1914, Messines 1914, 17, 18, Armentieres 1914, Givenchy 1914, Ypres 1914, 15, 17, 18, Langemarck 1914, 17, Gheluvelt, Nonne Bosschen, Festubert 1914, 15, Neuve Chapelle, Hill 60, Gravenstafel, St. Julien, Frezenberg

Bellewaarde, Aubers, Hooge 1915, Loos, Somme 1916,
18, Albert 1916, 18, Bazentin, Delville Wood, Pozieres,
Guillemont, Flers-Courcelette, Morval, Thiepval, Le
Transloy, Ancre Heights, Ancre 1916, 18, Bapaume
1917, 18, Arras 1917, 18, Vimy 1917, Scarpe 1917, 18,
Arleux, Oppy, Pilckem, Menin Road, Polygon Wood,
Broodseinde, Poelcappelle, Passchendaele, Cambrai
1917, 18, St. Quentin, Rosieres, Avre, Villers
Bretonneux, Lys, Estaires, Hazebrouck, Bailleul,
Kemmel, Bethune, Scherpenberg, Amiens, Drocourt-
Queant, Hindenburg Line, Havrincourt, Epehy, Canal
du Nord, St. Quentin Canal, Beaurevoir, Courtrai,
Selle, Valenciennes, Sambre, France and Flanders 1914–
18, Italy 1917–18, Helles, Landing at Helles, Struma,
Doiran 1918, Macedonia 1915–18, Krithia, Suvla,
Landing at Suvla, Scimitar Hill, Gallipoli 1915–16,
Rumani, Egypt 1915–17, Gaza, El Mughar, Nebi
Samwil, Jerusalem, Jaffa, Tell' Asur, Megiddo, Sharon,
Damascus, Palestine 1917–18, Tigris 1916, Shaiba, Kut
al Amara 1915, 17, Ctesiphon, Defence of Kut al
Amara, Baghdad, Mesopotamia 1914–18.

The Second World War—Vist, Norway 1940, Defence of
Escaut, St. Omer-La Bassee, Defence of Arras, Ypres-
Comines Canal, Dunkirk 1940, St. Valery-en-Caux,
Normandy Landing, Cambes, Tilly sur Seulles, Fontenay
le Pesnil, Odon, Defence of Rauray, Caen, Orne,
Bourguebus Ridge, Troarn, Le Perier Ridge, Brieux
Bridgehead, Falaise, Nederrijn, Le Havre, Antwerp-
Turnhout Canal, Scheldt, Venraij, Venlo Pocket,
Zetten, Rhineland, Hochwald, Lingen, Brinkum,
Bremen, Arnhem 1945, North-West Europe 1940, 44–
45, Abyssinia 1940, Falluja, Baghdad 1941, Iraq 1941,
Palmyra, Jebel Mazar, Syria 1941, Sidi Barrani, Tobruk
1941, Tobruk Sortie, Belhamed, Mersa Matruh, Defence
of Alamein Line, Deir El Shein, Ruweisat, Ruweisat
Ridge, El Alamein, Matmata Hills, Akarit, Enfidaville,
Djebel Garci, Djedeida, Djebel Djaffa, Montagne Farm,
Sedjenane I, Mine de Sedjenane, Oued Zarga, Djebel
Tanngoucha, Argoub Sellah, Sidi Ahmed, Tunis,
Ragoubet Souissi, North Africa 1940–43, Landing in
Sicily, Adrano, Sicily 1943, Trigno, Sangro, Villa
Grande, Salerno, Vietri Pass, Capture of Naples, Cava di
Tirreni, Volturno Crossing, Calabritto, Garigliano
Crossing, Monte Tuga, Anzio, Cassino I–II, Castle Hill,
Hangman's Hill, Monte Gabbione, Trasimene Line,
Gothic Line, Monte Gridolfo, Gemmano Ridge, Lamone

Crossing, Monte Colombo, San Marino, Monte La Pieve, Argenta Gap, Italy 1943–45, Athens, Greece 1944–45, Crete, Heraklion, Madagascar, Kampar, Johore, Muar, Batu Pahat, Singapore Island, Malaya 1941–42, Donbaik, Point 201 (Arakan), Yu, North Arakan, Buthidaung, Ngakyedauk Pass, Imphal, Tamu Road, Bishenpur, Kohima, Aradura, Monywa 1945, Mandalay, Myinmu Bridgehead, Irrawaddy, Ramree, Chindits 1944, Burma 1943–45.

Maryang-San, Korea 1951–52.

Uniform	Blue, piping scarlet, facings dark blue
Regimental marches [Quick]	Arrangement of *Rule Britannia* and *Speed the Plough*
[Slow]	*The Northamptonshire*
Regimental journal	*The Castle*
Regimental headquarters	The Keep, Gibraltar Barracks, Bury St. Edmunds, Suffolk IP33 3RN

1st EAST ANGLIAN REGIMENT
(ROYAL NORFOLK AND SUFFOLK)

Formed August 1959 by amalgamation of the Royal Norfolk Regiment with The Suffolk Regiment.

Uniform	Blue, piping and facings yellow
Regimental journal	*The Britannia & Castle*
Note	Since this Regiment existed for only five years under the above title before being amalgamated yet again, other details are not shown.

THE ROYAL NORFOLK REGIMENT
(9th)

Raised June 1685 as Colonel Henry Cornwall's Regiment of Foot.

Titles	1685 Colonel Henry Cornwall's Regiment of Foot *Title subsequently changed with Colonels' names*

1751 9th Regiment of Foot
1782 9th (or the East Norfolk) Regiment of Foot
1881 The Norfolk Regiment
1935 The Royal Norfolk Regiment
1959 Amalgamated with The Suffolk Regiment to form
1st East Anglian Regiment (Royal Norfolk and
Suffolk)

Battle honours Belleisle, Havannah, Martinique 1794, Rolica, Vimiera, Corunna, Busaco, Salamanca, Vittoria, St. Sebastian, Nive, Peninsula, Cabool 1842, Moodkee, Ferozeshah, Sobraon, Sevastopol, Kabul 1879, Afghanistan 1879–80, Paardeberg, South Africa 1900–02.

The Great War—20 *Battalions*—Mons, Le Cateau, Retreat from Mons, Marne 1914, Aisne 1914, La Bassee 1914, Ypres 1914, 15, 17, 18, Gravenstafel, St. Julien, Frezenberg, Bellewaarde, Loos, Somme 1916, 18, Albert 1916, 18, Delville Wood, Pozieres, Guillemont, Flers-Courcelette, Morval, Thiepval, Le Transloy, Ancre Heights, Ancre 1916, 18, Arras 1917, Vimy 1917, Scarpe 1917, Arleux, Oppy, Pilckem, Langemarck 1917, Polygon Wood, Broodseinde, Poelcappelle, Passchendaele, Cambrai 1917, 18, St. Quentin, Bapaume 1918, Lys, Bailleul, Kemmel, Scherpenberg, Amiens, Hindenburg Line, Epehy, Canal du Nord, St. Quentin Canal, Beaurevoir, Selle, Sambre, France and Flanders 1914–18, Italy 1917–18, Suvla, Landing at Suvla, Scimitar Hill, Gallipoli 1915, Egypt 1915–17, Gaza, El Mughar, Nebi Samwil, Jerusalem, Jaffa, Tel 'Asur, Megiddo, Sharon, Palestine 1917–18, Shaiba, Kut al Amara 1915, 17, Ctesiphon, Defence of Kut al Amara, Mesopotamia 1914–18.

The Second World War—Defence of Escaut, St. Omer-La Bassee, St. Valery-en-Caux, Normandy Landing, Caen, Le Perier Ridge, Brieux Bridgehead, Venraij, Rhineland, Hochwald, Lingen, Brinkum, North-West Europe 1940, 44–45, Johore, Muar, Batu Pahat, Singapore Island, Malaya 1942, Kohima, Aradura, Mandalay, Burma 1944–45.

Korea 1951–52.

Uniform Scarlet, piping and facings yellow

Regimental march [Quick] *Rule Britannia* (Arne)

Regimental journal *The Britannia*

Nicknames The Fighting Ninth. The Holy Boys

Remarks The Regimental Badge, incorporating the figure of Britannia, was granted by Queen Anne in recognition of the 9th's gallantry at the battle of Almanza in 1707.

THE SUFFOLK REGIMENT
(12th)

The Regiment originated as an independent company of Foot raised in 1660 as garrison for Windsor Castle, and commanded by Henry Howard, 7th Duke of Norfolk. In June 1685 this company was augmented as a Regiment of Foot, subsequently becoming the 12th Foot.

Titles 1685 The Duke of Norfolk's Regiment of Foot *Title subsequently changed with Colonels' names*
1751 12th Regiment of Foot
1782 12th (or the East Suffolk) Regiment of Foot
1881 The Suffolk Regiment
1959 Amalgamated with The Royal Norfolk Regiment to form 1st East Anglian Regiment (Royal Norfolk and Suffolk)

Battle honours Dettingen, Minden, Gibraltar 1779–83, Seringapatam, India, South Africa 1851–52–53, New Zealand, Afghanistan 1878–80, South Africa 1899–1902.

The Great War—22 *Battalions*—Mons, Le Cateau, Retreat from Mons, Marne 1914, Aisne 1914, La Bassee 1914, Givenchy 1914, Neuve Chapelle, Ypres 1915, 17, 18, Gravenstafel, St. Julien, Frezenberg, Bellewaarde, Aubers, Hooge 1915, Loos, Somme 1916, 18, Albert 1916, 18, Bazentin, Delville Wood, Pozieres, Flers-Courcelette, Morval, Thiepval, Le Transloy, Ancre Heights, Ancre 1916, 18, Arras 1917, 18, Scarpe 1917, 18, Arleux, Pilckem, Langemarck, 1917, Menin Road, Polygon Wood, Poelcappelle, Passchendaele, Cambrai 1917, 18, St. Quentin, Bapaume 1918, Lys, Estaires, Messines 1918, Hazebrouck, Bailleul, Kemmel, Bethune, Scherpenberg, Amiens, Hindenburg Line, Epehy, Canal du Nord, Courtrai, Selle, Valenciennes, Sambre, France and Flanders 1914–18, Struma, Doiran 1918, Macedonia 1915–18, Suvla, Landing at Suvla, Scimitar Hill, Gallipoli 1915, Egypt 1915–17, Gaza, El

Mughar, Nebi Samwil, Jerusalem, Jaffa, Tell 'Asur, Megiddo, Sharon, Palestine 1917–18.

The Second World War—Dunkirk 1940, Normandy Landing, Odon, Falaise, Venraij, Brinkum, North-West Europe 1940, 44–45, Singapore Island, Malaya 1942, North Arakan, Imphal, Burma 1943–45.

Motto *Montis Insignia Calpe* (from the Arms of Gibraltar)

Uniform Scarlet, piping yellow, facings yellow

Regimental marches [Quick] *Speed the Plough* (Tradit.)
[Slow] *The Slow March of the Suffolk Regiment*

Regimental journal *The Suffolk Regimental Gazette*

Nickname The Old Dozen

Remarks The Suffolks were proud of having been one of the 'Minden Regiments' who defeated the French cavalry at Minden (1759).

Their Badge incorporating a Castle and Key, and the Motto *Montis Insignia Calpe* (from the Arms of Gibraltar) were authorised in recognition of their part in the defence of Gibraltar during the siege of 1779–83.

2nd EAST ANGLIAN REGIMENT

(DUCHESS OF GLOUCESTER'S OWN ROYAL LINCOLNSHIRE AND NORTHAMPTONSHIRE)

Formed June 1960 by amalgamation of The Royal Lincolnshire Regiment with the Northamptonshire Regiment.

Uniform Blue, piping scarlet, facings blue

Regimental journal *The Poacher*

Note Since this Regiment existed for only four years under the above title before being amalgamated yet again, other details are not shown.

THE ROYAL LINCOLNSHIRE REGIMENT

(10th)

Raised at Plymouth, June 1685, from independent companies of Foot and commanded by Colonel John Granville, 1st Earl of Bath.

Titles 1685 The Earl of Bath's Regiment of Foot (or Granville's Regiment) *Title subsequently changed with Colonels' names*
1751 10th Regiment of Foot
1782 10th (or North Lincolnshire) Regiment of Foot
1881 The Lincolnshire Regiment
1946 The Royal Lincolnshire Regiment
1960 Amalgamated with The Northamptonshire Regiment to form 2nd East Anglian Regiment (Duchess of Gloucester's Own Royal Lincolnshire and Northamptonshire)

Battle honours Blenheim, Ramillies, Oudenarde, Malplaquet, Egypt (with the Sphinx), Peninsula, Sobraon, Mooltan, Goojarat, Punjaub, Lucknow, Atbara, Khartoum, Paardeberg, South Africa 1900–02.

The Great War—Mons, Le Cateau, Retreat from Mons, Marne 1914, Aisne 1914, 18, La Bassee 1914, Messines 1914, 17, 18, Armentieres 1914, Ypres 1914, 15, 17, Nonne Bosschen, Neuve Chapelle, Gravenstafel, St. Julien, Frezenberg, Bellewaarde, Aubers, Loos, Somme 1916, 18, Albert 1916, 18, Bazentin, Delville Wood, Pozieres, Flers-Courcelette, Morval, Thiepval, Ancre 1916, 18, Arras 1917, 18, Scarpe, 1917, 18, Arleux, Pilckem, Langemarck 1917, Menin Road, Polygon Wood, Broodseinde, Poelcappelle, Passchendaele, Cambrai 1917, 18, St. Quentin, Bapaume 1918, Lys, Estaires, Bailleul, Kemmel, Amiens, Drocourt-Queant, Hindenburg Line, Epehy, Canal du Nord, St. Quentin Canal, Beaurevoir, Selle, Sambre, France and Flanders 1914–18, Suvla, Landing at Suvla, Scimitar Hill, Gallipoli 1915, Egypt 1916.

The Second World War—Vist, Norway 1940, Dunkirk 1940, Normandy Landing, Cambes, Fontenay le Pesnil, Defence of Rauray, Caen, Orne, Bourguebus Ridge, Troarn, Nederrijn, Le Havre, Antwerp-Turnhout Canal, Venraij, Venlo Pocket, Rhineland, Hochwald, Lingen, Bremen, Arnhem 1945, North-West Europe 1940, 44–45, Sedjenane I, Mine de Sedjenane, Argoub Sellah, North Africa 1943, Salerno, Vietri Pass, Capture of Naples, Cava di Tirreni, Volturno Crossing, Garigliano Crossing, Monte Tuga, Gothic Line, Monte Gridolfo, Gemmano Ridge, Lamone Crossing, San Marino, Italy 1943–45, Donbaik, Point 201 (Arakan), North Arakan, Buthidaung, Ngakyedauk Pass, Ramree, Burma 1943–45.

Uniform Pre-1881, scarlet, facings yellow. 1881–1946, scarlet, facings white. With the granting of the 'Royal' prefix in 1946, facings were altered to blue.

Regimental march [Quick] *The Lincolnshire Poacher* (Tradit.)

Regimental journal *The Imps*

Nicknames The Poachers. The Springers

THE NORTHAMPTONSHIRE REGIMENT

(48th and 58th)

Formed 1881 by amalgamation of the 48th (Northamptonshire) Regiment of Foot with the 58th (Rutlandshire) Regiment of Foot.

Battle honours Louisburg, Quebec 1759, Martinique 1762, Havannah, Gibraltar 1779–83, Martinique 1794, Maida, Douro, Talavera, Albuhera, Badajoz, Salamanca, Vittoria, Pyrenees, Nivelle, Egypt (with the Sphinx), Orthes, Toulouse, Peninsula, New Zealand, Sevastopol, South Africa 1879, Tirah, Modder River, South Africa 1899–1902.

The Great War—13 *Battalions*—Mons, Retreat from Mons, Marne 1914, Aisne 1914, 18, Ypres 1914, 17, Langemarck 1914, 17, Gheluvelt, Nonne Bosschen, Givenchy 1914, Neuve Chapelle, Aubers, Loos, Somme 1916, 18, Albert 1916, 18, Bazentin, Delville Wood,

Pozieres, Flers-Courcelette, Morval, Thiepval, Le Transloy, Ancre Heights, Ancre 1916, 18, Bapaume 1917, 18, Arras 1917, 18, Vimy 1917, Scarpe 1917, 18, Arleux, Messines, 1917, Pilckem, Passchendaele, Cambrai 1917, 18, St. Quentin, Rosieres, Avre, Villers Bretonneux, Amiens, Drocourt-Queant, Hindenburg Line, Epehy, St. Quentin Canal, Selle, Sambre, France and Flanders 1914–18, Suvla, Landing at Suvla, Scimitar Hill, Gallipoli 1915, Egypt 1915–17, Gaza, El Mughar, Nebi Samwil, Jerusalem, Jaffa, Tell 'Asur, Megiddo, Sharon, Palestine 1917–18.

The Second World War—Defence of Escaut, Defence of Arras, Ypres-Comines Canal, North-West Europe 1940, 45, Djedeida, Djebel Djaffa, Oued Zarga, Djebel Tanngoucha, Sidi Ahmed, North Africa 1942–43, Landing in Sicily, Adrano, Sicily 1943, Sangro, Garigliano Crossing, Anzio, Cassino II, Monte Gabbione, Trasimene Line, Monte La Pieve, Argenta Gap, Italy 1943–45, Madagascar, Yu, Imphal, Tamu Road, Bishenpur, Monywa 1945, Myinmu Bridgehead, Irrawaddy, Burma 1943–45.

Motto	*Montis Insignia Calpe* (from the Arms of Gibraltar)
Uniform	Scarlet, piping and facings buff
Regimental marches [Quick]	*The Northamptonshire*
[Slow]	*The Duchess*
Regimental journal	*The Journal of The Northamptonshire Regiment*
Nicknames	The Steelbacks. The Black Cuffs

48th
(NORTHAMPTONSHIRE)
REGIMENT OF FOOT

Raised at Norwich, January 1741, as the 59th Regiment of Foot commanded by Colonel The Hon. James Cholmondeley. Renumbered 48th in 1748.

Titles   1741 Colonel Cholmondeley's Regiment of Foot *Title subsequently changed with Colonels' names*
1751 48th Regiment of Foot
1782 48th (or the Northamptonshire) Regiment of Foot

1881 Amalgamated with the 58th (Rutlandshire) Regiment of Foot to form The Northamptonshire Regiment

Battle honours Louisburg, Quebec, Douro, Talavera, Albuhera, Badajoz, Salamanca, Vittoria, Pyrenees, Nivelle, Orthes, Toulouse, Peninsula, Sevastopol.

Uniform Scarlet, facings buff

Regimental march [Quick] *The Northamptonshire*

58th (RUTLANDSHIRE) REGIMENT OF FOOT

Raised at Gloucester by Colonel Robert Anstruther, December 1755, as 60th Regiment of Foot. Renumbered 58th in 1757.

Titles 1755 60th Regiment of Foot
1757 58th Regiment of Foot
1782 58th (or the Rutlandshire) Regiment of Foot
1881 Amalgamated with the 48th (Northamptonshire) Regiment of Foot to form The Northamptonshire Regiment

Battle honours Louisburg, Quebec, Gibraltar (with Castle and Key), Egypt (with the Sphinx), Maida, Salamanca, Vittoria, Pyrenees, Nivelle, Orthes, Peninsula, New Zealand, South Africa 1879.

Motto *Montis Insignia Calpe* (from the Arms of Gibraltar)

Uniform Scarlet, facings black

Regimental march [Quick] *The Lincolnshire Poacher* (Tradit.)

Nicknames The Steelbacks. The Black Cuffs

Remarks The 58th were one of the five infantry regiments defending Gibraltar during the siege of 1779–83. Their Badge and Motto commemorated these services.

3rd EAST ANGLIAN REGIMENT

(16th/44th FOOT)

Formed June 1958 by amalgamation of The Bedfordshire and Hertfordshire Regiment with The Essex Regiment.

Uniform Blue, piping and facings yellow

Regimental journal *The Wasp and The Eagle*

Note Since this Regiment existed for only six years under the above title before a final amalgamation, further details are not shown.

THE BEDFORDSHIRE AND HERTFORDSHIRE REGIMENT

(16th)

Raised October 1688 by Colonel Archibald Douglas and mustered at Reading. After James II's abdication in December 1688, Douglas was removed by William of Orange and Colonel Robert Hodges was appointed in his place.

Titles 1688 Colonel Douglas's Regiment of Foot
Colonel Hodges' Regiment of Foot *Title subsequently changed with Colonels' names*
1751 16th Regiment of Foot
1782 16th (or the Buckinghamshire) Regiment of Foot
1809 16th (or Bedfordshire) Regiment of Foot
1881 The Bedfordshire Regiment
1919 The Bedfordshire and Hertfordshire Regiment
Note The 'Hertfordshire' subtitle had no connection with the true Hertfordshire Regiment (49th Foot) which had become absorbed in the Berkshire Regiment in 1881. It was added solely in recognition of the services of numerous Hertfordshire men in the 16th during the Great War.
1958 Amalgamated with The Essex Regiment to form 3rd East Anglian Regiment (16th/44th Foot)

Battle honours Namur, 1695, Blenheim, Ramillies, Oudenarde, Malplaquet, Surinam, Chitral, South Africa 1900–02.

The Great War—18 *Battalions*—Mons, Le Cateau, Retreat from Mons, Marne 1914, Aisne 1914, La Bassee 1914, Ypres 1914, 15, 17, Langemarck 1914, 17, Gheluvelt, Nonne Bosschen, Neuve Chapelle, Hill 60, St. Julien, Frezenberg, Bellewaarde, Aubers, Festubert 1915, Loos, Somme 1916, 18, Albert 1916, 18, Bazentin, Delville Wood, Pozieres, Guillemont, Flers-Courcelette, Morval, Thiepval, Le Transloy, Ancre Heights, Ancre 1916, 18, Arras 1917, 18, Vimy 1917, Scarpe 1917, Arleux, Oppy, Messines 1917, Pilckem, Polygon Wood, Broodseinde, Poelcappelle, Passchendaele, Cambrai 1917, 18, St. Quentin, Bapaume 1918, Rosieres, Avre, Villers Bretonneux, Lys, Hazebrouck, Scherpenberg, Amiens, Drocourt-Queant, Hindenberg Line, Epehy, Canal du Nord, St. Quentin Canal, Selle, Sambre, France and Flanders 1914–18, Italy 1917–18, Suvla, Landing at Suvla, Scimitar Hill, Gallipoli 1915, Egypt 1915–17, Gaza, El Mughar, Nebi Samwil, Jerusalem, Jaffa, Tell 'Asur, Megiddo, Sharon, Palestine 1917–18.

The Second World War—Dunkirk 1940, North-West Europe 1940, Tobruk 1941, Tobruk Sortie, Belhamed, Tunis, North Africa 1941, 43, Cassino II, Trasimene Line, Italy 1944–45, Athens, Greece 1944–45, Singapore Island, Malaya 1942, Chindits 1944, Burma 1944.

Uniform Scarlet, piping and facings white

Regimental march [Quick] *Mandolinata*

Regimental journal *The Wasp*

Nicknames The Old Bucks. The Peacemakers

THE ESSEX REGIMENT
(44th and 56th)

Formed 1881 by amalgamation of the 44th (East Essex) Regiment of Foot with the 56th (West Essex) Regiment of Foot.

Battle honours Moro, Havannah, Gibraltar 1779–83, Egypt (with the Sphinx), Badajoz, Salamanca, Peninsula, Bladensburg, Waterloo, Ava, Alma, Inkerman, Sevastopol, Taku Forts,

Nile 1884–85, Relief of Kimberley, Paardeberg, South Africa 1899–1902.

The Great War—31 *Battalions*—Le Cateau, Retreat from Mons, Marne 1914, Aisne 1914, Messines 1914, Armentieres 1914, Ypres 1915, 17, St. Julien, Frezenberg, Bellewaarde, Loos, Somme 1916, 18, Albert 1916, 18, Bazentin, Delville Wood, Pozieres, Flers-Courcelette, Morval, Thiepval, Le Transloy, Ancre Heights, Ancre 1916, 18, Bapaume 1917, 18, Arras 1917, 18, Scarpe 1917, 18, Arleux, Pilckem, Langemarck 1917, Menin Road, Broodseinde, Poelcappelle, Passchendaele, Cambrai 1917, 18, St. Quentin, Avre, Villers Bretonneux, Lys, Hazebrouck, Bethune, Amiens, Drocourt-Queant, Hindenburg Line, Havrincourt, Epehy, St. Quentin Canal, Selle, Sambre, France and Flanders 1914–18, Helles, Landing at Helles, Krithia, Suvla, Landing at Suvla, Scimitar Hill, Gallipoli 1915, 16, Rumani, Egypt 1915–17, Gaza, Jaffa, Megiddo, Sharon, Palestine 1917–18.

The Second World War—St. Omer-La Bassee, Tilly sur Seulles, Le Havre, Antwerp-Turnhout Canal, Scheldt, Zetten, Arnhem 1945, North-West Europe 1940, 44–45, Abyssinia 1940, Falluja, Baghdad 1941, Iraq 1941, Palmyra, Syria 1941, Tobruk 1941, Belhamed, Mersa Matruh, Defence of Alamein Line, Deir el Shein, Ruweisat, Ruweisat Ridge, El Alamein, Matmata Hills, Akarit, Enfidaville, Djebel Garci, Tunis, Ragoubet Souissi, North Africa 1941–43, Trigno, Sangro, Villa Grande, Cassino I, Castle Hill, Hangman's Hill, Italy 1943–44, Athens, Greece 1944–45, Kohima, Chindits 1944, Burma 1943–45.

Motto	*Montis Insignia Calpe* (from the Arms of Gibraltar)
Uniform	Scarlet, piping and facings purple
Regimental marches [Quick]	*The Hampshire*
[Slow]	*The Essex*
Regimental journal	*The Eagle*
Nicknames	The Pompadours. The Little Fighting Fours

44th (EAST ESSEX)
REGIMENT OF FOOT

Raised January 1741 by Colonel James Long and ranked as 55th Foot. Renumbered 44th in 1748.

Titles 1741 Colonel Long's Regiment of Foot *Title subsequently changed with Colonels' names*
1748 44th Regiment of Foot
1782 44th (or the East Essex) Regiment of Foot
1881 Amalgamated with 56th (West Essex) Regiment of Foot to form The Essex Regiment

Battle honours Egypt (with the Sphinx), Badajoz, Salamanca, Peninsula, Bladensburg, Waterloo, Ava, Alma, Inkerman, Sevastopol, Taku Forts.

Uniform Scarlet, facings yellow

Nickname The Little Fighting Fours

56th (WEST ESSEX)
REGIMENT OF FOOT

Raised December 1755 by Colonel Lord Charles Manners, as the 58th Regiment of Foot. Renumbered 56th in 1757.

Titles 1755 58th Regiment of Foot
1757 56th Regiment of Foot
1782 56th (or the West Essex) Regiment of Foot
1881 Amalgamated with 44th (East Essex) Regiment of Foot to form The Essex Regiment

Battle honours Moro, Gibraltar, Sevastopol, Havannah.

Motto *Montis Insignia Calpe* (from the Arms of Gibraltar)

Uniform Scarlet, facings purple

Nickname The Pompadours

Remarks The 56th were one of the five infantry regiments forming the garrison of Gibraltar during the siege of 1779–83. These services were commemorated by their Badge and Motto. The Regiment was the only one in the British Army to bear the Battle Honour *Moro*, gained in the West Indies, 1762.

THE ROYAL LEICESTERSHIRE REGIMENT

Raised in London, September 1688, by Colonel Solomon Richards.

Titles 1688 Colonel Richards's Regiment of Foot *Title subsequently changed with Colonels' names*
1751 17th Regiment of Foot
1782 17th (or the Leicestershire) Regiment of Foot
1881 The Leicestershire Regiment
1946 The Royal Leicestershire Regiment
1964 Amalgamated with 1st, 2nd and 3rd East Anglian Regiments to form The Royal Anglian Regiment

Battle honours Namur 1695, Louisburg, Martinique 1762, Havannah, Hindoostan, Ghuznee 1839, Khelat, Affghanistan 1839, Sevastopol, Ali Masjid, Afghanistan 1878–79, Defence of Ladysmith, South Africa 1899–1902.

The Great War— 19 *Battalions*—Aisne 1914, 18, La Bassee 1914, Armentieres 1914, Festubert 1914, 15, Neuve Chapelle, Aubers, Hooge 1915, Somme 1916, 18, Bazentin, Flers-Courcelette, Morval, Le Transloy, Ypres 1917, Polygon Wood, Cambrai 1917, 18, St. Quentin, Lys, Bailleul, Kemmel, Scherpenberg, Albert 1918, Bapaume 1918, Hindenburg Line, Epehy, St. Quentin Canal, Beaurevoir, Selle, Sambre, France and Flanders 1914–18, Megiddo, Sharon, Damascus, Palestine 1918, Tigris 1916, Kut al Amara 1917, Baghdad, Mesopotamia 1915–18.

The Second World War—Norway 1940, Antwerp-Turnhout Canal, Scheldt, Zetten, North-West Europe 1944–45, Jebel Mazar, Syria 1941, Sidi Barrani, Tobruk 1941, Montagne Farm, North Africa 1940–41, 43, Salerno, Calabritto, Gothic Line, Monte Gridolfo,

Monte Colombo, Italy 1943–45, Crete, Heraklion, Kampar, Malaya 1941–42, Chindits 1944.

Maryang-San, Korea 1951–52.

Motto *Veni et Vici* (Borne only from 1841 to 1845) (I came and I conquered)

Uniform Blue, piping and facings pearl grey

Regimental marches [Quick] *A Hunting Call* combined with 1772 and *Romaika*
[Slow] *General Monckton*

Regimental journal *The Green Tiger*

Nicknames The Tigers. The Bengal Tigers

Remarks The Regiment's Badge of a Royal Tiger superscribed 'Hindoostan' was authorised in 1825 in recognition of services in India, 1804–1823.

THE DEVONSHIRE AND DORSET REGIMENT
(11th, 39th and 54th)

Formed 17th May 1958 by amalgamation of The Devonshire Regiment with The Dorset Regiment.

Battle honours Dettingen, Plassey, Gibraltar 1779–83, Martinique 1794, Egypt (with the Sphinx), Marabout, Albuhera, Salamanca, Vittoria, Pyrenees, Nivelle, Nive, Orthes, Toulouse, Peninsula, Ava, Maharajpore, Sevastopol, Afghanistan 1879–80, Tirah, Defence of Ladysmith, Relief of Ladysmith, South Africa 1899–1902.

*The Great War—38 Battalions—*Mons, Le Cateau, Retreat from Mons, Marne 1914, Aisne 1914, 18, La Bassee, 1914, Armentieres 1914, Neuve Chapelle, Hill 60, Ypres 1915, 17, Gravenstafel, St. Julien, Frezenberg, Bellewaarde, Aubers, Loos, Somme 1916, 18, Albert 1916, 18, Bazentin, Delville Wood, Guillemont, Flers-Courcelette, Morval, Thiepval, Ancre 1916, 18, Arras 1917, Vimy 1917, Scarpe 1917, Bullecourt, Messines 1917, Pilckem, Langemarck 1917, Polygon Wood,

Broodseinde, Poelcappelle, Passchendaele, St. Quentin,
Rosieres, Villers Bretonneux, Lys, Hazebrouck, Bois des
Buttes, Marne 1918, Tardenois, Amiens, Bapaume 1918,
Hindenburg Line, Havrincourt, Epehy, Canal du Nord,
St. Quentin Canal, Beaurevoir, Cambrai 1918, Selle,
Sambre, France and Flanders 1914–18, Piave, Vittorio
Veneto, Italy 1917–18, Doiran 1917, 18, Macedonia
1915–18, Suvla, Landing at Suvla, Scimitar Hill,
Gallipoli 1915, Egypt 1916–17, Gaza, El Mughar, Nebi
Samwil, Jerusalem, Tell 'Asur, Megiddo, Sharon,
Palestine 1917–18, Basra, Shaiba, Kut al Amara 1915,
17, Ctesiphon, Defence of Kut al Amara, Tigris 1916,
Baghdad, Khan Baghdadi, Mesopotamia 1916–18.

The Second World War—St. Omer-La Bassee,
Normandy Landing, Port en Bessin, Villers Bocage, Tilly
sur Seulles, Caen, Mont Pincon, St. Pierre La Vielle,
Nederrijn, Arnhem 1944, Aam, Geilenkirchen, Roer,
Goch, Rhine, Ibbenburen, Twente Canal, North-West
Europe 1940, 44–45, Landing in Sicily, Agira,
Regalbuto, Sicily 1943, Landing at Porto San Venere,
Italy 1943, Malta 1940–42, Imphal, Shenam Pass, Tamu
Road, Kohima, Ukhrul, Mandalay, Myinmu Bridgehead,
Kyaukse 1945, Mt. Popa, Burma 1943–45.

Mottoes	*Semper Fidelis* (Ever faithful)
	Primus in Indis (First in India).
Uniform	Scarlet, piping and facings grass green*
Regimental marches [Quick]	*Widecombe Fair/We've Lived and Loved Together/Maid of Glenconnel*
[Slow]	*The Rose of Devon* and slow version of *Maid of Glenconnel*
Regimental journal	*The Journal of The Devonshire and Dorset Regiment*
Regimental headquarters	Wyvern Barracks, Barrack Road, Exeter, Devon EX2 6AE
Regimental museums	(Devonshire Regiment) As above
	(The Devonshire and Dorset Regiment and The Dorset Regiment) The Keep, Dorchester, Dorset DT1 1RN

*In formal orders of dress all ranks wear the 1914–18 Croix de Guerre ribbon on both
upper arms: see below under Devonshire Regiment.

THE DEVONSHIRE REGIMENT

(11th)

Raised at Bristol, 20th June 1685, as the Duke of Beaufort's Musketeers, by Colonel Henry Somerset, 1st Duke of Beaufort. In October the same year the Duke retired and command was assumed by his son, Charles, Marquess of Worcester.

Titles 1685 (June) The Duke of Beaufort's Musketeers
(October) The Marquess of Worcester's Regiment of Foot *Title subsequently changed by Colonels' names*
1751 11th Regiment of Foot
1782 11th (or the North Devonshire) Regiment of Foot
1881 The Devonshire Regiment
1958 Amalgamated with The Dorset Regiment to form The Devonshire and Dorset Regiment

Battle honours Dettingen, Salamanca, Pyrenees, Nivelle, Nive, Orthes, Toulouse, Peninsula, Afghanistan 1879–80, Tirah, Defence of Ladysmith, Relief of Ladysmith, South Africa 1899–1902.

The Great War—25 *Battalions*—Aisne 1914, 18, La Bassee, 1914, Armentieres, 1914, Neuve Chapelle, Hill 60, Ypres 1915, 17, Gravenstafel, St. Julien, Frezenberg, Aubers, Loos, Somme 1916, 18, Albert 1916, Bazentin, Delville Wood, Guillemont, Flers-Courcelette, Morval, Arras 1917, Vimy 1917, Scarpe 1917, Bullecourt, Pilckem, Langemarck 1917, Polygon Wood, Broodseinde, Poelcappelle, Passchendaele, Rosieres, Villers Bretonneux, Lys, Hazebrouck, Bois des Buttes, Marne 1918, Tardenois, Bapaume 1918, Hindenburg Line, Havrincourt, Epehy, Canal du Nord, Beaurevoir, Cambrai 1918, Selle, Sambre, France and Flanders 1914–18, Piave, Vittorio Veneto, Italy 1917–18, Doiran 1917, 18, Macedonia 1915–18, Egypt 1916–17, Gaza, Nebi Samwil, Jerusalem, Tell 'Asur, Palestine 1917–18, Tigris 1916, Kut al Amara 1917, Mesopotamia 1916–18.

The Second World War—Normandy Landing, Port en Bessin, Tilly sur Seulles, Caen, St. Pierre La Vielle, Nederrijn, Roer, Rhine, Ibbenburen, North-West Europe 1944–45, Landing in Sicily, Regalbuto, Sicily 1943,

Landing at Porto San Venere, Italy 1943, Malta 1940–42, Imphal, Shenam Pass, Tamu Road, Ukhrul, Myinmu Bridgehead, Kyaukse 1945, Burma 1943–45.

Motto *Semper Fidelis* (Ever faithful)

Uniform Scarlet, piping and facings Lincoln green

Regimental marches [Quick] *We've Lived and Loved Together* and *Widecombe Fair*
[Slow] *The Rose of Devon*

Regimental journal *The Journal of The Devonshire Regiment*

Nickname The Bloody Eleventh

Remarks In recognition of the 2nd Bn The Devonshire Regiment's heroic defence at Bois des Buttes, 27th May 1918, when they lost 23 officers and 528 other ranks, the French authorities awarded the Regiment the Croix de Guerre with Palm. As noted above, the ribbon continues to be worn by all ranks of the present Regiment in formal dress.

THE DORSET REGIMENT
(39th and 54th)

Formed 1881 by amalgamation of the 39th (Dorsetshire) Regiment of Foot with the 54th (West Norfolk) Regiment of Foot, to form The Dorsetshire Regiment. In 1951 the title was altered to The Dorset Regiment.

Battle honours Plassey, Gibraltar 1779–83, Martinique 1794, Marabout, Egypt (with the Sphinx), Albuhera, Vittoria, Pyrenees, Nivelle, Nive, Orthes, Peninsula, Ava, Maharajpore, Sevastopol, Tirah, Relief of Ladysmith, South Africa 1899–1902.

*The Great War—13 Battalions—*Mons, Le Cateau, Retreat from Mons, Marne 1914, Aisne 1914, La Bassee 1914, Armentieres 1914, Ypres 1915, 17, Gravenstafel, St. Julien, Bellewaarde, Somme 1916, 18, Albert 1916, 18, Flers-Courcelette, Thiepval, Ancre 1916, 18, Arras 1917, Scarpe 1917, Messines 1917, Langemarck 1917, Polygon Wood, Broodseinde, Poelcappelle, Passchendaele, St. Quentin, Amiens, Bapaume 1918, Hindenburg Line, Epehy, Canal du Nord, St. Quentin Canal, Beaurevoir, Cambrai 1918, Selle, Sambre, France and Flanders 1914–18, Suvla, Landing at Suvla, Scimitar

Hill, Gallipoli 1915, Egypt 1916, Gaza, El Mughar,
Nebi Samwil, Jerusalem, Tell 'Asur, Megiddo, Sharon,
Palestine 1917–18, Basra, Shaiba, Kut al Amara 1915,
17, Ctesiphon, Defence of Kut al Amara, Baghdad, Khan
Baghdadi, Mesopotamia 1914–18.

The Second World War—St. Omer-La Bassee,
Normandy Landing, Villers Bocage, Tilly sur Seulles,
Caen, Mont Pincon, St. Pierre La Vielle, Arnhem 1944,
Aam, Geilenkirchen, Goch, Rhine, Twente Canal,
North-West Europe 1940, 44–45, Landing in Sicily,
Agira, Regalbuto, Sicily 1943, Landing at Porto San
Venere, Italy 1943, Malta 1940–42, Kohima, Mandalay,
Mt. Popa, Burma 1944–45.

Motto   *Primus in Indis* (First in India)

Uniform   Scarlet, piping and facings grass green

Regimental marches [Quick]   *The Maid of Glenconnel*
[Slow]   The above in slow time

Regimental journal   *The Dorset Regimental Quarterly*

Nicknames   Sankey's Horse. The Green Linnets. The Flamers

39th (DORSETSHIRE) REGIMENT OF FOOT

Raised in Ireland, February 1702, by Colonel Richard
Coote.

Titles   1702 Colonel Richard Coote's Regiment of Foot *Title
subsequently changed with Colonels' names*
1751 39th Regiment of Foot
1782 39th (or East Middlesex) Regiment of Foot
1807 39th (or Dorsetshire) Regiment of Foot
1881 Amalgamated with 54th (West Norfolk) Regiment of
Foot to form The Dorsetshire Regiment

Battle honours   Plassey, Gibraltar (with Castle and Key), Albuhera,
Vittoria, Pyrenees, Nivelle, Nive, Orthes, Peninsula,
Maharajpore, Sevastopol.

Motto   *Primus in Indis* (First in India)

Uniform   Scarlet, facings grass green

Nicknames   Sankey's Horse. Green Linnets

Remarks The Motto *Primus in Indis* denotes the fact that the 39th Foot were the first 'King's' regiment (as opposed to the East India Company's) to land in India, in 1754, and were the only King's infantry under Clive at the Battle of Plassey (1757).

In November 1857 the 54th were en route for India in the troopship *Sarah Sands*, which caught fire and nearly foundered in the Indian Ocean. Thanks to the heroic efforts and superb discipline of the troops, the fire was brought under control and the damaged vessel was sailed into port at Mauritius.

The Regiment was one of the five infantry regiments defending Gibraltar during the siege of 1779–83.

54th (WEST NORFOLK) REGIMENT OF FOOT

Raised December 1755 by Lieut-Colonel John Campbell, Duke of Argyll, as the 56th Foot. Renumbered 54th in 1757.

Titles   1755 56th Regiment of Foot
1757 54th Regiment of Foot
1782 54th (or West Norfolk) Regiment of Foot
1881 Amalgamated with 39th Dorsetshire Regiment of Foot to form The Dorsetshire Regiment

Battle honours   Egypt (with the Sphinx), Marabout, Ava.

Uniform   Scarlet, facings grass green

Regimental marches [Quick] *The Maid of Glenconnel*
[Slow] The above in slow time

Nickname   The Flamers

Remarks   In November 1857 the 54th were en route for India in the troopship *Sarah Sands*, which caught fire and nearly foundered in the Indian Ocean. Thanks to the heroic efforts and superb discipline of the troops, the fire was brought under control and the damaged vessel was sailed into port at Mauritius.

The valour displayed by the soldiers of the 54th on this occasion resulted in an amendment to the terms of the Victoria Cross Warrant, hitherto restricted to bravery 'in the presence of the enemy'. In 1858 a new Warrant allowed the Award for '. . . courage and bravery displayed under circumstances of extreme danger, such as the occurrence of a fire on board ship, or of the foundering of a vessel at sea'.

'Sarah Sands Day' is still celebrated annually by The Devonshire and Dorset Regiment.

THE LIGHT INFANTRY

(13th, 32nd, 46th, 51st, 53rd, 68th, 85th, 105th, 106th)

One of the largest amalgamations in the British Army, The Light Infantry was formed in July 1968 by the amalgamation of the following four Regiments, which were themselves the results of mergers over the years.

The Somerset and Cornwall Light Infantry
The King's Own Yorkshire Light Infantry
The King's Shropshire Light Infantry
The Durham Light Infantry

Battle honours Gibraltar 1704–05, Dettingen, Minden, Nieuport, St. Lucia 1796, Tournay, Dominica, Egypt (with the Sphinx), Corunna, Rolica, Vimiera, Martinique 1809, Talavera, Fuentes d'Onor, Salamanca, Vittoria, Pyrenees, Nivelle, Nive, Orthes, Toulouse, Peninsula, Bladensburg, Waterloo, Ava, Aliwal, Sobraon, Ghuznee 1839, Affghanistan 1839, Cabool 1842, Jellalabad, Mooltan, Goojerat, Punjaub, Alma, Inkerman, Sevastopol, Reshire, Bushire, Koosh-ab, Persia, Lucknow, New Zealand, Pegu, Ali Masjid, South Africa 1878–79, Afghanistan 1878–80, Tel-el-Kebir, Egypt 1882, Nile 1884–85, Suakin 1885, Burma 1885–87, Modder River, Paardeberg, Relief of Ladysmith, South Africa 1899–1902.

The Great War—Mons, Le Cateau, Retreat from Mons, Marne 1914, 18, Aisne 1914, 18, La Bassee 1914, Messines 1914, 17, 18, Armentieres 1914, Ypres 1914, 15, 17, 18, Hill 60, Gravenstafel, St. Julien, Frezenberg, Bellewaarde, Hooge 1915, Loos, Mount Sorrel, Somme 1916, 18, Albert 1916, 18, Bazentin, Delville Wood, Pozieres, Guillemont, Flers-Courcelette, Morval, Le Transloy, Ancre Heights, Ancre 1916, 18, Bapaume 1917, 18, Arras 1917, 18, Vimy 1917, Scarpe 1917, 18, Arleux, Hill 70, Pilckem, Langemarck 1917, Menin Road, Polygon Wood, Broodseinde, Poelcappelle, Passchendaele, Cambrai 1917, 18, St. Quentin, Rosieres, Avre, Lys, Estaires, Hazebrouck, Bailleul, Kemmel, Bethune, Scherpenberg, Marne 1918, Soissonnais-

Ourcq, Tardenois, Amiens, Drocourt-Queant, Bligny, Hindenburg Line, Havrincourt, Epehy, Canal du Nord, St. Quentin Canal, Beaurevoir, Courtrai, Selle, Valenciennes, Sambre, France and Flanders 1914–18, Piave, Vittorio Veneto, Italy 1917–18, Struma, Doiran 1917, 18, Macedonia 1915–18, Suvla, Landing at Suvla, Scimitar Hill, Gallipoli 1915, Rumani, Egypt 1915–17, Gaza, El Mughar, Nebi Samwil, Jerusalem, Jericho, Tell 'Asur, Megiddo, Sharon, Palestine 1917–18, Tigris 1916, Sharqat, Mesopotamia 1916–18, N.W. Frontier India 1915, 16–17, Aden, Archangel 1918–19.

Afghanistan 1919.

The Second World War—Kvam, Norway 1940, Dyle, Defence of Escaut, Arras counter attack, St. Omer-La Bassee, Dunkirk 1940, Normandy Landing, Villers Bocage, Tilly sur Seulles, Odon, Fontenay le Pesnil, Cheux, Defence of Rauray, Caen, Hill 112, Bourgebus Ridge, Cagny, Troarn, Mont Pincon, Souleuvre, Le Perier Ridge, St. Pierre La Vielle, Noireau Crossing, Falaise, Seine 1944, Antwerp, Hechel, Gheel, Nederrijn, Le Havre, Antwerp-Turnhout Canal, Lower Maas, Opheusden, Venraij, Geilenkirchen, Venlo Pocket, Roer, Rhineland, Cleve, Goch, Hochwald, Xanten, Rhine, Ibbenburen, Lingen, Aller, Bremen, North-West Europe 1940, 44–45, Syria 1941, Halfaya 1941, Tobruk 1941, Relief of Tobruk, Gazala, Gabr el Fachri, Zt El Mrasses, Mersa Matruh, Point 174, El Alamein, Mareth, Sedjenane I, Mine de Sedjenane, El Kourzia, Argoub Sellah, Medjez Plain, Gueriat el Atach Ridge, Si Abdallah, Tunis, Djebel Bou Aoukaz 1943, I, North Africa 1940–43, Landing in Sicily, Solarino, Primosole Bridge, Sicily 1943, Salerno, Salerno Hills, Cava di Tirreni, Volturno Crossing, Monte Camino, Garigliano Crossing, Minturno, Monte Tuga, Anzio, Campoleone, Carroceto, Cassino II, Trasimene Line, Arezzo, Advance to Florence, Incontro, Gothic Line, Gemmano Ridge, Carpineta, Capture of Forli, Cosina Canal Crossing, Defence of Lamone Bridgehead, Pergola Ridge, Rimini Line, Cesena, Monte Ceco, Monte Grande, Sillaro Crossing, Italy 1943–45, Athens, Greece 1944–45, Cos, Middle East 1942, Sittang 1942, Donbaik, North Arakan, Buthidaung, Ngakyedauk Pass, Kohima, Mandalay, Burma 1942, 43–45.

Kowang-San, Hill 227, I, Korea 1951–53.

Mottoes *Aucto Splendore Resurgo* (I rise again with increased splendour)
Cede Nullis (Yield to none)
Faithful

Uniform Jacket, dark green; trousers, blue; piping white, facings blue

Regimental marches [Quick] *Light Infantry*
[Double] *The Keel Row* (Tradit.)

Regimental journal *The Silver Bugle*

Regimental headquarters Peninsula Barracks, Winchester, Hampshire

Regimental museums (The Somerset Light Infantry)
Somerset County Museum, Taunton Castle, Taunton, Somerset

(The Duke of Cornwall's Light Infantry)
The Keep, Bodmin, Cornwall

(The King's Own Yorkshire Light Infantry)
Light Infantry Office (Yorkshire), Wakefield Road, Pontefract, West Yorkshire

(The King's Shropshire Light Infantry)
Sir John Moore Barracks, Copthorne, Shrewsbury

(The Durham Light Infantry)
Aykley Heads, Durham City

Remarks Originally formed as lightly-equipped, highly mobile troops for skirmishing and scouting, Light Infantry regiments always marched at 140 paces per minute as opposed to the normal pace of 120. Instead of drums and fifes they had bugle bands, and their Badges always incorporated the curved bugle-horn, symbolic of the huntsman, or *Jäger*.

THE SOMERSET AND CORNWALL LIGHT INFANTRY

(13th, 32nd, 46th)

Formed October 1959 by amalgamation of The Somerset Light Infantry (Prince Albert's) with The Duke of Cornwall's Light Infantry.

Note Since this Regiment existed for only nine years under the above title, further details are not given.

THE SOMERSET LIGHT INFANTRY

(PRINCE ALBERT'S)
(13th)

Raised June 1685 by Colonel Theophilus, Earl of Huntingdon, and mustered at Buckingham.

Titles 1685 The Earl of Huntingdon's Regiment of Foot *Title subsequently changed with Colonels' names*

1706–13 The Earl of Barrymore's Regiment, converted to Pearce's Dragoons (see *Remarks* below)

1706 The Earl of Barrymore's Regiment (of Foot) reformed

1751 13th Regiment of Foot

1782 13th (1st Somersetshire) Regiment of Foot

1822 13th (or 1st Somersetshire) Regiment of Foot (Light Infantry)

1842 13th or Prince Albert's Regiment of Light Infantry

1881 Prince Albert's Light Infantry (Somersetshire Regiment) In the same year title altered to Prince Albert's (Somersetshire Light Infantry)

1912 Prince Albert's (Somerset Light Infantry)

1921 The Somerset Light Infantry (Prince Albert's)

1959 Amalgamated with The Duke of Cornwall's Light Infantry to form The Somerset and Cornwall Light Infantry

Battle honours Gibraltar 1704–05, Dettingen, Martinique 1809, Ava, Ghuznee 1839, Affghanistan 1839, Cabool, 1842, Jellalabad, Sevastopol, South Africa 1878–79, Burma 1885–87, Relief of Ladysmith, South Africa 1899–1902.

The Great War—16 *Battalions*—Le Cateau, Retreat from Mons, Marne 1914, 18, Aisne 1914, Armentieres 1914, Ypres 1915, 17, 18, St. Julien, Frezenberg, Bellewaarde, Hooge 1915, Loos, Mount Sorrel, Somme 1916, 18, Albert 1916, 18, Delville Wood, Guillemont, Flers-Courcelette, Morval, Le Transloy, Ancre 1916, 18, Arras 1917, 18, Vimy, 1917, Scarpe 1917, 18, Arleux, Langemarck 1917, Menin Road, Polygon Wood, Broodseinde, Poelcappelle, Passchendaele, Cambrai 1917, 18, St. Quentin, Bapaume 1918, Rosieres, Avre, Lys, Hazebrouck, Bethune, Soissonnais-Ourcq, Drocourt-Queant, Hindenburg Line, Havrincourt, Epehy, Canal du Nord, Courtrai, Selle, Valenciennes, Sambre, France and Flanders 1914–18, Gaza, El Mughar, Nebi Samwil, Jerusalem, Megiddo, Sharon, Palestine 1917–18, Tigris 1916, Sharqat, Mesopotamia 1916–18, N.W. Frontier, India 1915.

Afghanistan 1919.

The Second World War—Odon, Caen, Hill 112, Mont Pincon, Noireau Crossing, Seine 1944, Nederrijn, Geilenkirchen, Roer, Rhineland, Cleve, Goch, Hochwald, Xanten, Rhine, Bremen, North-West Europe 1944–45, Cassino II, Trasimene Line, Arezzo, Advance to Florence, Capture of Forli, Cosina Canal Crossing, Italy 1944–45, Athens, Greece 1944–45, North Arakan, Buthidaung, Ngakyedauk Pass, Burma 1943–44.

Uniform Jacket, dark green; piping white; trousers, blue; facings blue

Regimental marches [Quick] *Prince Albert* (Glover)
[Slow] *Palace Guard* (James)

Regimental journal *The Light Bob Gazette*

Nicknames The Illustrious Garrison. Jellalabad Heroes. The Bleeders

Remarks In January 1706, during the campaign in Spain, the Earl of Peterborough found himself in want of mounted troops and converted The Earl of Barrymore's Regiment (13th) into a separate regiment of dragoons under the temporary CO, Lieut-Colonel Edward Pearce. They served as such until the peace of 1713, when they were disbanded. In the meantime the Earl of Barrymore reformed the 13th Foot in 1706.

The Regiment's unique Battle Honour *Jellalabad* was awarded for the defence of that fort (in Afghanistan) during the winter of 1841–42 when, under General Sir Robert Sale, they earned their sobriquet 'The Illustrious Garrison'.

The sergeants of the 13th were unique among Line regiments in wearing their crimson sashes over the left shoulder instead of the right. Tradition ascribes this custom to the battle of Culloden when all the officers became casualties and the sergeants took over. The custom was officially recognised in 1865 and incorporated in Queen's Regulations. It is continued in the present Regiment.

The Regimental Journal, *The Light Bob Gazette*, was founded in 1893, but the Regiment had previously published a journal entitled *The Pal. Journal of the Camp Follower*, first issued in India, October 1857. This is claimed to be the earliest Regimental Journal of the British Army.

THE DUKE OF CORNWALL'S LIGHT INFANTRY

(32nd and 46th)

Formed 1881 by amalgamation of the 32nd (Cornwall) Light Infantry with the 46th (South Devonshire) Regiment of Foot.

Battle honours Gibraltar 1704–05, Dettingen, St. Lucia 1778, Dominica, Rolica, Vimiera, Corunna, Salamanca, Pyrenees, Nivelle, Nive, Orthes, Peninsula, Waterloo, Mooltan, Goojerat, Punjaub, Sevastopol, Lucknow, Tel-el-Kebir, Egypt 1882, Nile 1884–85, Paardeberg, South Africa 1899–1902.

The Great War—15 *Battalions*—Mons, Le Cateau, Retreat from Mons, Marne 1914, Aisne 1914, La Bassee 1914, Armentieres 1914, Ypres 1915, 17, Gravenstafel, St. Julien, Frezenberg, Bellewaarde, Hooge 1915, Mount Sorrel, Somme 1916, 18, Delville Wood, Guillemont, Flers-Courcelette, Morval, Le Transloy, Ancre 1916,

Bapaume 1917, 18, Arras 1917, Vimy 1917, Scarpe 1917, Arleux, Langemarck 1917, Menin Road, Polygon Wood, Broodseinde, Poelcappelle, Passchendaele, Cambrai 1917, 18, St. Quentin, Rosieres, Lys, Estaires, Hazebrouck, Albert 1918, Hindenburg Line, Havrincourt, Canal du Nord, Selle, Sambre, France and Flanders 1914–18, Italy 1917–18, Struma, Doiran 1917, 18, Macedonia, 1915–18, Gaza, Nebi Samwil, Jerusalem, Tell 'Asur, Megiddo, Sharon, Palestine 1917–18, Aden.

The Second World War—Defence of Escaut, Cheux, Hill 112, Mont Pincon, Noireau Crossing, Nederrijn, Opheusden, Geilenkirchen, Rhineland, Goch, Rhine, North-West Europe 1940, 44–45, Gazala, Medjez Plain, Si Abdallah, North Africa 1942–43, Cassino II, Trasimene Line, Advance to Florence, Incontro, Rimini Line, Italy 1944–45.

Motto	One and All (Motto of County of Cornwall)
Uniform	Jacket, scarlet; piping white; trousers, blue, facings white
Regimental march [Quick]	*One and All* and *Trelawny*
Regimental journal	*One and All*
Nicknames	The Docs. The Surprisers. Red Feathers. Murray's Bucks

32nd (CORNWALL) LIGHT INFANTRY

Raised February 1702 by Colonel Edward Fox as regiment of Marines.

Titles 1702 Colonel Edward Fox's Regiment of Marines
Continued as Marines until 1713, title changing with Colonels' names
1713 *Disbanded*
1715 *Re-raised* as 32nd Regiment of Foot
1782 32nd (or the Cornwall) Regiment of Foot
1858 32nd (Cornwall) Light Infantry
1881 Amalgamated with the 46th (South Devonshire) Regiment of Foot to form The Duke of Cornwall's Light Infantry

Battle honours Dettingen, Rolica, Vimiera, Corunna, Salamanca, Pyrenees, Nivelle, Nive, Orthes, Peninsula, Waterloo, Mooltan, Goojerat, Punjaub, Lucknow.

Uniform Scarlet, facings white

Regimental march [Quick] *One and All*

Remarks The 32nd Foot and one weak company of the 84th formed the British element of the garrison of Lucknow which defended the Residency during the 87-day siege in the Indian Mutiny, 1857. In recognition of their staunch defence, the 32nd were granted the title 'Light Infantry' by Royal Decree of 14th May 1858.

46th (SOUTH DEVONSHIRE) REGIMENT OF FOOT

Raised January 1741 by Colonel John Price, and ranked as 57th Foot until renumbered 46th in 1748.

Titles 1741 Colonel Price's Regiment of Foot *Title subsequently changed with Colonels' names*
1751 46th Regiment of Foot
1782 46th (or South Devonshire) Regiment of Foot
1881 Amalgamated with the 32nd (Cornwall) Light Infantry to form The Duke of Cornwall's Light Infantry

Battle honours Dominica, Sevastopol.

Uniform Scarlet, facings yellow

Regimental march [Quick] *Rosin the Beau*

Nicknames Red Feathers. Murray's Bucks. The Surprisers. The Lacedemonians

THE KING'S OWN YORKSHIRE LIGHT INFANTRY

(51st and 105th)

Formed 1881 by amalgamation of 51st (2nd Yorkshire West Riding) or The King's Own Light Infantry Regiment with the 105th (Madras Light Infantry) Regiment.

Title was originally The King's Own Light Infantry (South Yorkshire Regiment). Altered to The King's Own (Yorkshire Light Infantry) in 1887. Brackets discarded in 1921.

Battle honours Minden, Corunna, Fuentes d'Onor, Salamanca, Vittoria, Pyrenees, Nivelle, Orthes, Peninsula, Waterloo, Pegu, Ali Masjid, Afghanistan 1878–80, Burma 1885–87, Modder River, South Africa 1899–1902.

The Great War—26 *Battalions*—Mons, Le Cateau, Retreat from Mons, Marne 1914, 18, Aisne 1914, 18, La Bassee 1914, Messines 1914, 17, 18, Ypres 1914, 15, 17, 18, Hill 60, Gravenstafel, St. Julien, Frezenberg, Bellewaarde, Hooge 1915, Loos, Somme 1916, 18, Albert 1916, 18, Bazentin, Delville Wood, Pozieres, Guillemont, Flers-Courcelette, Morval, Le Transloy, Ancre 1916, Arras 1917, 18, Scarpe 1917, Langemarck 1917, Menin Road, Polygon Wood, Broodseinde, Poelcappelle, Passchendaele, Cambrai 1917, 18, St. Quentin, Bapaume 1918, Lys, Hazebrouck, Bailleul, Kemmel, Scherpenberg, Tardenois, Amiens, Hindenburg Line, Havrincourt, Epehy, Canal du Nord, St. Quentin Canal, Beaurevoir, Selle, Valenciennes, Sambre, France and Flanders 1914–18, Piave, Vittorio Veneto, Italy 1917–18, Struma, Macedonia 1915–17, Egypt 1915–16.

The Second World War—Kvam, Norway 1940, Fontenay le Pesnil, Le Havre, Antwerp-Turnhout Canal, Lower Maas, North-West Europe 1944–45, Mine de Sedjenane, Argoub Sellah, North Africa 1943, Sicily 1943, Salerno, Salerno Hills, Cava di Tirreni, Volturno Crossing, Garigliano Crossing, Minturno, Monte Tuga, Anzio, Gemmano Ridge, Carpineta, Lamone Bridgehead, Italy 1943–45, Sittang 1942, Burma 1942.

Motto *Cede Nullis* (Yield to none)

Uniform Jacket, dark green; trousers, blue; piping white, facings blue

Regimental marches [Quick] *Jockey to the Fair* (Tradit.)
[Double] *The Keel Row* (Tradit.)

Regimental journal *The Bugle*

Nickname The Koylis

51st (2nd YORKSHIRE WEST RIDING) THE KING'S OWN LIGHT INFANTRY REGIMENT

Raised December 1755 as the 53rd Regiment of Foot, commanded by Colonel Robert Napier. Renumbered 51st in 1757.

Titles 1755 53rd Regiment of Foot (or Napier's)
1757 51st Regiment of Foot (or Brudenell's)
1782 51st (2nd Yorkshire, West Riding) Regiment of Foot
1809 51st (2nd Yorkshire West Riding) Regiment of Foot (Light Infantry)
1821 51st (2nd Yorkshire West Riding) The King's Own Light Infantry Regiment
1881 Amalgamated with 105th (Madras Light Infantry) Regiment to form The King's Own Light Infantry (South Yorkshire Regiment)
1887 The King's Own (Yorkshire Light Infantry)

Battle honours Minden, Corunna, Fuentes d'Onor, Salamanca, Vittoria, Pyrenees, Nivelle, Orthes, Peninsula, Waterloo, Pegu, Ali Masjid, Afghanistan 1878–80.

Uniform Scarlet, facings blue

Regimental marches [Quick] *The Jockey of York* (Tradit.)
[Double] *The Keel Row* (Tradit.)

Remarks The 51st were one of the six 'Minden Regiments'.

105th (MADRAS LIGHT INFANTRY) REGIMENT

Raised 1839 as the 2nd Madras European Regiment (Light Infantry) of the Hon. East India Company's forces. Transferred to the British Army in 1861.

Titles 1839 2nd Madras European Regiment (Light Infantry)
1858 2nd Madras (Light Infantry) Regiment
1861 105th (Madras Light Infantry) Regiment
1881 Amalgamated with 51st (2nd Yorkshire West Riding) The King's Own Light Infantry Regiment to form The King's Own Light Infantry (South Yorkshire Regiment)

Motto *Cede Nullis* (Yield to none)

Uniform Scarlet, facings buff

THE KING'S SHROPSHIRE LIGHT INFANTRY
(53rd and 85th)

Formed 1881 by amalgamation of the 53rd (Shropshire) Regiment of Foot with the 85th King's Light Infantry.

Titles 1881 The Shropshire Regiment (King's Light Infantry). In the same year altered to The King's Light Infantry (Shropshire Regiment)
1882 The King's (Shropshire Light Infantry)
1920 The King's Shropshire Light Infantry

Battle honours Nieuport, Tournay, St. Lucia 1796, Talavera, Fuentes d'Onor, Salamanca, Vittoria, Pyrenees, Nivelle, Nive, Toulouse, Peninsula, Bladensburg, Aliwal, Sobraon, Goojerat, Punjaub, Lucknow, Afghanistan 1879–80, Egypt 1882, Suakin 1885, Paardeberg, South Africa 1899–1902.

The Great War—13 Battalions—Aisne 1914, 18, Armentieres 1914, Ypres 1915, 17, Gravenstafel, St. Julien, Frezenberg, Bellewaarde, Hooge 1915, Mount Sorrel, Somme 1916, 18, Albert 1916, 18, Bazentin,

Delville Wood, Guillemont, Flers-Courcelette, Morval, Le Transloy, Ancre 1916, Arras 1917, 18, Scarpe 1917, Arleux, Hill 70, Langemarck 1917, Menin Road, Polygon Wood, Passchendaele, Cambrai 1917, 18, St. Quentin, Bapaume 1918, Rosieres, Lys, Estaires, Messines 1918, Hazebrouck, Bailleul, Kemmel, Bethune, Bligny, Hindenburg Line, Epehy, Canal du Nord, Selle, Valenciennes, Sambre, France and Flanders 1914–18, Doiran 1917, 18, Macedonia 1915–18, Gaza, Jerusalem, Jericho, Tell 'Asur, Palestine 1917–18.

The Second World War—Defence of Escaut, Dunkirk 1940, Normandy Landing, Odon, Caen, Bourguebus Ridge, Troarn, Mont Pincon, Souleuvre, Le Perier Ridge, Falaise, Antwerp, Nederrijn, Venraij, Rhineland, Hochwald, Ibbenburen, Lingen, Aller, Bremen, North-West Europe 1940, 44–45, Gueriat el Atach Ridge, Tunis, Djebel Bou Aoukaz 1943, II, North Africa 1943, Anzio, Campoleone, Carroceto, Gothic Line, Monte Ceco, Monte Grande, Italy 1943–45.

Kowang-San, Hill 227 I, Korea 1951–52.

Motto	*Aucto Splendore Resurgo* (I rise again with increased splendour)
Uniform	Jacket, dark green, piping white; trousers, blue with dark green stripe
Regimental marches [Quick]	*Old Towler* (Shields)
[Slow]	*The 53rd March* (Anon) and *The Daughter of the Regiment* (Donizetti)
Note	The latter March was never officially approved, but was adopted by the 85th in 1846 and inherited by The King's Shropshire Light Infantry.
Regimental journal	*The K.S.L.I. and Herefordshire L.I. Regimental Journal*
Nicknames	The Brickdusts. The Old Five-and-Threepennies. The Elegant Extracts. The Young Bucks

53rd (SHROPSHIRE) REGIMENT OF FOOT

Raised December 1755 as the 55th Regiment of Foot. Renumbered 53rd in 1757.

Titles 1755 55th Regiment of Foot
1757 53rd Regiment of Foot
1782 53rd (or the Shropshire) Regiment of Foot
1881 Amalgamated with the 85th King's Light Infantry to form The Shropshire Regiment (King's Light Infantry)

Battle honours Nieuport, Tournay, St. Lucia, Talavera, Salamanca, Vittoria, Pyrenees, Nivelle, Toulouse, Peninsula, Aliwal, Sobraon, Punjaub, Goojerat, Lucknow.

Uniform Scarlet, facings scarlet

Regimental march [Quick] *Old Towler* (Shields)

Nicknames The Brickdusts. Five-and-Threepennies

85th KING'S LIGHT INFANTRY

Raised March 1793 by Colonel Sir George Nugent from employees on the Marquis (later Duke) of Buckingham's estates.

Titles 1793 85th Regiment of Foot (or Bucks Volunteers)
1808 85th Regiment of Foot (Bucks Volunteers) (Light Infantry)
1815 85th (or Duke of York's Own) Regiment of Light Infantry
1821 85th or King's Light Infantry Regiment
1827 85th King's Light Infantry
1881 Amalgamated with 53rd (Shropshire) Regiment of Foot to form The Shropshire Regiment (King's Light Infantry)

Battle honours Fuentes d'Onor, Nive, Peninsula, Bladensburg, Afghanistan 1879–80.

Motto *Aucto Splendore Resurgo* (I rise again with increased splendour)

Uniform Scarlet, facings blue

Regimental march [Quick] *The Daughter of the Regiment* (Donizetti)

Nicknames The Elegant Extracts. The Young Bucks

THE DURHAM LIGHT INFANTRY

(68th and 106th)

Formed 1881 by amalgamation of the 68th (Durham) Light Infantry with the 106th Bombay Light Infantry.

Battle honours Salamanca, Vittoria, Pyrenees, Nivelle, Orthes, Peninsula, Alma, Inkerman, Sevastopol, Reshire, Bushire, Koosh-ab, Persia, New Zealand, Relief of Ladysmith, South Africa 1899–1902.

The Great War— 37 *Battalions*—Aisne 1914, 18, Armentieres 1914, Ypres 1915, 17, 18, Gravenstafel, St. Julien, Frezenberg, Bellewaarde, Hooge 1915, Loos, Somme 1916, 18, Albert 1916, 18, Bazentin, Delville Wood, Pozieres, Guillemont, Flers-Courcelette, Morval, Le Transloy, Ancre Heights, Arras 1917, 18, Scarpe 1917, Arleux, Hill 70, Messines 1917, Pilckem, Langemarck 1917, Menin Road, Polygon Wood, Broodseinde, Passchendaele, Cambrai 1917, 18, St. Quentin, Rosieres, Lys, Estaires, Hazebrouck, Bailleul, Kemmel, Scherpenberg, Marne 1918, Tardenois, Bapaume 1918, Hindenburg Line, Havrincourt, Epehy, Canal du Nord, St. Quentin Canal, Beaurevoir, Courtrai, Selle, Sambre, France and Flanders 1914–18, Piave, Vittorio Veneto, Italy 1917–18, Macedonia 1916– 18, Egypt 1915–16, N.W. Frontier, India 1915, 1916– 17, Archangel 1918–19.

Afghanistan 1919.

The Second World War—Dyle, Arras counter attack, St. Omer-La Bassee, Dunkirk 1940, Villers Bocage, Tilly sur Seulles, Defence of Rauray, St. Pierre La Vielle, Gheel, Roer, Ibbenburen, North-West Europe 1940, 44–45, Syria 1941, Halfaya 1941, Tobruk 1941, Relief of Tobruk, Gazala, Gabr el Fachri, Zt el Mrasses, Mersa

Matruh, Point 174, El Alamein, Mareth, Sedjenane I, El Kourzia, North Africa 1940–43, Landing in Sicily, Solarino, Primosole Bridge, Sicily 1943, Salerno, Volturno Crossing, Teano, Monte Camino, Monte Tuga, Gothic Line, Gemmano Ridge, Cosina Canal Crossing, Pergola Ridge, Cesena, Sillaro Crossing, Italy 1943–45, Athens, Greece 1944–45, Cos, Middle East 1943, Malta 1942, Donbaik, Kohima, Mandalay, Burma 1943–45.

Korea 1952–53.

Motto	Faithful
Uniform	Jacket, dark green; trousers, blue; piping white, facings dark green.

Regimental marches	[Quick]	*The Light Barque*
	[Slow]	*Old 68th*
	[Double]	*The Keel Row* and *Monymusk*
Regimental journal		*Regimental Journal of The Durham Light Infantry*
Nickname		The Faithful Durhams

68th (DURHAM) LIGHT INFANTRY

Originally formed in 1756 as 2nd Battalion of the 23rd Regiment of Foot (Royal Welsh Fusiliers). In April 1758 separated as the 68th Regiment of Foot under Colonel John Lambton.

Titles	1758 68th Regiment of Foot
	1782 68th (or the Durham) Regiment of Foot
	1808 68th (Durham) Light Infantry
	1881 Amalgamated with 106th Bombay Light Infantry to form The Durham Light Infantry

Battle honours	Salamanca, Vittoria, Pyrenees, Nivelle, Orthes, Peninsula, Alma, Inkerman, Sevastopol, New Zealand.
Uniform	Scarlet, facings dark green

Regimental marches	[Quick]	*The Light Barque*
	[Slow]	*Prince Regent*
	[Double]	*The Keel Row* and *Monymusk*

Regimental journal *The Argo. The Durham Light Infantry Gazette*

Nickname The Faithfuls

106th BOMBAY LIGHT INFANTRY

Raised 1826 as 2nd Bombay European Regiment of Foot for service with the Hon. East India Company's forces. Transferred to British Army in 1861.

Titles 1826 2nd Bombay European Regiment of Foot (H.E.I.C.)
1840 2nd Bombay European Light Infantry (H.E.I.C.)
1855 2nd European Regiment, Bombay Light Infantry (H.E.I.C.)
1861 106th Bombay Light Infantry
1881 Amalgamated with 68th (Durham) Light Infantry to form The Durham Light Infantry

Battle honours Reshire, Bushire, Kooshab, Persia.

Uniform Scarlet, facings white

Regimental marches [Quick] *Paddy Carey* (to 1878) *Ap Shenkin* and *The Light Barque*
[Slow] *The Garb of Old Gaul*
[Double] *The Keel Row* and *Monymusk*

Nickname The Busters

THE PRINCE OF WALES'S OWN REGIMENT OF YORKSHIRE
(14th and 15th)

Formed April 1958 by amalgamation of The West Yorkshire Regiment (The Prince of Wales's Own) with The East Yorkshire Regiment (The Duke of York's Own).

Battle honours Namur 1695, Blenheim, Ramillies, Oudenarde, Malplaquet, Louisburg, Quebec 1759, Martinique 1762, Havannah, St. Lucia 1778, Martinique 1794, 1809, Tournay, Corunna, Guadaloupe 1810, Java, Waterloo, Bhurtpore, India, Sevastopol, New Zealand, Afghanistan 1879–80, Relief of Ladysmith, South Africa 1899–1902.

The Great War—Aisne 1914, 18, Armentieres 1914, Neuve Chapelle, Ypres 1915, 17, 18, Gravenstafel, St. Julien, Frezenberg, Bellewaarde, Aubers, Hooge 1915, Loos, Somme 1916, 18, Albert 1916, 18, Bazentin, Delville Wood, Pozieres, Flers-Courcelette, Morval, Thiepval, Le Transloy, Ancre Heights, Ancre 1916, Arras 1917, 18, Scarpe 1917, 18, Arleux, Oppy, Bullecourt, Hill 70, Messines 1917, 18, Pilckem, Langemarck 1917, Menin Road, Polygon Wood, Broodseinde, Poelcappelle, Passchendaele, Cambrai 1917, 18, St. Quentin, Bapaume 1918, Rosieres, Villers Bretonneux, Lys, Estaires, Hazebrouck, Bailleul, Kemmel, Scherpenberg, Marne 1918, Tardenois, Amiens, Drocourt-Queant, Hindenburg Line, Havrincourt, Epehy, Canal du Nord, St. Quentin Canal, Selle, Valenciennes, Sambre, France and Flanders, 1914–18, Piave, Vittorio Veneto, Italy 1917–18, Struma, Doiran 1917, Macedonia 1915–18, Suvla, Landing at Suvla, Scimitar Hill, Gallipoli 1915, Egypt 1915–16.

The Second World War—Withdrawal to Escaut, Defence of Escaut, Defence of Arras, French Frontier 1940, Ypres-Comines Canal, Dunkirk 1940, Normandy Landing, Tilly sur Seulles, Odon, Caen, Bourguebus Ridge, Troarn, Mont Pincon, St. Pierre la Vielle, Gheel, Nederrijn, Aam, Venraij, Rhineland, Schaddenhof, Brinkum, Bremen, North-West Europe 1940, 44–45, Jebel Dafeis, Keren, Ad Teclesan, Abyssinia 1940–41, Gazala, Cauldron, Mersa Matruh, Defence of Alamein Line, El Alamein, Mareth, Wadi Zigzaou, Akarit, North Africa 1940–43, Primosole Bridge, Sicily 1943, Pegu 1942, Yenangyaung 1942, North Arakan, Maungdaw, Defence of Sinzweya, Imphal, Bishenpur, Kanglatongbi, Meiktila, Capture of Meiktila, Defence of Meiktila, Rangoon Road, Pyawbwe, Sittang 1945, Burma 1942–45.

Motto *Nec Aspera Terrent* (Nor do difficulties deter)

Uniform Scarlet, piping and facings white

Regimental marches [Quick] *Ça Ira* (See below under West Yorkshire Regiment) followed by *The Yorkshire Lass*

[Slow] *God Bless the Prince of Wales* (Richards) and *The XV von England* (Anon—see below under The East Yorkshire Regiment)

Regimental journal *The White Rose*

Regimental headquarters 3/3A Tower Street, York YO1 1SB

Regimental Museum As above

THE WEST YORKSHIRE REGIMENT
(THE PRINCE OF WALES'S OWN)
(14th)

Raised at Canterbury, June 1685, by Colonel Sir Edward Hales.

Titles 1685 Sir Edward Hales's Regiment of Foot *Title subsequently changed with Colonels' names*

1751 14th Regiment of Foot

1782 14th (or the Bedfordshire) Regiment of Foot

1809 14th (or the Buckinghamshire) Regiment of Foot

1876 14th (Buckinghamshire) (Prince of Wales's Own) Regiment of Foot

1881 The Prince of Wales's Own (West Yorkshire Regiment)

1920 The West Yorkshire Regiment (The Prince of Wales's Own)

1958 Amalgamated with The East Yorkshire Regiment (Duke of York's Own) to form The Prince of Wales's Own Regiment of Yorkshire

Battle honours Namur 1695, Tournay, Corunna, Java, Waterloo, Bhurtpore, India, Sevastopol, New Zealand, Afghanistan 1879–80, Relief of Ladysmith, South Africa 1899–1902.

The Great War—31 *Battalions*—Aisne 1914, 18, Armentieres 1914, Neuve Chapelle, Aubers, Hooge

1915, Loos, Somme 1916, 18, Albert 1916, 18,
Bazentin, Pozieres, Flers-Courcelette, Morval, Thiepval,
Le Transloy, Ancre Heights, Ancre 1916, Arras 1917,
18, Scarpe 1917, 18, Bullecourt, Hill 70, Messines 1917,
18, Ypres 1917, 18, Pilckem, Langemarck 1917, Menin
Road, Polygon Wood, Poelcappelle, Passchendaele,
Cambrai 1917, 18, St. Quentin, Rosieres, Villers
Bretonneux, Lys, Hazebrouck, Bailleul, Kemmel, Marne
1918, Tardenois, Amiens, Bapaume 1918, Drocourt-
Queant, Hindenburg Line, Havrincourt, Epehy, Canal
du Nord, Selle, Valenciennes, Sambre, France and
Flanders 1914–18, Piave, Vittorio Veneto, Italy 1917–18,
Suvla, Landing at Suvla, Scimitar Hill, Gallipoli 1915,
Egypt 1915–16.

The Second World War—North-West Europe 1940, Jebel
Dafeis, Keren, Ad Teclesan, Abyssinia 1940–41,
Cauldron, Defence of Alamein Line, North Africa 1940–
42, Pegu 1942, Yenangyaung 1942, North Arakan,
Maungdaw, Defence of Sinzweya, Imphal, Bishenpur,
Kanglatongbi, Meiktila, Capture of Meiktila, Defence of
Meiktila, Rangoon Road, Pyawbwe, Sittang 1945, Burma
1942–45.

Motto *Nec Aspera Terrent* (Nor do difficulties deter)

Uniform Scarlet, piping and facings buff

Regimental marches [Quick] *Ça Ira* (Bécourt)
[Slow] *God Bless the Prince of Wales* (Richards)

Regimental journal *Ça Ira*

Nicknames The Old and Bold. Calvert's Entire

Remarks The Regimental March *Ça Ira* was a French
revolutionary song dating from 1789, to music composed
by one Bécourt, violinist in a Paris theatre orchestra. At
Famars in 1793 when the 14th were heavily attacked, the
Colonel ordered his Drummers to strike up the enemy
air, saying 'We'll beat them to their own damned tune!'
They did, and by order of the Duke of York the tune was
adopted as the Regimental quickstep in 1793, and has
remained so ever since.

THE EAST YORKSHIRE REGIMENT
(THE DUKE OF YORK'S OWN)
(15th)

Raised at Nottingham, June 1685, by Colonel Sir William Clifton, Bt.

Titles 1685 Sir William Clifton's Regiment of Foot *Title subsequently changed with Colonels' names*
1751 15th Regiment of Foot
1782 15th (or the Yorkshire East Riding) Regiment of Foot
1881 The East Yorkshire Regiment
1935 The East Yorkshire Regiment (The Duke of York's Own)
1958 Amalgamated with The West Yorkshire Regiment (The Prince of Wales's Own) to form The Prince of Wales's Own Regiment of Yorkshire

Battle honours Blenheim, Ramillies, Oudenarde, Malplaquet, Louisburg, Quebec 1759, Martinique 1762, Havannah, St. Lucia 1778, Martinique 1794, 1809, Guadaloupe 1810, Afghanistan 1879–80, South Africa 1900–02.

The Great War—21 *Battalions*—Aisne 1914, 18, Armentieres 1914, Ypres 1915, 17, 18, Gravenstafel, St. Julien, Frezenberg, Bellewaarde, Hooge 1915, Loos, Somme 1916, 18, Albert 1916, 18, Bazentin, Delville Wood, Pozieres, Flers-Courcelette, Morval, Thiepval, Ancre Heights, Ancre 1916, Arras 1917, 18, Scarpe 1917, 18, Arleux, Oppy, Messines 1917, 18, Pilckem, Langemarck 1917, Menin Road, Polygon Wood, Broodseinde, Poelcappelle, Passchendaele, Cambrai 1917, 18, St. Quentin, Bapaume 1918, Rosieres, Lys, Estaires, Hazebrouck, Kemmel, Scherpenberg, Amiens, Hindenburg Line, Epehy, Canal du Nord, St. Quentin Canal, Selle, Sambre, France and Flanders 1914–18, Struma, Doiran 1917, Macedonia 1915–18, Suvla, Landing at Suvla, Scimitar Hill, Gallipoli 1915, Egypt 1915–16.

The Second World War—Withdrawal to Escaut, Defence of Escaut, Defence of Arras, French Frontier 1940,

Ypres-Comines Canal, Dunkirk 1940, Normandy
Landing, Tilly sur Seulles, Odon, Caen, Bourguebus
Ridge, Troarn, Mont Pincon, St. Pierre la Vielle, Gheel,
Nederrijn, Aam, Venraij, Rhineland, Schaddenhof,
Brinkum, Bremen, North-West Europe 1940, 44–45,
Gazala, Mersa Matruh, Defence of Alamein Line, El
Alamein, Mareth, Wadi Zigzaou, Akarit, North Africa
1942–43, Primosole Bridge, Sicily 1943, Sittang 1945,
Burma 1945.

Uniform Scarlet, piping and facings white

Regimental marches [Quick] *The Yorkshire Lass*
[Slow] *The XV von England*

Regimental journal *The Snapper*

Nicknames The Snappers. Poona Guards

Remarks The Regiment fought at the capture of Quebec under
Wolfe, and in mourning for his death in that action the
officers thereafter wore a black line in their gold lace.
Later a black backing was incorporated in the Regimental
Badge.

The curiously-titled Slow March *The XV von England*
dates from about 1790, and Regimental records merely
state that it 'was received from the War Office in
Dresden, Saxony'. No further explanation is forthcoming.

THE GREEN
HOWARDS
(ALEXANDRA, PRINCESS OF WALES'S
OWN YORKSHIRE REGIMENT)
(19th)

One of the few Infantry regiments never to have been
amalgamated, The Green Howards trace their origin to
independent companies of Foot raised in November 1688
by Colonel Francis Luttrell to support Prince William of
Orange and the 'Glorious Revolution'. These companies
were not actually augmented into a Regiment of Foot
until February 1689.

Titles 1688 Colonel Luttrell's Companies of Foot
1689 Colonel Luttrell's Regiment of Foot *Title subsequently changed with Colonels' names*
1751 19th Regiment of Foot
1782 19th (1st Yorkshire North Riding) Regiment of Foot
1875 19th (1st Yorkshire North Riding Regiment) (The Princess of Wales's Own)
1881 The Princess of Wales's Own (Yorkshire Regiment)
1902 Alexandra, Princess of Wales's Own Yorkshire Regiment
1921 The Green Howards (Alexandra, Princess of Wales's Own Yorkshire Regiment)

Battle honours Malplaquet, Belleisle, Alma, Inkerman, Sevastopol, Tirah, Relief of Kimberley, Paardeberg, South Africa 1899–1902.

The Great War—Ypres 1914, 15, 17, Langemarck 1914, 17, Gheluvelt, Neuve Chapelle, St. Julien, Frezenberg, Bellewaarde, Aubers, Festubert 1915, Loos, Somme 1916, 18, Albert 1916, Bazentin, Pozieres, Flers-Courcelette, Morval, Thiepval, Le Transloy, Ancre Heights, Ancre 1916, Arras 1917, 18, Scarpe 1917, 18, Messines 1917, 18, Pilckem, Menin Road, Polygon Wood, Broodseinde, Poelcappelle, Passchendaele, Cambrai 1917, 18, St. Quentin, Bapaume 1918, Rosieres, Lys, Estaires, Hazebrouck, Kemmel, Scherpenberg, Aisne 1918, Drocourt-Queant, Hindenburg Line, Canal du Nord, Beaurevoir, Selle, Valenciennes, Sambre, France and Flanders 1914–18, Piave, Vittorio Veneto, Italy 1917–18, Suvla, Landing at Suvla, Scimitar Hill, Gallipoli 1915, Egypt 1916, Archangel 1918.

Afghanistan 1919.

The Second World War—Otta, Norway 1940, Defence of Arras, Dunkirk 1940, Normandy Landing, Tilly sur Seulles, St. Pierre La Vielle, Gheel, Nederrijn, North-West Europe 1940, 44–45, Gazala, Defence of Alamein Line, El Alamein, Mareth, Akarit, North Africa 1942–43, Landing in Sicily, Lentini, Sicily 1943, Minturno, Anzio, Italy 1943–44, Arakan Beaches, Burma 1945.

Uniform Scarlet, piping and facings grass green

Regimental marches [Quick] *The Bonnie English Rose*
[Slow] *Maria Theresa*

Regimental journal *Green Howards Gazette*

Regimental headquarters Trinity Church Square, The Market Place, Richmond, North Yorkshire DL10 4QN

Regimental museum As above

Nicknames The present official title, The Green Howards, was originally a nickname, first appearing as Howard's Greens. In 1740 two Colonels Howard were commanding regiments, and as the 19th wore green facings they were dubbed 'Green Howards' to distinguish them from the 3rd Foot with their buff facings—'Howard's Buffs'.

Remarks Since 1875 the Regimental Badge has incorporated the Cross or *Dannebrog* of the Danish Royal Family and the Cypher of Alexandra, Princess of Wales (later Queen Alexandra), who was the daughter of King Christian IX of Denmark.

The Slow March *Maria Theresa* is said to have been presented to the Regiment by that Austrian Empress at the time of the Wars of the Austrian Succession (1740–48).

THE ROYAL HIGHLAND FUSILIERS
(PRINCESS MARGARET'S OWN GLASGOW AND AYRSHIRE REGIMENT)
(21st, 71st, 74th)

Formed 20th January 1959 by amalgamation of The Royal Scots Fusiliers with The Highland Light Infantry (City of Glasgow Regiment).

Battle honours Blenheim, Ramillies, Oudenarde, Malplaquet, Dettingen, Belleisle, Carnatic, Hindoostan, Sholinghur, Mysore, Gibraltar 1780–83, Martinique 1794, Seringapatam, Assaye, Cape of Good Hope 1806, Rolica, Vimiera, Corunna, Busaco, Fuentes d'Onor, Almaraz, Ciudad Rodrigo, Badajoz, Salamanca, Vittoria, Pyrenees, Nivelle, Nive, Orthes, Toulouse, Peninsula,

Bladensburg, Waterloo, South Africa 1851–53, Alma, Inkerman, Sevastopol, Central India, South Africa 1879, Tel-el-Kebir, Egypt 1882, Burma 1885–87, Tirah, Modder River, Relief of Ladysmith, South Africa 1899–1902.

The Great War—Mons, Le Cateau, Retreat from Mons, Marne 1914, Aisne 1914, La Bassee 1914, Ypres 1914, 15, 17, 18, Langemarck 1914, 17, Gheluvelt, Nonne Bosschen, Givenchy 1914, Neuve Chapelle, St. Julien, Aubers, Festubert 1915, Loos, Somme 1916, 18, Albert 1916, 18, Bazentin, Delville Wood, Pozieres, Flers-Courcelette, Le Transloy, Ancre Heights, Ancre 1916, 18, Arras 1917, 18, Vimy 1917, Scarpe 1917, 18, Arleux, Messines 1917, 18, Pilckem, Menin Road, Polygon Wood, Passchendaele, Cambrai 1917, 18, St. Quentin, Bapaume 1918, Rosieres, Lys, Estaires, Hazebrouck, Bailleul, Kemmel, Bethune, Scherpenberg, Amiens, Drocourt-Queant, Hindenburg Line, Havrincourt, Canal Du Nord, St. Quentin Canal, Beaurevoir, Courtrai, Selle, Sambre, France and Flanders 1914–18, Doiran 1917, 18, Macedonia 1916–18, Helles, Gallipoli 1915–16, Rumani, Egypt 1916–17, Gaza, El Mughar, Nebi Samwil, Jerusalem, Jaffa, Tell 'Asur, Palestine 1917–18, Tigris 1916, Kut al Amara 1917, Sharqat, Mesopotamia 1916–18, Murman 1919, Archangel 1919.

The Second World War—Defence of Arras, Ypres-Comines Canal, Somme 1940, Withdrawal to Seine, Withdrawal to Cherbourg, Odon, Fontenay Le Pesnil, Cheux, Defence of Rauray, Esquay, Mont Pincon, Quarry Hill, Estry Falaise, La Vie Crossing, La Touques Crossing, Seine 1944, Aart, Nederrijn, Best, Le Havre, Antwerp-Turnhout Canal, Scheldt, South Beveland, Walcheren Causeway, Lower Maas, Meijel, Venlo Pocket, Roer, Ourthe, Rhineland, Reichswald, Cleve, Goch, Moyland Wood, Weeze, Rhine, Ibbenburen, Dreirwalde, Aller, Uelzen, Bremen, Artlenberg, North-West Europe 1940, 44–45, Jebel Shiba, Barentu, Keren, Massawa, Abyssinia 1941, Gazala, Cauldron, Mersa Matruh, Fuka, North Africa 1940–42, Landing in Sicily, Sicily 1943, Sangro, Garigliano Crossing, Minturno, Anzio, Advance to Tiber, Italy 1943, 44, 45, Madagascar, Adriatic, Middle East 1942, 44, Athens Greece 1944–45, North Arakan, Razabil, Pinwe, Shweli, Mandalay, Burma 1944–45.

Motto *Nemo Nos Impune Lacessit* (No one provokes us with impunity)

Uniform Doublet, blue; trews, Mackenzie tartan; facings blue

Regimental marches [Quick] *The British Grenadiers* and *Whistle o'er the Lave o't*
[Slow] *The Garb of Old Gaul* and *March of the 21st Regiment*

Regimental journal *The Journal of The Royal Highland Fusiliers*

Regimental headquarters 518 Sauchiehall Street, Glasgow G2 3LW

Regimental museum As above

THE ROYAL SCOTS
FUSILIERS
(21st)

Raised September 1678 by Colonel Charles Erskine, 5th Earl of Mar.

Titles 1678 The Earl of Mar's Regiment of Foot

Title subsequently changed with Colonels' names. The first recorded mention of the 'Fusilier' (or 'Fuzileer') title dates from 1691, when the Regiment was styled 'Colonel O'Farrell's Fuzileers'.

1707 North British Fuzileers*
1713 Royal Regiment of North British Fuzileers
1751 21st Regiment of Foot (or Royal North British Fuzileers)
1877 21st (Royal Scots Fusiliers) Regiment of Foot
1881 The Royal Scots Fusiliers
1959 Amalgamated with The Highland Light Infantry (City of Glasgow Regiment) to form The Royal Highland Fusiliers (Princess Margaret's Own Glasgow and Ayrshire Regiment)

Battle honours Blenheim, Ramillies, Oudenarde, Malplaquet, Dettingen, Belleisle, Martinique 1794, Bladensburg, Alma, Inkerman, Sevastopol, South Africa 1879, Burma

---

*The style 'North British', officially bestowed after the Union of England and Scotland (1707), was never popular within the Regiment, who preferred 'Scots' and later 'Royal Scots', and this variant was often used outside the Regiment before it became officially sanctioned in 1877.

1885–87, Tirah, Relief of Ladysmith, South Africa
1899–1902.

The Great War—18 *Battalions*—Mons, Le Cateau,
Retreat from Mons, Marne 1914, Aisne 1914, La Bassee
1914, Ypres 1914, 17, 18, Langemarck 1914, Gheluvelt,
Nonne Bosschen, Neuve Chapelle, Aubers, Festubert
1915, Loos, Somme 1916, 18, Albert 1916, 18,
Bazentin, Delville Wood, Pozieres, Flers-Courcelette, Le
Transloy, Ancre Heights, Ancre 1916, Arras 1917, 18,
Scarpe 1917, 18, Arleux, Messines 1917, Pilckem,
Menin Road, Polygon Wood, St. Quentin, Bapaume
1918, Rosieres, Lys, Estaires, Hazebrouck, Bailleul,
Bethune, Scherpenberg, Drocourt-Queant, Hindenburg
Line, Canal du Nord, Courtrai, Selle, France and
Flanders 1914–18, Doiran 1917, 18, Macedonia 1916–
18, Helles, Gallipoli 1915–16, Rumani, Egypt 1916–17,
Gaza, El Mughar, Nebi Samwil, Jerusalem, Jaffa, Tell
'Asur, Palestine 1917–18.

The Second World War—Defence of Arras, Ypres-
Comines Canal, Somme 1940, Withdrawal to Seine,
Odon, Fontenay le Pesnil, Cheux, Defence of Rauray,
Mont Pincon, Estry, Falaise, La Vie Crossing, La
Touques Crossing, Aart, Nederrijn, Best, Le Havre,
Antwerp-Turnhout Canal, Scheldt, South Beveland,
Lower Maas, Meijel, Venlo Pocket, Roer, Rhineland,
Reichswald, Cleve, Goch, Rhine, Dreirwalde, Uelzen,
Bremen, Artlenberg, North-West Europe 1940, 44–45,
Landing in Sicily, Sicily 1943, Sangro, Garigliano
Crossing, Minturno, Anzio, Advance to Tiber, Italy
1943–44, Madagascar, Middle East 1942, North Arakan,
Razabil, Pinwe, Shweli, Mandalay, Burma 1944–45.

Uniform Doublet, blue; trews, Hunting (Erskine) tartan, facings
blue

Regimental marches [Quick] *The British Grenadiers* (Tradit.)
[Slow] *The Garb of Old Gaul* (Reid)

Regimental journal *The Journal of The Royal Scots Fusiliers*

Nicknames The Earl of Mar's Greybreeks. Fusil Jocks

Remarks Although ranking as the 21st Foot, The Royal Scots
Fusiliers were actually 4th in terms of age. But in 1694 it
was decreed that Scottish and Irish regiments should take
precedence from the dates they were first placed on the
English establishment, and as The Scots Fusiliers did not
cross the border until 1688 their precedence was fixed

from that date, and not the date of their raising.

The Regiment was the second in the British Army to be armed and equipped as Fusiliers (the first being The Royal Fusiliers). The Fusilier was armed with the flintlock 'fusil' or musket in place of the clumsy matchlock or wheel-lock, and carried a bayonet. The Fusilier regiments had no pikemen as in other contemporary infantry regiments.

THE HIGHLAND LIGHT INFANTRY
(CITY OF GLASGOW REGIMENT)
(71st and 74th)

Formed 1881 by amalgamation of the 71st (Highland Light Infantry) Regiment of Foot with the 74th (Highlanders) Regiment of Foot, to form The Highland Light Infantry. '(City of Glasgow Regiment)' added in 1923.

Battle honours Carnatic, Hindoostan, Sholinghur, Mysore, Gibraltar 1780–83, Seringapatam, Assaye, Cape of Good Hope 1806, Rolica, Vimiera, Corunna, Busaco, Fuentes d'Onor, Ciudad Rodrigo, Badajoz, Almaraz, Salamanca, Vittoria, Pyrenees, Nivelle, Nive, Orthes, Toulouse, Peninsula, Waterloo, South Africa 1851–52–53, Sevastopol, Central India, Tel-el-Kebir, Egypt 1882, Modder River, South Africa 1899–1902.

*The Great War—26 Battalions—*Mons, Retreat from Mons, Marne 1914, Aisne 1914, Ypres 1914, 15, 17, 18, Langemarck 1914, 17, Gheluvelt, Nonne Bosschen, Givenchy 1914, Neuve Chapelle, St. Julien, Aubers, Festubert 1915, Loos, Somme 1916, 18, Albert 1916, 18, Bazentin, Delville Wood, Pozieres, Flers-Courcelette, Le Transloy, Ancre Heights, Ancre 1916, 18, Arras 1917, 18, Vimy 1917, Scarpe 1917, 18, Arleux, Pilckem, Menin Road, Polygon Wood, Passchendaele, Cambrai 1917, 18, St. Quentin, Bapaume 1918, Lys, Estaires, Messines 1918, Hazebrouck, Ballieul, Kemmel, Amiens, Drocourt-Queant, Hindenburg Line, Havrincourt, Canal du Nord, St. Quentin Canal, Beaurevoir, Courtrai, Selle, Sambre, France and Flanders 1914–18, Gallipoli 1915–16,

Rumani, Egypt 1916, Gaza, El Mughar, Nebi Samwil, Jaffa, Palestine 1917–18, Tigris 1916, Kut al Amara 1917, Sharqat, Mesopotamia 1916–18, Murman 1919, Archangel 1919.

The Second World War—Withdrawal to Cherbourg, Odon, Cheux, Esquay, Mont Pincon, Quarry Hill, Estry, Falaise, Seine 1944, Alart, Nederrijn, Best, Scheldt, Lower Maas, South Beveland, Walcheren Causeway, Asten, Roer, Ourthe, Rhineland, Reichswald, Goch, Moyland Wood, Weeze, Rhine, Ibbenburen, Dreirwalde, Aller, Uelzen, Bremen, Artlenberg, North-West Europe 1940, 44–45, Jebel Shiba, Barentu, Keren, Massawa, Abyssinia 1941, Gazala, Cauldron, Mersa Matruh, Fuka, North Africa 1940–42, Landing in Sicily, Sicily 1943, Italy 1943, 45, Athens, Greece 1944–45, Adriatic, Middle East 1944.

Uniform Doublet, piper green; kilt, MacKenzie tartan, facings buff

Regimental march [Quick] *Whistle o'er the Lave o't*

Regimental journal *The H.L.I. Chronicle*

Nicknames The Glesca Keelies. Pig-and-Whistle Light Infantry

71st (HIGHLAND LIGHT INFANTRY) REGIMENT OF FOOT

Raised December 1777 by Colonel John Mackenzie, Lord Macleod, and ranked as the 73rd (Highland) Regiment of Foot. Re-ranked as 71st in 1786.

Titles 1777 73rd (Highland) Regiment of Foot (or 'MacLeod's Highlanders')
1786 71st (Highland) Regiment of Foot
1808 71st (Glasgow Highland) Regiment of Foot
1809 71st (Glasgow Highland) Regiment of Foot (Light Infantry)
1810 71st (Highland) Regiment of Foot (Light Infantry)
1855 71st (Highland Light Infantry) *This style, with or without brackets, had been in popular use since about 1810.*

1881 Amalgamated with the 74th (Highlanders) Regiment to form The Highland Light Infantry ('City of Glasgow Regiment' added in 1923)

Battle honours Carnatic, Sholinghur, Mysore, Hindoostan, Cape of Good Hope 1806, Rolica, Vimiera, Corunna, Fuentes d'Onor, Almaraz, Vittoria, Pyrenees, Nive, Orthes, Peninsula, Waterloo, Sevastopol, Central India.

Uniform Scarlet, facings buff

Nicknames The Glesca Keelies. The Pig-and-Whistle Light Infantry

74th (HIGHLANDERS) REGIMENT OF FOOT

Raised October 1787 by Major-General Sir Archibald Campbell, as the 74th (Highland) Regiment of Foot.

Titles 1787 74th (Highland) Regiment of Foot (In 1803 was known as 'The Assaye Regiment')
1816 74th Regiment of Foot
1845 74th (Highland) Regiment of Foot
1847 74th (Highlanders) Regiment of Foot
1881 Amalgamated with 71st (Highland Light Infantry) Regiment of Foot to form The Highland Light Infantry

Battle honours Assaye (with the Elephant), Seringapatam, Busaco, Fuentes d'Onor, Ciudad Rodrigo, Badajoz, Salamanca, Vittoria, Pyrenees, Nivelle, Orthes, Toulouse, Peninsula, South Africa 1851–52–53.

Uniform Scarlet, facings white

Nickname The Assayes

Remarks The distinguished conduct of the 74th at the battle of Assaye (1803) when all the officers were killed or wounded, was recognised by the East India Company's granting of a third, honorary, Colour in addition to the normal King's and Regimental Colours. This Colour, renewed at Regimental expense, is still carried by the present Regiment.

THE CHESHIRE REGIMENT

(22nd)

One of the few Regiments never to have been amalgamated, The 22nd was raised at Chester, March 1689, by Colonel Henry Howard, 7th Duke of Norfolk.

Titles   1689 The Duke of Norfolk's Regiment of Foot *Title subsequently changed with Colonels' names*
1751 22nd Regiment of Foot
1782 22nd (or the Cheshire) Regiment of Foot
1881 The Cheshire Regiment

Although the above remains the official title, the Regiment itself invariably uses the old numerical title, 'The 22nd (Cheshire) Regiment'.

Battle honours   Louisburg, Martinique 1762, Havannah, Meeanee, Hyderabad, Scinde, South Africa 1900–02.

The Great War—Mons, Le Cateau, Retreat from Mons, Marne 1914, 18, Aisne 1914, 18, La Bassee 1914, Armentieres 1914, Ypres 1914, 15, 17, 18, Nonne Bosschen, Hill 60, Gravenstafel, St. Julien, Frezenberg, Bellewaarde, Loos, Somme 1916, 18, Albert 1916, 18, Bazentin, Delville Wood, Pozieres, Guillemont, Flers-Courcelette, Morval, Thiepval, Le Transloy, Ancre Heights, Ancre 1916, Arras 1917, 18, Vimy 1917, Scarpe 1917, 18, Oppy, Messines 1917, 18, Pilckem, Langemarck 1917, Menin Road, Polygon Wood, Broodseinde, Poelcapelle, Passchendaele, Cambrai 1917, 18, St. Quentin, Bapaume 1918, Rosieres, Lys, Estaires, Hazebrouck, Bailleul, Kemmel, Scherpenberg, Soissonnais-Ourcq, Hindenburg Line, Canal du Nord, Courtrai, Selle, Valenciennes, Sambre, France and Flanders 1914–18, Italy 1917–18, Struma, Doiran 1917, 18, Macedonia 1915–18, Suvla, Sari Bair, Landing at Suvla, Scimitar Hill, Gallipoli 1915, Egypt 1915–17, Gaza, El Mughar, Jerusalem, Jericho, Tell 'Asur, Palestine 1917–18, Tigris 1916, Kut al Amara 1917, Baghdad, Mesopotamia 1916–18.

The Second World War—Dyle, Withdrawal to Escaut, St. Omer-La Bassee, Wormhoudt, Cassel, Dunkirk 1940, Normandy Landing, Mont Pincon, St. Pierre La Vielle, Gheel, Nederrijn, Aam, Aller, North-West Europe 1940, 44–45, Sidi Barrani, Capture of Tobruk, Gazala, Mersa Matruh, Defence of Alamein Line, Deir el Shein, El Alamein, Mareth, Wadi Zeus East, Wadi Zigzaou, Akarit, Wadi Akarit East, Enfidaville, North Africa 1940–43, Landing in Sicily, Primosole Bridge, Simeto Bridgehead, Sicily 1943, Sangro, Salerno, Santa Lucia, Battipaglia, Volturno Crossing, Monte Maro, Teano, Monte Camino, Garigliano Crossing, Minturno, Damiano, Anzio, Rome, Gothic Line, Coriano, Gemmano Ridge, Savignano, Senio Floodbank, Rimini Line, Ceriano Ridge, Valli di Comacchio, Italy 1943–45, Malta 1941–42.

Uniform	Scarlet, piping and facings buff
Regimental marches [Quick]	*Wha wadna fecht for Charlie?*
[Slow]	*The 22nd Regiment Slow March 1772*
Regimental journal	*The Oak Tree*
Regimental headquarters	The Castle, Chester CH1 2DN
Regimental museum	As above
Nicknames	The Lightning Conductors. The Red Knights. The Old Two Twos. The Peep-of-Day Boys. The Specimens
Remarks	The 'leaved acorn' Badge is claimed to commemorate the saving of King George II from capture at Dettingen (1743) by a draft detachment of 22nd soldiers. The King is said to have plucked an oak twig and handed it to them, desiring the Regiment to wear the emblem in memory of their gallant conduct.

The 22nd are the only Regiment of the British Army to bear the Battle Honours *Meeanee, Hyderabad, Scinde*, gained for their services with General Sir Charles Napier's forces in the conquest of Scinde (1843).

THE ROYAL WELCH FUSILIERS
(23rd)

Raised at Ludlow, March 1689 by Colonel Henry Herbert, 4th Lord Herbert. One of the few Regiments never amalgamated.

Titles 1689 Lord Herbert of Cherbury's Regiment of Foot *Title subsequently changed with Colonels' names*
1702 Welsh Regiment of Fuzileers
1713 The Royal Regiment of Welsh Fuzileers
1714 The Prince of Wales's Own Royal Regiment of Welsh Fuzileers
1727 The Royal Welch Fusiliers
1751 23rd (Royal Welch Fusiliers) Regiment of Foot
1881 The Royal Welsh Fusiliers
1920 The Royal Welch Fusiliers

Battle honours Namur 1695, Blenheim, Ramillies, Oudenarde, Malplaquet, Dettingen, Minden, Egypt (with the Sphinx), Corunna, Martinique 1809, Albuhera, Badajoz, Salamanca, Vittoria, Pyrenees, Nivelle, Orthes, Toulouse, Peninsula, Waterloo, Alma, Inkerman, Sevastopol, Lucknow, Ashantee 1873–74, Burma 1885–87, Relief of Ladysmith, South Africa 1899–1902, Pekin 1900.

The Great War—Mons, Le Cateau, Retreat from Mons, Marne 1914, Aisne 1914, 18, La Bassee 1914, Messines 1914, 17, 18, Armentieres 1914, Ypres 1914, 17, 18, Langemarck 1914, 17, Gheluvelt, Givenchy 1914, Neuve Chapelle, Aubers, Festubert 1915, Loos, Somme 1916, 18, Albert 1916, 18, Bazentin, Delville Wood, Pozieres, Guillemont, Flers-Courcelette, Morval, Le Transloy, Ancre Heights, Ancre 1916, 18, Arras 1917, Scarpe 1917, Arleux, Bullecourt, Pilckem, Menin Road, Polygon Wood, Broodseinde, Poelcappelle, Passchendaele, Cambrai 1917, 18, St. Quentin, Bapaume 1918, Lys, Bailleul, Kemmel, Scherpenberg, Hindenburg Line, Havrincourt, Epehy, St. Quentin Canal, Beaurevoir, Selle, Valenciennes, Sambre, France and Flanders 1914–18, Piave, Vittorio Veneto, Italy 1917–18, Doiran 1917, 18, Macedonia 1915–18, Suvla, Sari Bair, Landing at Suvla, Scimitar Hill, Gallipoli 1915–16, Rumani, Egypt 1915–17, Gaza, El Mughar, Jerusalem, Jericho, Tell 'Asur, Megiddo, Nablus, Palestine 1917–18, Tigris 1916, Kut al Amara 1917, Baghdad, Mesopotamia 1916–18.

The Second World War—Dyle, Defence of Escaut, St. Omer-La Bassee, Caen, Esquay, Falaise, Nederrijn, Lower Maas, Venlo Pocket, Ourthe, Rhineland, Reichswald, Goch, Weeze, Rhine, Ibbenburen, Aller, North-West Europe 1940, 44–45, Madagascar, Middle East 1942, Donbaik, North Arakan, Kohima, Mandalay, Ava, Burma 1943–45.

Uniform Scarlet, facings blue (See below under *Remarks*)

Regimental marches [Quick] *The British Grenadiers* (Tradit.)
[Slow] *War March of the Men of Glamorgan* (Tradit.)

Regimental journal *Y Ddraig Goch* (The Red Dragon)

Regimental headquarters Hightown Barracks, Wrexham, Clwyd LL13 8RD

Regimental museum Queen's Tower, The Castle, Caernarfon, Gwynedd

Remarks The 23rd were one of the six British infantry regiments who distinguished themselves at Minden (1759) by defeating the French cavalry.

A distinctive and unique feature of the uniform is the black 'Flash' or knot of ribbons worn at the back of the collar by all ranks. The 23rd was the last Regiment in the British Army to wear the pigtail, or queue, and the Flash symbolises the black leather bag sheathing the pigtail. Its wear was officially sanctioned by King William IV in 1834.

On the reorganisation of the infantry in 1881 the War Office proposed to retitle the 23rd 'The North Wales Regiment', but on the intervention of the Earl of Powis it was permitted to retain the title of 'The Royal Welsh Fusiliers'. The former spelling of 'Welch' was restored in 1920.

THE ROYAL REGIMENT OF WALES
(24th/41st FOOT)

Formed June 1969 by amalgamation of The South Wales Borderers (24th Foot) with The Welch Regiment (41st and 69th Foot).

Battle honours Blenheim, Ramillies, Oudenarde, Malplaquet, Belleisle, Martinique 1762, St. Vincent 1797, Egypt (with the Sphinx), Cape of Good Hope 1806, India, Talavera, Bourbon, Busaco, Fuentes d'Onor, Java, Salamanca, Detroit, Queenstown, Miami, Vittoria, Pyrenees, Nivelle, Niagara, Orthes, Peninsula, Waterloo, Ava, Candahar 1842, Ghuznee 1842, Cabool 1842, Chillianwallah, Goojerat, Punjaub, Alma, Inkerman, Sevastopol, South Africa 1877–78–79, Burma 1885–87, Relief of Kimberley, Paardeberg, South Africa 1899–1902.

The Great War—Mons, Retreat from Mons, Marne 1914, Aisne 1914, 18, Ypres 1914, 15, 17, 18, Langemarck 1914, 17, Gheluvelt, Nonne Bosschen, Givenchy 1914, Gravenstafel, St. Julien, Frezenberg, Bellewaarde, Aubers, Loos, Somme 1916, 18, Albert 1916, 18, Bazentin, Pozieres, Flers-Courcelette, Morval, Ancre Heights, Ancre 1916, 18, Arras 1917, 18, Scarpe 1917, Messines 1917, 18, Pilckem, Menin Road, Polygon Wood, Broodseinde, Poelcappelle, Passchendaele, Cambrai 1917, 18, St. Quentin, Bapaume 1918, Lys, Estaires, Hazebrouck, Bailleul, Kemmel, Bethune, Scherpenberg, Drocourt-Queant, Hindenburg Line, Havrincourt, Epehy, St. Quentin Canal, Beaurevoir, Courtrai, Selle, Valenciennes, Sambre, France and Flanders 1914–18, Struma, Doiran 1917, 18, Macedonia 1915–18, Helles, Landing at Helles, Krithia, Suvla, Sari Bair, Landing at Suvla, Scimitar Hill, Gallipoli 1915–16, Egypt 1915–17, Gaza, El Mughar, Jerusalem, Jericho, Tell 'Asur, Megiddo, Nablus, Palestine 1917–18, Aden, Tigris 1916, Kut al Amara 1917, Baghdad, Mesopotamia 1916–18, Tsingtao.

The Second World War—Norway 1940, Normandy Landing, Sully, Odon, Caen, Bourguebus Ridge, Mont Pincon, Souleuvre, Le Perier Ridge, Falaise, Risle Crossing, Antwerp, Nederrijn, Le Havre, Antwerp-Turnhout Canal, Scheldt, Lower Maas, Venlo Pocket, Zetten, Ourthe, Rhineland, Reichswald, Weeze, Hochwald, Rhine, Ibbenburen, Aller, Arnhem 1945, North-West Europe 1944–45, Benghazi, Gazala, North Africa 1940–42, Sicily 1943, Coriano, Croce, Rimini Line, Ceriano Ridge, Argenta Gap, Italy 1943–45, Crete, Canea, Withdrawal to Sphakia, Middle East 1941, North Arakan, Mayu Tunnels, Pinwe, Kyaukmyaung Bridgehead, Shweli, Myitson, Maymyo, Rangoon Road, Sittang 1945, Burma 1944–45.

Korea 1951–52.

Motto	*Gwell Angau Na Chywilydd* (Better death than dishonour)
Uniform	Scarlet, piping and facings grass green
Regimental marches [Quick]	*Men of Harlech* (Tradit.)
[Slow]	*Scipio* (Handel)
Regimental journal	*The Men of Harlech*
Regimental headquarters	Maindy Barracks, Cardiff CF4 3YE
Regimental museums	(South Wales Borderers) The Barracks, Brecon, Powys
	(The Welch Regiment) The Castle, Cardiff
Remarks	A silver wreath of immortelles is borne on the Queen's Colour pike (see 'South Wales Borderers').

THE SOUTH WALES BORDERERS
(24th FOOT)

Raised in Kent, March 1689, as Sir Edward Dering's Regiment of Foot. In 1747 ranked as 24th Foot.

Titles	1689 Sir Edward Dering's Regiment of Foot *Title subsequently changed with Colonels' names*
	1751 24th Regiment of Foot

1782 24th (or 2nd Warwickshire) Regiment of Foot
1881 The South Wales Borderers
1969 Amalgamated with The Welch Regiment to form
The Royal Regiment of Wales

Battle honours Blenheim, Ramillies, Oudenarde, Malplaquet, Egypt (with the Sphinx), Cape of Good Hope 1806, Talavera, Busaco, Fuentes d'Onor, Salamanca, Vittoria, Pyrenees, Nivelle, Orthes, Peninsula, Chillianwallah, Goojerat, Punjaub, South Africa 1877–78–79, Burma 1885–87, South Africa 1900–02.

The Great War—18 *Battalions*—Mons, Retreat from Mons, Marne 1914, Aisne 1914, 18, Ypres 1914, 17, 18, Langemarck 1914, 17, Gheluvelt, Nonne Bosschen, Givenchy 1914, Aubers, Loos, Somme 1916, 18, Albert 1916, 18, Bazentin, Pozieres, Flers-Courcelette, Morval, Ancre Heights, Ancre 1916, Arras 1917, 18, Scarpe 1917, Messines 1917, 18, Pilckem, Menin Road, Polygon Wood, Broodseinde, Poelcappelle, Passchendaele, Cambrai 1917, 18, St. Quentin, Bapaume 1918, Lys, Estaires, Hazebrouck, Bailleul, Kemmel, Bethune, Scherpenberg, Drocourt-Queant, Hindenburg Line, Havrincourt, Epehy, St. Quentin Canal, Beaurevoir, Courtrai, Selle, Valenciennes, Sambre, France and Flanders 1914–18, Doiran 1917, 18, Macedonia 1915–18, Helles, Landing at Helles, Krithia, Suvla, Sari Bair, Scimitar Hill, Gallipoli 1915–16, Egypt, 1916, Tigris 1916, Kut al Amara 1917, Baghdad, Mesopotamia 1916–18, Tsingtao.

The Second World War—Norway 1940, Normandy Landing, Sully, Caen, Falaise, Risle Crossing, Le Havre, Antwerp-Turnhout Canal, Scheldt, Zetten, Arnhem 1945, North-West Europe 1944–45, Gazala, North Africa 1942, North Arakan, Mayu Tunnels, Pinwe, Shweli, Myitson, Burma 1944–45.

Uniform Scarlet, facings grass green (from 1881 to 1905 facings were white)

Regimental march [Quick] *March of the Men of Harlech* (Tradit.)

Regimental journal *The XXIV. Journal of The South Wales Borderers*

Nicknames Howard's Greens (Not to be confused with the Green Howards—see p. 159). The Bengal Tigers

Remarks In recognition of the 24th's gallantry at Isandhlwana and Rorke's Drift during the Zulu War of 1879 (when the

Regiment won nine VCs), in 1880 Queen Victoria presented a silver wreath of immortelles to be borne 'for ever' on the pike of the Queen's Colour. The original wreath is now preserved in the South Wales Borderers' Regimental Chapel in Brecon Cathedral, the present Regiment carrying a replica on the Queen's Colour.

THE WELCH REGIMENT
(41st and 69th)

Formed 1881 by amalgamation of the 41st (The Welsh) Regiment with the 69th (South Lincolnshire) Regiment, which became respectively the 1st and 2nd Battalions of The Welch Regiment.

Note Prior to 1921 there was constant variation in the spelling of 'Welsh'. Between 1831 and 1862 official publications used 'Welsh' and 'Welch' indiscriminately as the spirit moved them. After the latter date the 's' spelling was officially adopted, but the Regiment continued to prefer 'c'. This was finally authorised in 1921.

Battle honours Belleisle, Martinique 1762, St. Vincent 1797, India, Bourbon, Java, Detroit, Queenstown, Miami, Niagara, Waterloo, Ava, Candahar 1842, Ghuznee 1842, Cabool 1842, Alma, Inkerman, Sevastopol, Relief of Kimberley, Paardeberg, South Africa 1899–1902.

The Great War—34 Battalions—Mons, Retreat from Mons, Marne 1914, Aisne 1914, 18, Ypres 1914, 15, 17, Langemarck 1914, 17, Gheluvelt, Nonne Bosschen, Givenchy 1914, Gravenstafel, St. Julien, Frezenberg, Bellewaarde, Aubers, Loos, Somme 1916, 18, Albert 1916, 18, Bazentin, Pozieres, Flers-Courcelette, Morval, Ancre Heights, Ancre 1916, 18, Messines 1917, 18, Pilckem, Menin Road, Polygon Wood, Broodseinde, Poelcappelle, Passchendaele, Cambrai 1917, 18, St. Quentin, Bapaume 1918, Lys, Estaires, Hazebrouck, Bailleul, Kemmel, Bethune, Scherpenberg, Arras 1918, Drocourt-Queant, Hindenburg Line, Epehy, St. Quentin Canal, Beaurevoir, Selle, Valenciennes, Sambre, France and Flanders 1914–18, Struma, Doiran 1917, 18, Macedonia 1915–18, Suvla, Sari Bair, Landing at Suvla, Scimitar Hill, Gallipoli 1915, Egypt 1915–17, Gaza, El Mughar, Jerusalem, Jericho, Tell 'Asur, Megiddo,

Nablus, Palestine 1917–18, Tigris 1916, Kut al Amara 1917, Baghdad, Mesopotamia 1916–18.

The Second World War—Falaise, Lower Maas, Reichswald, North-West Europe 1944–45, Benghazi, North Africa 1940–42, Sicily 1943, Coriano, Croce, Rimini Line, Ceriano Ridge, Argenta Gap, Italy 1943–45, Crete, Canea, Withdrawal to Sphakia, Middle East 1941, Kyaukmyaung Bridgehead, Maymyo, Rangoon Road, Sittang 1945, Burma 1944–45.

Korea, 1951–52.

Motto	*Gwell Angau Na Chywilydd* (Better death than dishonour)
Uniform	Scarlet, facings white
Regimental march [Quick]	*Ap Shenkin* (Tradit.)
Regimental journal	*Men of Harlech*

41st (THE WELSH) REGIMENT

Raised March 1719 by Colonel Edmund Fielding, as regiment of Invalids.

Titles	1719 Colonel Fielding's Regiment of Foot *Title subsequently changed with Colonels' names*
	1747 The Royal Invalids (41st Regiment of Foot)
	1751 41st Regiment of Foot, or Invalids
	1782 41st (Royal Invalids) Regiment of Foot
	1787 41st Regiment of Foot
	1831 41st (The Welsh) Regiment of Foot (spelling later altered to 'Welch')
	1881 Amalgamated with 69th (South Lincolnshire) Regiment of Foot to form The Welch Regiment
Battle honours	Detroit, Queenstown, Miami, Niagara, Ava, Candahar 1842, Ghuznee 1842, Cabool 1842, Alma, Inkerman, Sevastopol.
Motto	*Gwell Angau Na Chywilydd* (Better death than dishonour)
Uniform	Scarlet, facings white
Regimental march [Quick]	*Ap Shenkin* (Tradit.)

69th (SOUTH LINCOLNSHIRE) REGIMENT

Raised August 1756 as 2nd Battalion 24th Foot. Became 69th Regiment of Foot in April 1758.

Titles   1756 2nd Battalion 24th Regiment of Foot
1758 69th Regiment of Foot
1782 69th (the South Lincolnshire) Regiment of Foot
1881 Amalgamated with 41st (The Welsh) Regiment of Foot to form The Welch Regiment

Battle honours   St. Vincent, Bourbon, Java, Waterloo, India.

Uniform   Scarlet, facings Lincoln green

Regimental march [Quick]   *The Lincolnshire Poacher* (Tradit.)

Nicknames   The Ups and Downs. (Numeral '69' reads the same upside down). The Old Agamemnons

THE KING'S OWN SCOTTISH BORDERERS
(25th)

The Regiment was raised on 18th March 1689 by Act of the Scottish Parliament, with David Melville, 3rd Earl of Leven as Colonel. Its task was the defence of Edinburgh against the forces of ex-King James II commanded by the Earl of Claverhouse. The Regiment mustered within four hours and mounted guard on the gates of the town the same night. It was brought on to the regular establishment by King William III in April 1689.

The King's Own Scottish Borderers is one of the few Regiments never to have been amalgamated.

Titles 1689 The Earl of Leven's Regiment of Foot (also known as 'The Edinburgh Regiment') *Title subsequently changed with Colonels' names*
1751 25th (Edinburgh) Regiment of Foot
1782 25th (or the Sussex) Regiment of Foot
1805 25th (or King's Own Borderers) Regiment of Foot
1881 The King's Own Borderers
1887 The King's Own Scottish Borderers

Battle honours Namur 1695, Minden, Egmont-op-Zee, Egypt (with the Sphinx), Martinique 1809, Afghanistan 1878–80, Chitral, Tirah, Paardeberg, South Africa 1900–02.

The Great War—Mons, Le Cateau, Retreat from Mons, Marne 1914, 18, Aisne 1914, La Bassee 1914, Messines 1914, Ypres 1914, 15, 17, 18, Nonne Bosschen, Hill 60, Gravenstafel, St. Julien, Frezenberg, Bellewaarde, Loos, Somme 1916, 18, Albert 1916, 18, Bazentin, Delville Wood, Pozieres, Guillemont, Flers-Courcelette, Morval, Le Transloy, Ancre Heights, Arras 1917, 18, Vimy 1917, Scarpe 1917, 18, Arleux, Pilckem, Langemarck 1917, Menin Road, Polygon Wood, Broodseinde, Poelcapelle, Passchendaele, Cambrai 1917, 18, St. Quentin, Lys, Estaires, Hazebrouck, Kemmel, Soissonnais-Ourcq, Bapaume 1918, Drocourt-Queant, Hindenburg Line, Epehy, Canal du Nord, Courtrai, Selle, Sambre, France and Flanders 1914–18, Italy 1917–18, Helles, Landing at Helles, Krithia, Suvla, Scimitar Hill, Gallipoli 1915–16, Rumani, Egypt 1916, Gaza, El Mughar, Nebi Samwil, Jaffa, Palestine 1917–18.

The Second World War—Dunkirk 1940, Cambes, Odon, Cheux, Defence of Rauray, Caen, Esquay, Troarn, Mont Pincon, Estry, Aart, Nederrijn, Arnhem 1944, Best, Scheldt, Flushing, Venraij, Meijel, Venlo Pocket, Roer, Rhineland, Reichswald, Cleve, Goch, Rhine, Ibbenburen, Lingen, Dreirwalde, Uelzen, Bremen, Artlenberg, North-West Europe 1940, 44–45, North Arakan, Buthidaung, Ngakyedauk Pass, Imphal, Kanglatongbi, Ukhrul, Meiktila, Irrawaddy, Kama, Burma 1943, 45.

Kowang-San, Maryang-San, Korea 1951–52.

Mottoes *In Veritate Religionis Confido* (I trust in the truth of religion)
Nisi Dominus Frustra (Unless the Lord be with us all is in vain)

Uniform Doublet, blue; trews, No. 7 (Leslie) tartan; facings blue

Regimental marches [Quick] *Blue Bonnets o'er the Border*
[Slow] *The Standard on the Braes of Mar*

Regimental journal *The Borderers Chronicle*

Regimental headquarters The Barracks, Berwick-on-Tweed, Northumberland
TD15 1DG

Regimental museum As above

Nicknames The KOSBs. The Botherers. Kokky-Olly-Birds

Remarks Originally raised and recruited in Edinburgh, the 25th
were early granted the privilege of marching through that
city's streets with bayonets fixed, drums beating, Colours
flying, and were accorded the right to raise recruits in the
Scottish capital without the formality of seeking
permission from the Lord Provost. They remain the only
Regiment in the British Army to enjoy these privileges.

THE CAMERONIANS
(SCOTTISH RIFLES)
(26th and 90th)

Formed 1881 by amalgamation of the 26th (Cameronian)
Regiment of Foot with the 90th Light Infantry Regiment,
Perthshire Volunteers.

This distinguished Regiment—Scotland's only Rifle
Regiment—is now represented solely by a small
Regimental Headquarters and two Territorial Army
Companies. In the defence cuts of 1968 the Regiment
was given the option of amalgamation or disbandment,
and having chosen the latter, its single Regular Battalion
was accordingly disbanded.

The Regiment's title and Battle Honours continue to
be shown in the Army List.

Battle honours Blenheim, Ramillies, Oudenarde, Malplaquet, Mandora,
Egypt (with the Sphinx), Corunna, Martinique 1809,
Guadaloupe 1810, China, South Africa 1846–47,
Sevastopol, Lucknow, Abyssinia, South Africa 1877–78–
79, Relief of Ladysmith, South Africa 1899–1902.

The Great War—Mons, Le Cateau, Retreat from Mons, Marne 1914, 18, Aisne 1914, La Bassee 1914, Armentieres 1914, Neuve Chapelle, Aubers, Loos, Somme 1916, 18, Albert 1916, Bazentin, Pozieres, Flers-Courcelette, Le Transloy, Ancre Heights, Arras 1917, 18, Scarpe 1917, 18, Arleux, Ypres 1917, 18, Pilckem, Langemarck 1917, Menin Road, Polygon Wood, Passchendaele, St. Quentin, Rosieres, Avre, Lys, Hazebrouck, Bailleul, Kemmel, Scherpenberg, Soissonnais-Ourcq, Drocourt-Queant, Hindenburg Line, Epehy, Canal du Nord, St. Quentin Canal, Cambrai 1918, Courtrai, Selle, Sambre, France and Flanders 1914–18, Doiran 1917, 18, Macedonia 1915–18, Gallipoli 1915–16, Rumani, Egypt 1916–17, Gaza, El Mughar, Nebi Samwil, Jaffa, Palestine 1917–18.

The Second World War—Ypres-Comines Canal, Odon, Cheux, Caen, Mont Pincon, Estry, Nederrijn, Best, Scheldt, South Beveland, Walcheren Causeway, Asten, Roer, Rhineland, Reichswald, Moyland, Rhine, Dreirwalde, Bremen, Artenburg, North-West Europe 1940, 44–45, Landing in Sicily, Simeto Bridgehead, Sicily 1943, Garigliano Crossing, Anzio, Advance to Tiber, Italy 1943–44, Pegu 1942, Paungde, Yenagyaung 1942, Chindits 1944, Burma 1942, 44.

Uniform Doublet, rifle green; trews, No. 6 (Douglas) tartan

Regimental marches [Quick] *Within a Mile of Edinboro' Town*
[Slow] *In the Garb of Old Gaul* (Reid) (When required—Rifle Regiments do not normally march past in slow time)

Regimental journal *The Covenanter*

Regimental headquarters Mote Hill, off Muir Street, Hamilton, Lanarkshire ML3 6BJ

Regimental museum As above

26th (CAMERONIAN) REGIMENT OF FOOT

Raised at Douglas (Lanarkshire), May 1689, by Colonel James Douglas, Earl of Angus, from Scottish Covenanters, followers of Richard Cameron, killed at Airds Moss, Ayrshire, 1680.

Titles 1689 The Earl of Angus's Regiment of Foot *Official title subsequently changed with Colonels' names, but the Regiment was referred to as 'Cameronians'*
1751 26th Regiment of Foot
1786 26th (or Cameronian) Regiment of Foot
1881 Amalgamated with 90th Light Infantry Regiment Perthshire Volunteers to form The Cameronians (Scottish Rifles)

Battle honours Blenheim, Ramillies, Oudenarde, Malplaquet, Egypt (with the Sphinx), Corunna, China (with the Dragon), Abyssinia, South Africa 1846–47.

Uniform Scarlet, facings yellow

Regimental march [Quick] *Within a Mile of Edinboro' Town*

90th LIGHT INFANTRY REGIMENT, PERTHSHIRE VOLUNTEERS

Raised May 1794 by Lieutenant-Colonel Thomas Graham (later 1st Lord Lynedoch) as a regiment of Foot.

Titles 1794 90th Regiment of Foot (or Perthshire Volunteers)
1815 90th Light Infantry Regiment, Perthshire Volunteers
1881 Amalgamated with 26th (or Cameronian) Regiment of Foot to form The Cameronians (Scottish Rifles)

Battle honours Mandora, Egypt (with the Sphinx), Martinique, Guadaloupe, Sevastopol, Lucknow.

Uniform Scarlet, facings buff

Regimental marches [Quick] *The Gathering of the Grahams* (Also known as *Athole Highlanders*)
[Slow] *In the Garb of Old Gaul* (Reid)

Nickname The Perthshire Greybreeks

Remarks Although the distinction 'Light Infantry' was not officially conferred until 1815, the 90th had been equipped and drilled as Light Infantry since its formation in 1794.

THE ROYAL IRISH RANGERS

(27th (INNISKILLING) 83rd and 87th)

Formed July 1968 by amalgamation of The Royal Inniskilling Fusiliers, The Royal Ulster Rifles and The Royal Irish Fusiliers (Princess Victoria's).

Battle honours Martinique 1762, Havannah, St. Lucia 1778, 1796, India, Cape of Good Hope 1806, Maida, Monte Video, Talavera, Bourbon, Busaco, Barrosa, Fuentes d'Onor, Java, Tarifa, Ciudad Rodrigo, Badajoz, Salamanca, Vittoria, Pyrenees, Nivelle, Niagara, Orthes, Toulouse, Peninsula, Waterloo, Ava, South Africa 1835, 1846–47, Sevastopol, Central India, Tel-el-Kebir, Egypt 1882, 1884, Relief of Ladysmith, South Africa 1899–1902.

The Great War—Mons, Le Cateau, Retreat from Mons, Marne 1914, Aisne 1914, La Bassee 1914, Messines 1914, 17, 18, Armentieres 1914, Ypres 1914, 15, 17, 18, Nonne Bosschen, Neuve Chapelle, Loos, Frezenberg, Aubers, Festubert 1915, Gravenstafel, St. Julien, Bellewaarde, Somme 1916, 18, Albert 1916, Bazentin, Pozieres, Guillemont, Ginchy, Le Transloy, Ancre, Ancre Heights, Arras 1917, Scarpe 1917, Pilckem, Langemarck 1917, Polygon Wood, Broodseinde, Poelcappelle, Cambrai 1917, 18, St. Quentin, Rosieres, Hindenburg Line, Lys, Bailleul, Beaurevoir, Kemmel, Courtrai, Selle, Sambre, France and Flanders 1914–18, Kosturino, Struma, Macedonia 1915–17, Helles, Landing at Helles, Krithia, Suvla, Sari Bair, Landing at Suvla, Scimitar Hill, Gallipoli 1915–16, Egypt 1916, Gaza, Jerusalem, Tell 'Asur, Megiddo, Nablus, Palestine 1917–18.

The Second World War—Dyle, Withdrawal to Escaut, Defence of Arras, St. Omer-La Bassee, Ypres-Comines Canal, Dunkirk 1940, Normandy Landing, Cambes, Caen, Troarn, Venlo Pocket, Rhine, Bremen, North-West Europe 1940, 44–45, Two Tree Hill, Bou Arada, Stuka Farm, Oued Zarga, Djebel Bel Mahdi, Djebel Ang, Djebel Tanngoucha, North Africa 1942–43, Landing in Sicily, Solarino, Simeto Bridgehead, Adrano,

Centuripe, Salso Crossing, Simeto Crossing, Malleto, Pursuit to Messina, Sicily 1943, Termoli, Trigno, San Salvo, Sangro, Fossacesia, Garigliano Crossing, Minturno, Anzio, Cassino II, Massa Tambourini, Liri Valley, Rome, Advance to Tiber, Trasimene Line, Monte Spaduro, Monte Grande, Argenta Gap, San Nicolo Canal, Italy 1943–45, Leros, Middle East 1942, Malta 1940, Yenangyaung 1942, Donbaik, Burma 1942–43.

Seoul, Imjin, Korea 1950–51.

Motto	*Faugh-a-Ballagh* (Clear the way)
Uniform	Piper green, piping and facings piper green
Regimental marches [Quick]	*Killaloe*
[Slow]	*Eileen Allanagh*
Regimental journal	*The Blackthorn*
Regimental headquarters	5 Waring Street, Belfast BT1 2EW
Regimental museums	(Royal Inniskilling Fusiliers) The Castle, Enniskillen, Co. Fermanagh, N. Ireland
	(Royal Ulster Rifles) 5 Waring Street, Belfast BT1 2EW
	(Royal Irish Fusiliers) Sovereign's House, The Mall, Armagh, N. Ireland

THE ROYAL INNISKILLING FUSILIERS

Formed in 1881 by amalgamation of the 27th (Inniskilling) Regiment of Foot with the 108th (Madras Infantry) Regiment of Foot.

Battle honours Egypt (with the Sphinx), Martinique 1762, Havannah, St. Lucia 1778, 1796, Maida, Badajoz, Salamanca, Vittoria, Pyrenees, Nivelle, Orthes, Toulouse, Peninsula, Waterloo, South Africa 1835, 1846–47, Central India, Relief of Ladysmith, South Africa, 1899–1902.

The Great War—13 *Battalions*—Le Cateau, Retreat from Mons, Marne 1914, Aisne 1914, Messines 1914, 17, Armentieres 1914, Aubers, Festubert 1915, Somme 1916, 18, Albert 1916, Bazentin, Guillemont, Ginchy,

Ancre, 1916, Arras 1917, Scarpe 1917, Ypres 1917, 18, Pilckem, Langemarck 1917, Polygon Wood, Broodseinde, Poelcappelle, Cambrai 1917, 18, St. Quentin, Rosieres, Hindenburg Line, Beaurevoir, Courtrai, Selle, Sambre, France and Flanders 1914–18, Kosturino, Struma, Macedonia 1915–17, Helles, Landing at Helles, Krithia, Suvla, Landing at Suvla, Scimitar Hill, Gallipoli 1915–16, Egypt 1916, Gaza, Jerusalem, Tell 'Asur, Palestine 1917–18.

The Second World War—Defence of Arras, Ypres-Comines Canal, North-West Europe 1940, Two Tree Hill, Bou Arada, Oued Zarga, Djebel Bel Mahdi, Djebel Tanngoucha, North Africa 1942–43, Landing in Sicily, Solarino, Simeto Bridgehead, Adrano, Centuripe, Simeto Crossing, Pursuit to Messina, Sicily 1943, Termoli, Trigno, San Salvo, Sangro, Garigliano Crossing, Minturno, Anzio, Cassino II, Massa Tambourini, Liri Valley, Rome, Advance to Tiber, Trasimene Line, Monte Spaduro, Argenta Gap, Italy 1943–45, Middle East 1942, Yenangyaung 1942, Donbaik, Burma 1942–43.

Motto	*Nec Aspera Terrent* (Neither do difficulties deter)
Uniform	Scarlet, piping and facings blue
Regimental marches [Quick]	*The Sprig of Shillelagh* (Code) and *Rory O'More* (Lover)
Regimental journal	*Sprig of Shillelagh*
Nickname	The Skins

27th (INNISKILLING) REGIMENT OF FOOT

Raised June 1689 by Colonel Zachariah Tiffin, from independent companies of the Enniskillen garrison, but not taken on the Regular establishment until January 1690.

Titles	1690 Colonel Zachariah Tiffin's Enniskillen Regiment of Foot *Title subsequently changed with Colonels' names*
	1751 27th (or Inniskilling) Regiment of Foot
	1881 Amalgamated with the 108th (Madras Infantry) Regiment of Foot to form The Royal Inniskilling Fusiliers

Battle honours St. Lucia 1778, 1796, Egypt (with the Sphinx), Maida, Badajoz, Salamanca, Vittoria, Pyrenees, Nivelle, Orthes, Toulouse, Peninsula, Waterloo, South Africa 1835, 1846–47.

Motto *Nec Aspera Terrent* (Neither do difficulties deter)

Uniform Scarlet, facings buff

Regimental march [Quick] *The Sprig of Shillelagh* (Code)

Nickname The Skins

108th (MADRAS INFANTRY) REGIMENT OF FOOT

Raised in India, 1854, as the 3rd Madras European Regiment of the Hon. East India Company's forces. Transferred to the British Army in 1861 and title changed to 108th (Madras Infantry) Regiment of Foot.

In 1881 amalgamated with 27th (Inniskilling) Regiment of Foot to form The Royal Inniskilling Fusiliers.

Battle honours Central India.

Uniform Scarlet, facings yellow

Regimental march [Quick] *Rory O'More* (Lover)

THE ROYAL ULSTER RIFLES

Formed 1881 by amalgamation of the 83rd (County of Dublin) Regiment of Foot with the 86th (Royal County Down) Regiment of Foot, to form The Royal Irish Rifles. After the formation of the Irish Free State the title was altered, in 1921, to The Royal Ulster Rifles.

Battle honours Egypt (with the Sphinx), India, Cape of Good Hope 1806, Talavera, Bourbon, Busaco, Fuentes d'Onor, Ciudad Rodrigo, Badajoz, Salamanca, Vittoria, Nivelle, Orthes, Toulouse, Peninsula, Central India, South Africa 1899–1902.

The Great War—21 *Battalions*—Mons, Le Cateau, Retreat from Mons, Marne 1914, Aisne 1914, La Bassee

1914, Messines 1914, 17, 18, Armentieres 1914, Ypres 1914, 15, 17, 18, Nonne Bosschen, Neuve Chapelle, Frezenberg, Aubers, Somme 1916, 18, Albert 1916, Bazentin, Pozieres, Guillemont, Ginchy, Ancre Heights, Pilckem, Langemarck 1917, Cambrai 1917, St. Quentin, Rosieres, Lys, Bailleul, Kemmel, Courtrai, France and Flanders 1914–18, Kosturino, Struma, Macedonia 1915–17, Suvla, Sari Bair, Gallipoli 1915, Gaza, Jerusalem, Tell 'Asur, Palestine 1917–18.

The Second World War—Dyle, Dunkirk 1940, Normandy Landing, Cambes, Caen, Troarn, Venlo Pocket, Rhine, Bremen, North-West Europe 1940, 44–45.

Seoul, Imjin, Korea 1950–51.

Motto	*Quis Separabit* (Who shall separate?)
Uniform	Jacket, rifle green; trousers, black; piping and facings rifle green.
Regimental marches [Quick]	*Off Off Said the Stranger* (Craven) and *The South Down Militia* (Anon.)
Regimental journal	*Quis Separabit*
Nickname	The Stickies

83rd (COUNTY OF DUBLIN) REGIMENT OF FOOT

Raised Dublin, September 1793, by Colonel William Fitch and ranked as 83rd Foot.

Titles	1793 83rd Regiment of Foot (Popularly known as 'Fitch's Grenadiers')
	1859 83rd (County of Dublin) Regiment of Foot
	1881 Amalgamated with 86th (Royal County Down) Regiment of Foot to form The Royal Irish Rifles (Title changed to The Royal Ulster Rifles in 1921)
Battle honours	Cape of Good Hope 1806, Talavera, Busaco, Fuentes d'Onor, Ciudad Rodrigo, Badajoz, Salamanca, Vittoria, Nivelle, Orthes, Toulouse, Peninsula, Central India.
Uniform	Scarlet, facings yellow
Regimental marches [Quick]	*Garry Owen* (Tradit.) and *Off Off Said the Stranger* (Craven)

86th (ROYAL COUNTY DOWN) REGIMENT OF FOOT

Raised at Shrewsbury October, 1793, by Major-General Sir Cornelius Cuyler, as the 86th Regiment of Foot.

Titles 1793 86th Regiment of Foot (Also known as 'The Shropshire Volunteers')
1809 86th (or Leinster) Regiment of Foot
1812 86th (or The Royal County Down) Regiment of Foot
1881 Amalgamated with 83rd (County of Dublin) Regiment to form The Royal Irish Rifles (Title changed to The Royal Ulster Rifles in 1921)

Battle honours Egypt (with the Sphinx), India, Bourbon, Central India.

Motto *Quis Separabit* (Who shall separate?)

Uniform Scarlet, facings blue

Regimental march [Quick] *St. Patrick's Day* (Tradit.)

Nickname The Irish Giants

THE ROYAL IRISH FUSILIERS
(PRINCESS VICTORIA'S)

Formed 1881 by amalgamation of 87th (Royal Irish Fusiliers) Regiment of Foot with 89th (Princess Victoria's) Regiment of Foot.

Battle honours Egypt (with the Sphinx), Monte Video, Talavera, Barrosa, Java, Tarifa, Vittoria, Nivelle, Niagara, Orthes, Toulouse, Peninsula, Ava, Sevastopol, Tel-el-Kebir, Egypt 1882, 1884, Relief of Ladysmith, South Africa 1899–1902.

The Great War—14 *Battalions*—Le Cateau, Retreat from Mons, Marne 1914, Aisne 1914, Armentieres 1914, Ypres 1915, 17, 18, Gravenstafel, St. Julien, Frezenberg, Bellewaarde, Somme 1916, 18, Albert 1916, Guillemont,

Ginchy, Le Transloy, Arras 1917, Scarpe 1917, Messines 1917, 18, Langemarck 1917, Cambrai 1917, St. Quentin, Rosieres, Lys, Bailleul, Kemmel, Courtrai, France and Flanders 1914–18, Kosturino, Struma, Macedonia 1915–17, Suvla, Landing at Suvla, Scimitar Hill, Gallipoli 1915, Gaza, Jerusalem, Tell 'Asur, Megiddo, Nablus, Palestine 1917–18.

The Second World War—Withdrawal to Escaut, St. Omer-La Bassee, Bou Arada, Stuka Farm, Oued Zarga, Djebel Bel Mahdi, Djebel Ang, Djebel Tanngoucha, Adrano, Centuripe, Salso Crossing, Simeto Crossing, Malleto, Termoli, Trigno, Sangro, Fossacesia, Cassino II, Liri Valley, Trasimene Line, Monte Spaduro, Monte Grande, Argenta Gap, San Nicolo Canal, Leros, Malta, 1940.

Motto	*Faugh-a-Ballagh* (Clear the way)
Uniform	Scarlet, piping scarlet, facings blue
Regimental marches [Quick]	*The British Grenadiers* and combination of *St. Patrick's Day*, *Barrosa* and *Garry Owen*
Regimental journal	*Faugh-a-Ballagh*
Nicknames	Blayney's Bloodhounds. Aiglers. Eagle Takers. The Faughs

87th (ROYAL IRISH FUSILIERS) REGIMENT OF FOOT

Raised in Ireland, September 1793, by Colonel John Doyle, as the 87th (or Prince of Wales's Irish) Regiment of Foot.

Titles	1793 87th (or Prince of Wales's Irish) Regiment of Foot
	1811 87th (or Prince of Wales's Own Irish) Regiment of Foot
	1827 (January) 87th (Prince of Wales's Own Irish Fusiliers) Regiment of Foot
	(November) 87th (or Royal Irish Fusiliers) Regiment of Foot
	1881 Amalgamated with 89th (Princess Victoria's) Regiment of Foot to form Princess Victoria's (Royal Irish Fusiliers)

1921 Title changed to The Royal Irish Fusiliers (Princess Victoria's)

Battle honours Monte Video, Talavera, Barrosa, Tarifa, Vittoria, Nivelle, Orthes, Toulouse, Peninsula.

Motto *Faugh-a-Ballagh* (Clear the way)

Uniform Scarlet, facings blue

Regimental marches [Quick] *St. Patrick's Day* and *The British Grenadiers* (Tradit.)

Nicknames The Eagle Takers. The Faugh-a-Ballagh Boys

89th (PRINCESS VICTORIA'S) REGIMENT OF FOOT

Raised December 1793 by Colonel William Crosbie, and ranked as 89th Foot.

Titles 1793 89th Regiment of Foot
1866 89th (Princess Victoria's) Regiment of Foot
1881 Amalgamated with 87th (Royal Irish Fusiliers) to form Princess Victoria's (Royal Irish Fusiliers)

Battle honours Egypt (with the Sphinx), Java, Niagara, Ava, Sevastopol.

Uniform Scarlet, facings black

Regimental marches [Quick] *Garry Owen* (Tradit.) and *Barrosa*

Nicknames Blayney's Bloodhounds. The Rollickers

THE GLOUCESTERSHIRE REGIMENT
(28th and 61st)

Formed 1881 by amalgamation of the 28th (North Gloucestershire) Regiment with the 61st (South Gloucestershire) Regiment, which became 1st and 2nd Battalions, respectively.

189

Battle honours Ramillies, Louisburg, Guadaloupe 1759, Quebec 1759, Martinique 1762, Havannah, St. Lucia 1778, Egypt (with the Sphinx), Maida, Corunna, Talavera, Busaco, Barrosa, Albuhera, Salamanca, Vittoria, Pyrenees, Nivelle, Nive, Orthes, Toulouse, Peninsula, Waterloo, Chillianwallah, Goojerat, Punjaub, Alma, Inkerman, Sevastopol, Delhi 1857, Defence of Ladysmith, Relief of Kimberley, Paardeberg, South Africa 1899–1902.

The Great War—Mons, Retreat from Mons, Marne 1914, Aisne 1914, 18, Ypres 1914, 15, 17, Langemarck 1914, 17, Gheluvelt, Nonne Bosschen, Givenchy 1914, Gravenstafel, St. Julien, Frezenberg, Bellewaarde, Aubers, Loos, Somme 1916, 18, Albert 1916, 18, Bazentin, Delville Wood, Pozieres, Guillemont, Flers-Courcelette, Morval, Ancre Heights, Ancre 1916, Arras 1917, 18, Vimy 1917, Scarpe 1917, Messines 1917, 18, Pilckem, Menin Road, Polygon Wood, Broodseinde, Poelcappelle, Passchendaele, Cambrai 1917, 18, St. Quentin, Bapaume 1918, Rosieres, Avre, Lys, Estaires, Hazebrouck, Bailleul, Kemmel, Bethune, Drocourt-Queant, Hindenburg Line, Epehy, Canal du Nord, St. Quentin Canal, Beaurevoir, Selle, Valenciennes, Sambre, France and Flanders 1914–18, Piave, Vittorio Veneto, Italy 1917–18, Struma, Doiran 1917, Macedonia 1915–18, Suvla, Sari Bair, Scimitar Hill, Gallipoli 1915–16, Egypt 1916, Tigris 1916, Kut al Amara 1917, Baghdad, Mesopotamia 1916–18, Persia 1918.

The Second World War—Defence of Escaut, St. Omer-La-Bassee, Wormhoudt, Cassel, Villers Bocage, Mont Pincon, Falaise, Risle Crossing, Le Havre, Zetten, North-West Europe 1940, 44–45, Taukyan, Paungde, Monywa 1942, North Arakan, Mayu Tunnels, Pinwe, Shweli, Myitson, Burma 1942, 44–45.

Hill 327, Imjin, Korea 1950–51.

Uniform Scarlet, piping primrose, facings primrose

Regimental marches [Quick] *Kinnegad Slashers* (Tradit.)
[Slow] *Regimental Slow March 28th/61st*

Regimental journal *The Back Badge*

Regimental headquarters Custom House, 31 Commercial Road, Gloucester GL1 2HE

Regimental museum As above

Nicknames The Back Numbers. The Fore and Aft. The Glorious Glosters

Remarks The Gloucestershire Regiment enjoys the unique privilege of wearing a Badge at the back of the head-dress as well as at the front. This commemorates the action of the 28th Foot at Alexandria in March, 1801, when, attacked in front and rear, the two ranks of the Regiment fought back to back. The privilege was first officially confirmed in May 1830.

In May 1951, the 1st Battalion The Gloucestershire Regiment was awarded the United States Presidential Citation in recognition of its valorous action in the battle of Imjin, Korea, during the previous month, when two VCs were won. The only other British Army unit to be accorded this honour was 170 Light Battery Royal Artillery, which fought under command of the Gloucesters at Imjin. The Presidential Citation is commemorated by the wearing of a small flash of watered dark blue ribbon, enclosed in a gilt frame, beneath the shoulders of the tunic.

28th (NORTH GLOUCESTERSHIRE) REGIMENT

Raised March 1694 by Colonel John Gibson.

Titles 1694 Colonel Gibson's Regiment of Foot *Title subsequently changed with Colonels' names*
1742 28th Regiment of Foot
1782 28th (or North Gloucestershire) Regiment of Foot
1881 Amalgamated with 61st (South Gloucestershire) Regiment of Foot to form The Gloucestershire Regiment

Battle honours Ramillies, Louisburg, Quebec 1759, Martinique 1762, Havannah, St. Lucia 1778, Egypt (with the Sphinx), Corunna, Barrosa, Albuhera, Vittoria, Pyrenees, Nivelle, Nive, Orthes, Toulouse, Peninsula, Waterloo, Alma, Inkerman, Sevastopol.

Uniform Scarlet, facings yellow

Regimental march [Quick] *Kinnegad Slashers* (Tradit.)

Nicknames The Back Numbers. The Fore and Aft. The Old Braggs. The Slashers

Remarks For Back Badge, see main entry above.

61st (SOUTH GLOUCESTERSHIRE) REGIMENT

Raised 1756 as 2nd Battalion 3rd Foot (The Buffs). Reconstituted as 61st Foot in 1758.

Titles 1756 2nd Battalion 3rd (or East Kent) Regiment of Foot (The Buffs)
1758 61st Regiment of Foot
1782 61st (or South Gloucestershire) Regiment of Foot
1881 Amalgamated with 28th (North Gloucestershire) Regiment to form The Gloucestershire Regiment

Battle honours Egypt (with the Sphinx), Maida, Guadaloupe 1759, Talavera, Salamanca, Pyrenees, Nivelle, Nive, Orthes, Toulouse, Peninsula, Chillianwallah, Goojerat, Punjaub, Delhi 1857.

Uniform Scarlet, facings buff

Regimental march [Quick] *The Highland Pipers*

Nicknames The Flowers of Toulouse. Silver-tailed Dandies

THE WORCESTERSHIRE AND SHERWOOD FORESTERS REGIMENT

(29th/45th FOOT)

(29th, 36th, 45th, 95th)

Formed February 1970 by amalgamation of The Worcestershire Regiment with The Sherwood Foresters (Nottinghamshire and Derbyshire Regiment).

Battle honours Ramillies, Belleisle, Mysore, Hindoostan, Louisburg, Rolica, Vimiera, Corunna, Talavera, Busaco, Fuentes d'Onor, Albuhera, Ciudad Rodrigo, Badajoz, Salamanca, Vittoria, Pyrenees, Nivelle, Nive, Orthes, Toulouse, Peninsula, Ava, Ferozeshah, Sobraon, South Africa 1846–47, Chillianwallah, Goojerat, Punjaub, Alma, Inkerman, Sevastopol, Central India, Abyssinia, Egypt 1882, Tirah, South Africa 1899–1902.

The Great War—Mons, Le Cateau, Retreat from Mons, Marne 1914, Aisne 1914, 18, La Bassee 1914, Armentieres 1914, Ypres 1914, 15, 17, 18, Langemarck 1914, 17, Gheluvelt, Nonne Bosschen, Neuve Chapelle, Aubers, Festubert 1915, Hooge 1915, Loos, Somme 1916, 18, Albert 1916, 18, Bazentin, Delville Wood, Pozieres, Ginchy, Flers-Courcelette, Morval, Thiepval, Le Transloy, Ancre Heights, Ancre 1916, Arras 1917, 18, Vimy 1917, Scarpe 1917, 18, Arleux, Messines 1917, 18, Pilckem, Langemarck 1917, Menin Road, Polygon Wood, Broodseinde, Poelcappelle, Passchendaele, Cambrai 1917, 18, St. Quentin, Bapaume 1918, Rosieres, Villers Bretonneux, Lys, Estaires, Hazebrouck, Bailleul, Kemmel, Scherpenberg, Amiens, Drocourt-Queant, Hindenburg Line, Epehy, Canal du Nord, St. Quentin Canal, Beaurevoir, Courtrai, Selle, Valenciennes, Sambre, France and Flanders 1914–18, Piave, Vittorio Veneto, Italy 1917–18, Doiran 1917–18, Macedonia 1915–18, Helles, Landing at Helles, Krithia, Suvla, Sari Bair, Landing at Suvla, Scimitar Hill, Gallipoli 1915–16, Egypt 1916, Tigris 1916, Kut al Amara 1917, Baghdad, Mesopotamia 1916–18, Baku, Persia 1918.

The Second World War—Norway 1940, Defence of Escaut, St. Omer-La Bassee, Ypres-Comines Canal, Wormhoudt, Dunkirk 1940, Odon, Bourguebus Ridge, Maltot, Mont Pincon, Jurques, La Variniere, Noirau Crossing, Seine 1944, Nederrijn, Geilenkirchen, Rhineland, Goch, Rhine, North-West Europe 1940, 44–45, Gogni Barentu, Keren, Amba Alagi, Abyssinia 1940–41, Gazala, Via Balbia, El Alamein, Djebel Guerba, Tamera, Medjez Plain, Tunis, North Africa 1941–43, Salerno, Volturno Crossing, Monte Camino, Anzio, Campoleone, Advance to Tiber, Gothic Line, Coriano, Cosina Canal Crossing, Monte Ceco, Italy 1943–45, Singapore Island, Malaya 1942, Kohima, Relief of Kohima, Naga Village, Mao Songsang, Shwebo, Mandalay, Irrawaddy, Mt. Popa, Burma 1944–45.

Motto	Firm
Uniform	Scarlet, piping and facings Lincoln green
Regimental marches [Quick]	*Royal Windsor** and *Young May Moon*
[Slow]	*Duchess of Kent* (Duchess of Kent)*
Regimental journal	*Firm and Forester*
Regimental headquarters	Norton Barracks, Worcester WR5 2PA

Regimental museums (Worcestershire Regiment)
City Museum, Foregate Street, Worcester

(Sherwood Foresters)
The Castle, Nottingham
City Museum, Strand, Derby

Nicknames The Woofers (the official abbreviation of Regiment's title is WFR)

Remarks The Regiment possesses an official mascot in the form of a live Ram, traditionally named 'Derby', which on ceremonial occasions is paraded with the Ram Major and Ram Orderly as escort. The first ram was 'captured' by the 95th (Derbyshire) Regiment at the siege of Kotah in Central India, 1858, and marched 3000 miles with them, being present at six actions. It is claimed that before his death in 1863 'Derby I' fought 33 personal battles with

---

*See below under 29th (Worcestershire) Regiment of Foot.

other rams and was never defeated. There have been a succession of 23 Rams since that date, and it has become customary for His Grace the Duke of Devonshire to present the replacements.

THE WORCESTERSHIRE REGIMENT
(29th and 36th)

Formed 1881 by amalgamation of the 29th (Worcestershire) Regiment of Foot with the 36th (Herefordshire) Regiment of Foot.

Battle honours Ramillies, Belleisle, Mysore, Hindoostan, Rolica, Vimiera, Corunna, Talavera, Albuhera, Salamanca, Pyrenees, Nivelle, Nive, Orthes, Toulouse, Peninsula, Ferozeshah, Sobraon, Chillianwallah, Goojerat, Punjaub, South Africa 1900–02.

The Great War—22 Battalions—Mons, Le Cateau, Retreat from Mons, Marne 1914, Aisne 1914, 18, La Bassee 1914, Armentieres 1914, Ypres 1914, 15, 17, 18, Langemarck 1914, 17, Gheluvelt, Nonne Bosschen, Neuve Chapelle, Aubers, Festubert 1915, Loos, Somme 1916, 18, Albert 1916, Bazentin, Delville Wood, Pozieres, Le Transloy, Ancre Heights, Ancre 1916, Arras 1917, Scarpe 1917, Arleux, Messines 1917, 18, Pilckem, Menin Road, Polygon Wood, Broodseinde, Poelcappelle, Passchendaele, Cambrai 1917, 18, St. Quentin, Bapaume 1918, Rosieres, Villers Bretonneux, Lys, Estaires, Hazebrouck, Bailleul, Kemmel, Scherpenberg, Hindenburg Line, Canal du Nord, St. Quentin Canal, Beaurevoir, Courtrai, Selle, Valenciennes, Sambre, France and Flanders 1914–18, Piave, Vittorio Veneto, Italy 1917–18, Doiran 1917–18, Macedonia 1915–18, Helles, Landing at Helles, Krithia, Suvla, Sari Bair, Scimitar Hill, Gallipoli 1915–16, Egypt 1916, Tigris 1916, Kut al Amara 1917, Baghdad, Mesopotamia 1916–18, Baku, Persia 1918.

The Second World War—Defence of Escaut, St. Omer-La Bassee, Wormhoudt, Odon, Bourguebus Ridge, Maltot, Mont Pincon, Jurques, La Variniere, Noireau Crossing, Seine 1944, Nederrijn, Geilenkirchen, Rhineland, Goch, Rhine, North-West Europe 1940, 44–

45, Gogni, Barentu, Keren, Amba Alagi, Abyssinia
1940–41, Gazala, Via Balbia, North Africa 1941–42,
Kohima, Relief of Kohima, Naga Village, Mao
Songsang, Shwebo, Mandalay, Irrawaddy, Mt. Popa,
Burma 1944–45.

Motto	Firm
Uniform	Scarlet, piping and facings grass green (emerald)
Regimental marches [Quick]	*Royal Windsor* (Princess Augusta)
[Slow]	*Duchess of Kent* (the Duchess)
Regimental journal	*Firm*
Nicknames	The Firms. Guards of the Line. Old and Bold

29th (WORCESTERSHIRE) REGIMENT OF FOOT

Originated as a regiment of Foot raised in February 1694
by Colonel Thomas Farrington. This regiment was
reduced in 1698, the officers being placed on half-pay. It
was reformed, under the same Colonel, in February
1702.

Titles	1694–98 Colonel Farrington's Regiment of Foot
	1702 Brigadier-General Farrington's Regiment of Foot
	Title subsequently changed with Colonel's names
	1751 29th Regiment of Foot
	1782 29th (or the Worcestershire) Regiment of Foot
	1881 Amalgamated with 36th (Herefordshire) Regiment of Foot to form The Worcestershire Regiment
Battle honours	Ramillies, Rolica, Vimiera, Talavera, Albuhera, Peninsula, Ferozeshah, Sobraon, Chillianwallah, Goojerat, Punjaub.
Uniform	Scarlet, facings yellow
Regimental marches [Quick]	*Royal Windsor* (Princess Augusta)
[Slow]	*Duchess of Kent* (the Duchess)
Nicknames	The Old and Bold. The Ever-Sworded 29th
Remarks	The Regimental Quick March *Royal Windsor* was presented to the 29th by Princess Augusta Sophia, daughter of George III, while the Regiment was stationed at Windsor, 1791–93. The Princess was musically

talented and tradition says the march was arranged, if not actually composed, by her. It is one of the oldest Regimental Marches in the British Army. The Slow March, *Duchess of Kent*, is also of Royal origin. Tradition ascribes it to Princess Victoria Mary Louisa, Duchess of Kent (and mother of Queen Victoria).

36th (HEREFORDSHIRE) REGIMENT OF FOOT

Raised in Ireland, June 1701, by Colonel William Caulfield, Viscount Charlemont.

Titles 1701 Viscount Charlemont's Regiment of Foot *Title subsequently changed with Colonels' names*
1751 36th Regiment of Foot
1782 36th (or Herefordshire) Regiment of Foot
1881 Amalgamated with 29th (Worcestershire) Regiment of Foot to form The Worcestershire Regiment

Battle honours Mysore, Hindoostan, Rolica, Vimiera, Corunna, Salamanca, Pyrenees, Nivelle, Nive, Orthes, Toulouse, Peninsula.

Motto Firm

Uniform Scarlet, facings grass green

Regimental march [Quick] *The Lincolnshire Poacher* (Tradit.)

Nicknames The Firms. The Saucy Greens

THE SHERWOOD FORESTERS
(NOTTINGHAMSHIRE AND DERBYSHIRE REGIMENT)
(45th and 95th)

Formed 1881 by amalgamation of 45th (Nottinghamshire-Sherwood Foresters) Regiment of Foot with 95th (Derbyshire) Regiment of Foot.

Titles 1881 (May) The Derbyshire Regiment (Sherwood Foresters)

(July) The Sherwood Foresters (Derbyshire Regiment)

1902 The Sherwood Foresters (Nottinghamshire and Derbyshire Regiment)

Battle honours Louisburg, Rolica, Vimiera, Talavera, Busaco, Fuentes d'Onor, Ciudad Rodrigo, Badajoz, Salamanca, Vittoria, Pyrenees, Nivelle, Orthes, Toulouse, Peninsula, Ava, South Africa, 1846–47, Alma, Inkerman, Sevastopol, Central India, Abyssinia, Egypt 1882, Tirah, South Africa 1899–1902.

The Great War— 30 *Battalions*—Aisne 1914, 18, Armentieres 1914, Neuve Chapelle, Aubers, Hooge 1915, Loos, Somme 1916, 18, Albert 1916, 18, Bazentin, Delville Wood, Pozieres, Ginchy, Flers-Courcelette, Morval, Thiepval, Le Transloy, Ancre Heights, Ancre 1916, Arras 1917, 18, Vimy 1917, Scarpe 1917, 18, Messines 1917, Ypres 1917, 18, Pilckem, Langemarck 1917, Menin Road, Polygon Wood, Broodseinde, Poelcappelle, Passchendaele, Cambrai 1917, 18, St. Quentin, Bapaume 1918, Rosieres, Villers Bretoneux, Lys, Bailleul, Kemmel, Scherpenberg, Amiens, Drocourt-Queant, Hindenburg Line, Epehy, Canal du Nord, St. Quentin Canal, Beaurevoir, Courtrai, Selle, Sambre, France and Flanders 1914–18, Piave, Italy 1917–18, Suvla, Landing at Suvla, Scimitar Hill, Gallipoli 1915, Egypt 1916.

The Second World War—Norway 1940, St. Omer-La Bassee, Ypres-Comines Canal, Dunkirk 1940, North-West Europe 1940, Gazala, El Alamein, Djebel Guerba, Tamera, Medjez Plain, Tunis, North Africa 1942–43, Salerno, Volturno Crossing, Monte Camino, Anzio, Campoleone, Advance to Tiber, Gothic Line, Coriano, Cosina Canal Crossing, Monte Ceco, Italy 1943–45, Singapore Island, Malaya 1942.

Uniform Scarlet, piping and facings, Lincoln green

Regimental marches [Quick] *The Young May Moon/I'm 95*
[Slow] *The Crich Memorial* (See below)

Regimental journal *The Foresters Journal*

Nickname The Old Stubborns

Remarks The Slow March, *The Crich Memorial*, was adopted in 1957. The Crich Memorial is a war memorial standing high above the Derbyshire countryside at Crich, near the border with Nottinghamshire. It was dedicated in 1923 to the memory of 11,409 men of The Sherwood Foresters who fell in World War I.

45th (NOTTINGHAMSHIRE— SHERWOOD FORESTERS) REGIMENT OF FOOT

Raised January 1741 by Colonel Daniel Houghton and ranked as 56th Regiment of Foot. Renumbered 45th Foot in 1748.

Titles 1741 Colonel Houghton's Regiment of Foot *Title subsequently changed with Colonels' names*
1751 45th Regiment of Foot
1779 45th (or Nottinghamshire) Regiment of Foot
1866 45th (Nottinghamshire-Sherwood Foresters) Regiment of Foot
1881 Amalgamated with the 95th (Derbyshire) Regiment of Foot to form the Derbyshire Regiment (Sherwood Foresters)

Battle honours Louisburg, Rolica, Vimiera, Talavera, Busaco, Fuentes d'Onor, Ciudad Rodrigo, Badajoz, Salamanca, Vittoria, Pyrenees, Nivelle, Orthes, Toulouse, Peninsula, Ava, South Africa 1846–47, Abyssinia.

Uniform Scarlet, facings Lincoln green

Regimental march [Quick] *The Young May Moon*

Nicknames The Old Stubborns. ('Sherwood Foresters' was a nickname before becoming officially incorporated in the title.)

95th (DERBYSHIRE) REGIMENT OF FOOT

Raised December 1823 by Colonel Sir Colin Halkett, as 95th Regiment of Foot.

Titles 1823 95th Regiment of Foot
1825 95th (or Derbyshire) Regiment of Foot
1881 Amalgamated with 45th (Nottinghamshire-Sherwood Foresters) Regiment of Foot to form The Derbyshire Regiment (Sherwood Foresters)

Battle honours Alma, Inkerman, Sevastopol, Central India.

Uniform Scarlet, facings yellow

Regimental march [Quick] *I'm Ninety-Five*

Nickname The Nails

Remarks The Maltese Cross of the Regimental Badge (inherited by The Sherwood Foresters) is said to have been adopted because many officers and men of the original Regiment had served in the former 95th Regiment which became The Rifle Brigade in 1816 and bore the same Cross. The Quick March, *I'm Ninety-Five*, was also that of The Rifle Brigade.

THE QUEEN'S LANCASHIRE REGIMENT
(30th, 40th, 47th, 59th, 81st, 82nd)

Formed 25th March 1970 by amalgamation of The Lancashire Regiment (Prince of Wales's Volunteers) with The Loyal Regiment (North Lancashire).

Battle honours Gibraltar 1704–05, Louisburg, Quebec 1759, Bellisle, Martinique 1762, Havannah, St. Lucia 1778, Egypt (with the Sphinx), Cape of Good Hope 1806, Maida, Monte Video, Rolica, Vimiera, Corunna, Talavera, Java, Tarifa, Badajoz, Salamanca, Vittoria, St. Sebastian, Pyrenees, Nivelle, Nive, Niagara, Orthes, Toulouse, Peninsula, Waterloo, Ava, Bhurtpore, Candahar 1842, Ghuznee 1842, Cabool 1842, Maharajpore, Alma, Inkerman, Sevastopol, Lucknow, Canton, New Zealand, Ali Masjid, Ahmad Khel, Afghanistan 1878–80, Chitral, Defence of Kimberley, Relief of Ladysmith, South Africa 1899–1902.

The Great War—Mons, Le Cateau, Retreat from Mons,
Marne 1914, 18, Aisne 1914, 18, La Bassee 1914,
Messines 1914, 17, 18, Armentieres 1914, Ypres 1914,
15, 17, 18, Langemarck 1914, 17, Gheluvelt, Nonne
Bosschen, Givenchy 1914, Neuve Chapelle, St. Julien,
Frezenberg, Bellewaarde, Aubers, Festubert 1915, Loos,
Somme 1916, 18, Albert 1916, 18, Bazentin, Pozieres,
Guillemont, Ginchy, Flers-Courcelette, Morval, Le
Transloy, Ancre Heights, Ancre 1916, 18, Arras 1917,
18, Vimy 1917, Scarpe 1917, 18, Arleux, Oppy,
Pilckem, Menin Road, Polygon Wood, Broodseinde,
Poelcappelle, Passchendaele, Cambrai 1917, 18, St.
Quentin, Bapaume 1918, Rosieres, Villers-Bretonneux,
Lys, Estaires, Hazebrouck, Bailleul, Kemmel, Bethune,
Scherpenberg, Soissonnais-Ourcq, Drocourt-Queant,
Hindenburg Line, Epehy, Canal du Nord, St. Quentin
Canal, Courtrai, Selle, Valenciennes, Sambre, France
and Flanders 1914–18, Kosturino, Doiran 1917, 18,
Macedonia 1915–18, Helles, Krithia, Suvla, Sari Bair,
Gallipoli 1915, Rumani, Egypt 1915–17, Gaza, Nebi
Samwil, Jerusalem, Jaffa, Tell 'Asur, Palestine 1917–18,
Tigris 1916, Kut al Amara 1917, Baghdad, Mesopotamia
1916–18, Kilimanjaro, E. Africa 1914–16, Baluchistan
1918.

Afghanistan 1919.

The Second World War—Defence of Escaut, Dunkirk
1940, Normandy Landing, Odon, Caen, Bourguebus
Ridge, Troarn, Falaise, Nederrijn, Lower Maas, Venraij,
Ourthe, Rhineland, Reichswald, Weeze, Hochwald,
Rhine, Ibbenburen, Aller, Bremen, North-West Europe
1940, 44–45, Banana Ridge, Djebel Kesskiss, Medjez
Plain, Gueriat el Atach Ridge, Gab Gab Gap, Djebel
Bou Aoukaz 1943, I, North Africa 1943, Anzio, Rome,
Fiesole, Gothic Line, Monte Gamberaldi, Monte Ceco,
Monte Grande, Italy 1944–45, Madagascar, Middle East
1942, Johore, Batu Pahat, Singapore Island, Malaya
1941–42, North Arakan, Mayu Tunnels, Kohima,
Pinwe, Meiktila, Nyaungu Bridgehead, Letse, Irrawaddy,
Burma 1943–45.

Motto	Loyally I Serve
Uniform	Scarlet, piping and facings blue
Regimental marches [Quick]	*L'Attaque/The Red Rose*
[Slow]	*Long Live Elizabeth*

Regimental journal *The Lancashire Lad*

Regimental headquarters Fulwood Barracks, Preston, Lancashire PR2 4AA

Regimental museum As above

THE LANCASHIRE REGIMENT
(PRINCE OF WALES'S VOLUNTEERS)

Formed 1st July 1958 by amalgamation of The East Lancashire Regiment with The South Lancashire Regiment (The Prince of Wales's Volunteers).

Uniform Scarlet, piping and facings white

Regimental marches [Quick] Arrangement of *L'Attaque* and *God Bless the Prince of Wales*

Regimental journal *The Regimental Magazine of The Lancashire Regiment (PWV)*

THE EAST LANCASHIRE REGIMENT
(30th and 59th)

Formed 1881 by amalgamation of 30th (1st Cambridgeshire) Regiment of Foot with the 59th (2nd Nottinghamshire) Regiment of Foot to form The West Lancashire Regiment. Later in the same year the title was altered to The East Lancashire Regiment.

Battle honours Gibraltar 1704–05, Belleisle, Egypt (with the Sphinx), Cape of Good Hope 1806, Corunna, Java, Badajoz, Salamanca, Vittoria, St. Sebastian, Nive, Peninsula, Waterloo, Bhurtpore, Alma, Inkerman, Sevastopol, Canton, Ahmad Khel, Afghanistan 1878–80, Chitral, South Africa, 1900–02.

The Great War—17 *Battalions*—Le Cateau, Retreat from Mons, Marne 1914, Aisne 1914, 18, Armentieres 1914, Neuve Chapelle, Ypres 1915, 17, 18, St. Julien, Frezenberg, Bellewaarde, Aubers, Somme 1916, 18,

Albert 1916, 18, Bazentin, Pozieres, Le Transloy, Ancre Heights, Ancre 1916, 18, Arras 1917, 18, Vimy, 1917, Scarpe 1917, 18, Arleux, Oppy, Messines 1917, Pilckem, Langemarck 1917, Menin Road, Polygon Wood, Broodseinde, Poelcappelle, Passchendaele, St. Quentin, Bapaume 1918, Rosieres, Villers Bretonneux, Lys, Estaires, Hazebrouck, Bailleul, Kemmel, Hindenburg Line, Canal du Nord, Cambrai 1918, Selle, Valenciennes, Sambre, France and Flanders 1914–18, Kosturino, Doiran 1917, 18, Macedonia 1915–18, Helles, Krithia, Suvla, Sari Bair, Gallipoli 1915, Rumani, Egypt 1915–17, Tigris 1916, Kut al Amara 1917, Baghdad, Mesopotamia 1916–17.

The Second World War—Defence of Escaut, Dunkirk 1940, Caen, Falaise, Nederrijn, Lower Maas, Ourthe, Rhineland, Reichswald, Weeze, Rhine, Ibbenburen, Aller, North-West Europe 1940, 44–45, Madagascar, North Arakan, Pinwe, Burma 1944–45.

Motto	*Spectamur Agendo* (By our deeds we are known)
Uniform	Scarlet, piping and facings white
Regimental marches [Quick]	*L'Attaque*
[Slow]	*God Bless the Prince of Wales* (Richards)
Regimental journal	*East Lancashire Regimental Journal*
Nicknames	The Three Tens. The Lillywhites

30th (1st CAMBRIDGESHIRE) REGIMENT OF FOOT*

This Regiment was originally raised 8th March 1689 by George Visct. Castleton, and styled Lord Castleton's Regiment of Foot. In 1698 it was disbanded as Colonel Thomas Saunderson's Regiment of Foot, but in 1702 was re-raised as Colonel Saunderson's Regiment of Marines.

Titles	1689 Lord Castleton's Regiment of Foot
	1694 Colonel Saunderson's Regiment of Foot
	1698 *Disbanded*

---

*This was the official title, but the Regiment always preferred '30th of Foot (1st Cambridgeshire Regiment)'.

1702 *Re-raised* as Colonel Saunderson's Regiment of
Marines *Title subsequently changed with Colonels'
names*

1714 General Wills's Regiment of Foot *Title subsequently
changed with Colonels' names*

1751 30th Regiment of Foot

1782 30th of Foot (1st Cambridgeshire Regiment)

1881 Amalgamated with 59th of Foot (2nd
Nottinghamshire Regiment) to form The East
Lancashire Regiment

Battle honours Egypt (with the Sphinx), Badajoz, Salamanca, Peninsula,
Waterloo, Alma, Inkerman, Sevastopol.

Motto *Spectamur Agendo* (By our deeds we are known)

Uniform Scarlet, facings yellow

Regimental march [Quick] *L'Attaque*

Nicknames The Three Tens. The Yellow Bellies (after facings)

59th
(2nd NOTTINGHAMSHIRE)
REGIMENT OF FOOT

Raised December 1755 by Colonel Sir Charles Montagu
as the 61st Regiment of Foot. Renumbered 59th in 1757.

Titles 1755 61st Regiment of Foot

1757 59th Regiment of Foot

1782 59th (2nd Nottinghamshire) Regiment of Foot

1881 Amalgamated with 30th (1st Cambridgeshire)
Regiment of Foot to form The East Lancashire
Regiment

Battle honours Cape of Good Hope 1806, Corunna, Java, Vittoria, St.
Sebastian, Nive, Peninsula, Bhurtpore, Canton, Ahmed
Khel, Afghanistan 1878–80.

Uniform Scarlet, facings white

Regimental march [Quick] *Lancashire Lad*

Nickname The Lillywhites

Remarks The 59th were the only regiment to bear the Battle
Honour *Canton*, awarded for the storming and capture of
that city in December 1857.

THE SOUTH LANCASHIRE REGIMENT
(THE PRINCE OF WALES'S VOLUNTEERS)
(40th and 82nd)

Formed 1881 by amalgamation of the 40th (2nd Somersetshire) Regiment of Foot with the 82nd Regiment of Foot (Prince of Wales's Volunteers) to form The Prince of Wales's Volunteers (South Lancashire). In 1938 the title was altered to The South Lancashire Regiment (The Prince of Wales's Volunteers).

Battle honours Louisburg, Martinique 1762, Havannah, St. Lucia 1778, Egypt (with the Sphinx), Monte Video, Rolica, Vimiera, Corunna, Talavera, Badajoz, Salamanca, Vittoria, Pyrenees, Nivelle, Orthes, Toulouse, Peninsula, Niagara, Waterloo, Candahar 1842, Ghuznee 1842, Cabool 1842, Maharajpore, Sevastopol, Lucknow, New Zealand, Relief of Ladysmith, South Africa 1899–1902.

The Great War—20 *Battalions*—Mons, Le Cateau, Retreat from Mons, Marne 1914, Aisne 1914, 18, La Bassee 1914, Messines 1914, 17, 18, Armentieres 1914, Ypres 1914, 15, 17, 18, Nonne Bosschen, St. Julien, Frezenberg, Bellewaarde, Somme 1916, 18, Albert 1916, Bazentin, Pozieres, Guillemont, Ginchy, Flers-Courcelette, Morval, Le Transloy, Ancre Heights, Ancre 1916, Arras 1917, 18, Scarpe 1917, 18 Pilckem, Langemarck 1917, Menin Road, Polygon Wood, Passchendale, Cambrai 1917, 18, St. Quentin, Bapaume 1918, Rosieres, Lys, Estaires, Hazebrouck, Bailleul, Kemmel, Scherpenberg, Drocourt-Queant, Hindenburg Line, Canal du Nord, Courtrai, Selle, Sambre, France and Flanders 1914–18, Doiran 1917, 18, Macedonia 1915–18, Suvla, Sari Bair, Gallipoli 1915, Egypt 1916, Tigris 1916, Kut al Amara 1917, Baghdad, Mesopotamia 1916–18, Baluchistan 1918.

Afghanistan 1919.

The Second World War—Dunkirk 1940, Normandy Landing, Odon, Bourguebus Ridge, Troarn, Falaise, Venraij, Rhineland, Hochwald, Bremen, North-West Europe 1940, 44–45, Madagascar, Middle East 1942,

North Arakan, Mayu Tunnels, Kohima, Meiktila, Nyaungu Bridgehead, Letse, Irrawaddy, Burma 1943–45.

Motto *Ich Dien* (I Serve)

Uniform Scarlet, piping and facings buff

Regimental marches [Quick] *God Bless the Prince of Wales* (Richards)
[Slow] *The Lancashire Witches*

Regimental journal *Regimental Chronicle The South Lancashire Regiment*

Nicknames The Fighting Fortieth. The Excellers

40th (2nd SOMERSET) REGIMENT OF FOOT

Raised 25th August 1717 by Colonel Richard Phillips, from independent companies of Foot in Nova Scotia.

Titles 1717 Colonel Phillips's Regiment of Foot *Title subsequently changed with Colonels' names*
1751 40th Regiment of Foot
1782 40th (2nd Somersetshire) Regiment of Foot
1881 Amalgamated with 82nd Regiment of Foot (Prince of Wales's Volunteers) to form The Prince of Wales's Volunteers (South Lancashire)

Battle honours Louisburg, Egypt (with the Sphinx), Monte Video, Rolica, Vimiera, Talavera, Badajoz, Salamanca, Vittoria, Pyrenees, Nivelle, Orthes, Toulouse, Peninsula, Waterloo, Candahar, Ghuzhee 1842, Cabool 1842, Maharajpore, New Zealand.

Uniform Scarlet, facings buff

Regimental march [Quick] *The Somerset Poacher*

Nicknames The Fighting Fortieth. The Excellers

82nd REGIMENT OF FOOT
(PRINCE OF WALES'S VOLUNTEERS)

Raised 27th September 1793 by Colonel Charles Leigh and styled 82nd Regiment of Foot (or Prince of Wales's Volunteers). This title remained unchanged until

amalgamation with the 40th (2nd Somersetshire)
Regiment of Foot in 1881.

Battle honours Rolica, Vimiera, Vittoria, Pyrenees, Nivelle, Orthes,
Peninsula, Niagara, Sevastopol, Lucknow.

Motto *Ich Dien* (I Serve)

Uniform Scarlet, facings yellow

Regimental march [Quick] *God Bless the Prince of Wales* (Richards)

THE LOYAL REGIMENT
(NORTH LANCASHIRE)
(47th and 81st)

Formed 1881 by amalgamation of the 47th (Lancashire)
Regiment of Foot with the 81st (Loyal Lincoln
Volunteers) Regiment of Foot.
Original title was The Loyal North Lancashire Regiment.
Altered as above in 1921.

Battle honours Louisburg, Quebec 1759, Maida, Corunna, Tarifa,
Vittoria, St. Sebastian, Nive, Peninsula, Ava, Alma,
Inkerman, Sevastopol, Ali Masjid, Afghanistan 1878–79,
Defence of Kimberley, South Africa 1899–1902.

The Great War— 21 *Battalions*—Mons, Retreat from
Mons, Marne 1914, 18, Aisne 1914, 18, Ypres 1914, 17,
18, Langemarck, 1914, Gheluvelt, Nonne Bosschen,
Givenchy 1914, Aubers, Festubert 1915, Loos, Somme
1916, 18, Albert 1916, Bazentin, Pozieres, Guillemont,
Ginchy, Flers-Courcelette, Morval, Ancre Heights,
Ancre 1916, Arras 1917, 18, Scarpe 1917, Arleux,
Messines 1917, Pilckem, Menin Road, Polygon Wood,
Poelcappelle, Passchendaele, Cambrai 1917, 18, St.
Quentin, Bapaume 1918, Lys, Estaires, Bailleul,
Kemmel, Bethune, Scherpenberg, Soissonnais-Ourcq,
Drocourt-Queant, Hindenburg Line, Epehy, Canal du
Nord, St. Quentin Canal, Courtrai, Selle, Sambre,
France and Flanders 1914–18, Doiran 1917, Macedonia
1917, Suvla, Sari Bair, Gallipoli 1915, Egypt 1916,
Gaza, Nebi Samwil, Jerusalem, Jaffa, Tell 'Asur,
Palestine 1917–18, Tigris 1916, Kut al Amara 1917,
Baghdad, Mesopotamia 1916–18, Kilimanjaro, E. Africa
1914–16.

The Second World War—Dunkirk 1940, North-West Europe 1940, Banana Ridge, Djebel Kesskiss, Medjez Plain, Gueriat el Atach Ridge, Djebel Bou Aoukaz 1943, I, Gab Gab Gap, North Africa 1943, Anzio, Rome, Fiesole, Gothic Line, Monte Gamberaldi, Monte Ceco, Monte Grande, Italy 1944–45, Johore, Batu Pahat, Singapore Island, Malaya 1941–42.

Motto *Loyauté M'Oblige* (Loyalty binds me)

Uniform Scarlet, piping and facings white

Regimental marches [Quick] *The Red Rose*
[Slow] Untitled (resembles *The Mountain Rose*)

Regimental journal *The Lancashire Lad*

Nickname The Lancashire Lads

Remarks The Loyal Regiment's antecedent, the 47th Foot, was the first unit to be officially associated with Lancashire (in 1782), and The Loyal Regiment itself was the last of the Lancashire regiments to lose its separate identity, in 1970.
The Battle Honours *Defence of Kimberley* and *Kilimanjaro* are unique to the Regiment.

47th (LANCASHIRE) REGIMENT OF FOOT

Raised January 1741 by Colonel John Mordaunt and ranked as 58th Regiment of Foot. Renumbered 47th in 1748.

Titles 1741 Colonel Mordaunt's Regiment of Foot *Title subsequently changed with Colonels' names*
1751 47th Regiment of Foot
1782 47th (or The Lancashire) Regiment of Foot
1881 Amalgamated with 81st (Loyal Lincoln Volunteers) Regiment of Foot to form The Loyal North Lancashire Regiment

Battle honours Louisburg, Quebec 1759, Tarifa, Vittoria, St. Sebastian, Peninsula, Ava, Alma, Inkerman, Sevastopol

Uniform Scarlet, facings white

Regimental marches [Quick] *The Mountain Rose*
[Slow] Untitled

Nicknames Wolfe's Own. The Cauliflowers

81st (LOYAL LINCOLN VOLUNTEERS) REGIMENT OF FOOT

Raised 23rd September 1793 by Major-General Albemarle Bertie, as the 83rd (Loyal Lincolnshire Volunteer) Regiment of Foot. Renumbered 81st in 1794.

Titles 1793 83rd (Loyal Lincolnshire Volunteer) Regiment of Foot
1794 81st Regiment of Foot
1832 81st (Loyal Lincoln Volunteers) Regiment of Foot
1881 Amalgamated with 47th (Lancashire) Regiment of Foot to form The Loyal North Lancashire Regiment

Battle honours Maida, Corunna, Peninsula, Ali Masjid, Afghanistan 1878–80.

Motto *Mox Surgere Victor* (Soon to arise as victor)

Uniform Scarlet, facings buff

Regimental march [Quick] *The Lincolnshire Poacher* (Tradit.)

Nickname The Loyals

Remarks Although four other short-lived Foot regiments bore the subtitle 'Loyal', these were all disbanded by 1796 and thenceforth only the 81st, and subsequently The Loyal Regiment, were so distinguished. Tradition relates the term to the enthusiasm with which the Lincolnshire recruits came forward for the original Regiment in 1793, while there is also a play on the Motto *Loyauté M'Oblige*, borne by the first Colonel, Major-General Albemarle Bertie (later 9th Earl of Lindsey).

THE DUKE OF WELLINGTON'S REGIMENT
(WEST RIDING)
(33rd and 76th)

Formed 1881 by amalgamation of the 33rd (Duke of Wellington's Regiment) with the 76th Regiment of Foot to form The Duke of Wellington's (West Riding Regiment). In 1920 title varied to The Duke of Wellington's Regiment (West Riding).

Battle honours Dettingen, Mysore, Seringapatam, Ally Ghur, Delhi 1803, Leswarree, Deig, Hindoostan (with the Elephant), Corunna, Nive, Peninsula, Waterloo, Alma, Inkerman, Sevastopol, Abyssinia, Relief of Kimberley, Paardeberg, South Africa 1900–02.

The Great War—Mons, Le Cateau, Retreat from Mons, Marne 1914, 18, Aisne 1914, La Bassee 1914, Ypres 1914, 15, 17, Nonne Bosschen, Hill 60, Gravenstafel, St. Julien, Aubers, Somme 1916, 18, Albert 1916, 18, Bazentin, Delville Wood, Pozieres, Flers-Courcelette, Morval, Thiepval, Le Transloy, Ancre Heights, Arras 1917, 18, Scarpe 1917, 18, Arleux, Bullecourt, Messines 1917, 18, Langemarck 1917, Menin Road, Polygon Wood, Broodseinde, Poelcappelle, Passchendaele, Cambrai 1917, 18, St. Quentin, Ancre 1918, Lys, Estaires, Hazebrouck, Bailleul, Kemmel, Bethune, Scherpenberg, Tardenois, Amiens, Bapaume 1918, Drocourt-Queant, Hindenburg Line, Havrincourt, Epehy, Canal du Nord, Selle, Valenciennes, Sambre, France and Flanders 1914–18, Piave, Vittorio Veneto, Italy 1917–18, Suvla, Landing at Suvla, Scimitar Hill, Gallipoli 1915, Egypt 1916.

Afghanistan 1919.

The Second World War—Dunkirk 1940, St. Valery-en-Caux, Tilly sur Seulles, Odon, Fontenay Le Pesnil, North-West Europe 1940, 44–45, Banana Ridge, Medjez Plain, Gueriat el Atach Ridge, Tunis, Djebel Bou Aoukaz 1943, North Africa 1943, Anzio, Campoleone,

Rome, Monte Ceco, Italy 1943–45, Sittang 1942, Paungde, Kohima, Chindits 1944, Burma 1942–44.

The Hook 1953, Korea 1952–53.

Motto *Virtutis Fortuna Comes* (Fortune is the companion of valour)
(Motto of the Dukes of Wellington)

Uniform Scarlet, piping and facings scarlet

Regimental march [Quick] *The Wellesley**

Regimental journal *The Iron Duke*

Regimental headquarters Wellesley Park, Highroad Well, Halifax, West Yorkshire HX2 0BA

Regimental museum Bankfield Museum, Boothtown Road, Halifax, West Yorkshire HX3 3RA

Nicknames The Havercake Lads. The Dukies

Remarks The Duke of Wellington's is the only Regiment named after a personage not of the Blood Royal (see below, p. 212).

33rd (DUKE OF WELLINGTON'S REGIMENT)

Raised February 1702 by Colonel George Hastings, Earl of Huntingdon.

Titles 1702 The Earl of Huntingdon's Regiment of Foot
1751 33rd Regiment of Foot
1782 33rd (or 1st Yorkshire West Riding) Regiment of Foot
1853 33rd (Duke of Wellington's Regiment)
1881 Amalgamated with the 76th Regiment of Foot to form The Duke of Wellington's (West Riding Regiment)
1920 Title varied to The Duke of Wellington's Regiment (West Riding)

The Wellesley is the authorised Quick March, but within the Regiment the following unofficial Marches are also played: *I'm Ninety-Five, Scotland the Brave* and *Ilkla Moor.*

Battle honours Dettingen, Seringapatam, Waterloo, Alma, Inkerman, Sevastopol, Abyssinia.

Motto *Virtutis Fortuna Comes* (Fortune is the companion of valour)
(Motto of the Dukes of Wellington)

Uniform Scarlet, facings scarlet

Regimental march [Quick] *The Wellesley*

Nicknames The Dukes. The Havercake Lads

Remarks The 1st Duke of Wellington was long associated with the Regiment. As the Hon. Arthur Wellesley he joined the 33rd in 1793, as a major, and later the same year became its Commanding Officer. He was Colonel of the Regiment 1806–1813, and after his death Queen Victoria granted permission for the Regiment to be named after him (1853). The Duke's Crest and Motto formed the Badge of the 33rd, which has been inherited by the present Regiment as its Cap Badge.

76th REGIMENT OF FOOT

Raised October 1787 for service with the Hon. East India Company. Commanded by Colonel Thomas Musgrave.

Titles 1787 76th Regiment of Foot (Also known until 1812 as 'The Hindoostan Regiment')
1881 Amalgamated with the 33rd (Duke of Wellington's Regiment) to form The Duke of Wellington's (West Riding Regiment)

Battle honours Hindoostan (with the Elephant), Mysore, Ally Ghur, Delhi 1803, Leswarree, Deig, Corunna, Nive, Peninsula.

Uniform Scarlet, facings scarlet

Regimental marches [Quick] *Scotland the Brave*
[Slow] *Logie o'Buchan*

Nicknames The Immortals. The Hindoostan Regiment. The Seven-and-Sixpennies

Remarks The 76th served with distinction in India from 1787 to 1807. During Lord Lake's campaigns of 1803–05 it was the only British infantry unit engaged, and its actions won it the Honour Badge of the Elephant and Howdah, and the Honour title of 'Hindoostan'. In addition, the

Governor-General of India directed that the 76th should be presented with a pair of Honorary Colours. The 76th was, and the present Regiment is, the only infantry Regiment of the Line to carry four Colours on parade.

THE ROYAL HAMPSHIRE REGIMENT

(37th and 67th)

Formed 1881 by amalgamation of the 37th (North Hampshire) Regiment of Foot with the 67th (South Hampshire) Regiment of Foot to form The Hampshire Regiment. 'Royal' prefix granted in 1946.

Battle honours Blenheim, Ramillies, Oudenarde, Malplaquet, Dettingen, Minden, Belleisle, Tournay, Barrosa, Peninsula, India (with the Tiger), Taku Forts, Pekin 1860, Charasiah, Kabul 1879, Afghanistan 1879–80, Burma 1885–87, Paardeberg, South Africa 1900–02.

The Great War—Le Cateau, Retreat from Mons, Marne 1914, 18, Aisne 1914, Armentieres 1914, Ypres 1915, 17, 18, St. Julien, Frezenberg, Bellewaarde, Somme 1916, 18, Albert 1916, Guillemont, Ginchy, Flers-Courcelette, Thiepval, Le Transloy, Ancre Heights, Ancre 1916, Arras 1917, 18, Vimy 1917, Scarpe 1917, 18, Messines 1917, 18, Pilckem, Langemarck 1917, Menin Road, Polygon Wood, Broodseinde, Poelcappelle, Passchendaele, Cambrai 1917, 18, St. Quentin, Bapaume 1918, Rosieres, Lys, Estaires, Hazebrouck, Bailleul, Kemmel, Bethune, Tardenois, Drocourt-Queant, Hindenburg Line, Havrincourt, Canal du Nord, Courtrai, Selle, Valenciennes, Sambre, France and Flanders 1914–18, Italy 1917–18, Kosturino, Struma, Doiran 1917, 18, Macedonia 1915–18, Helles, Landing at Helles, Krithia, Suvla, Sari Bair, Landing at Suvla, Scimitar Hill, Gallipoli 1915–16, Egypt 1915–17, Gaza, El Mughar, Nebi Samwil, Jerusalem, Jaffa, Tell 'Asur, Megiddo, Sharon, Palestine 1917–18, Aden, Shaiba, Kut al Amara 1915, 17, Tigris 1916, Baghdad, Sharqat,

Mesopotamia 1915–18, Persia, 1918–19, Archangel 1919, Siberia 1918–19.

The Second World War—Dunkirk 1940, Normandy Landing, Tilly sur Seulles, Caen, Hill 112, Mont Pincon, Jurques, St. Pierre La Vielle, Nederrijn, Roer, Rhineland, Goch, Rhine, North-West Europe 1940, 44–45, Tebourba Gap, Sidi Nsir, Hunt's Gap, Montagne Farm, Fondouk, Pichon, El Kourzia, Ber Rabai, North Africa 1940–43, Landing in Sicily, Regalbuto, Sicily 1943, Landing at Porto San Venere, Salerno, Salerno Hills, Battipaglia, Cava di Tirreni, Volturno Crossing, Garigliano Crossing, Damiano, Monte Ornito, Cerasola, Cassino II, Massa Vertecchi, Trasimene Line, Advance to Florence, Gothic Line, Monte Gridolfo, Montegaudio, Coriano, Montilgallo, Capture of Forli, Cosina Canal Crossing, Lamone Crossing, Pideura, Rimini Line, Montescudo, Frisoni, Italy 1943–45, Athens, Greece 1944–45, Malta 1941–42.

Uniform Scarlet, piping and facings yellow

Regimental march [Quick] *The Hampshire*

Regimental journal *Royal Hampshire Regimental Journal*

Regimental headquarters Serle's House, Southgate Street, Winchester, Hampshire SO23 9EZ

Regimental museum As above

Nickname The Tigers

Remarks In the defence reductions of 1969 The Royal Hampshire Regiment was scheduled for amalgamation with The Gloucestershire Regiment to form 'The Royal Regiment of Gloucestershire and Hampshire'. But by voluntarily reducing to one company ('The Minden Company') The Hampshires preserved their separate identity, and later regained battalion strength.

37th (NORTH HAMPSHIRE) REGIMENT OF FOOT

Raised in Ireland, February 1702, by Colonel Thomas Meredith.

Titles 1702 Colonel Meredith's Regiment of Foot
1751 37th Regiment of Foot

1782 37th (or North Hampshire) Regiment of Foot
1881 Amalgamated with 67th (South Hampshire)
     Regiment of Foot to form The Hampshire
     Regiment

Battle honours Blenheim, Ramillies, Oudenarde, Malplaquet,
Dettingen, Minden, Peninsula.

Uniform Scarlet, facings yellow

Regimental march [Quick] *The Highland Piper*

Remarks The 37th were one of the 'Glorious Six' Minden
Regiments.

67th (SOUTH HAMPSHIRE) REGIMENT OF FOOT

Originated in 1756 as 2nd Battalion of 20th Foot.
Augmented as separate regiment in April 1758, with
Brigadier-General (later Major-General) James Wolfe as
Colonel.

Titles 1758 67th Regiment of Foot
1782 67th (or South Hampshire) Regiment of Foot
1881 Amalgamated with 37th (North Hampshire)
     Regiment of Foot to form The Hampshire
     Regiment

Battle honours Belleisle, Barrosa, Peninsula, India (with the Tiger),
Taku Forts, Pekin 1860, Charasiah, Kabul 1879,
Afghanistan 1879–80.

Uniform Scarlet, facings yellow

Regimental march [Quick] *We'll gang nae mair to Yon Toon*

Nickname The Royal Tigers

Remarks The Royal Tiger superscribed 'India', borne on the
Regimental Colour and appointments, was granted for
the Regiment's services in the Indian campaigns of
1805–1826.

THE STAFFORDSHIRE REGIMENT
(THE PRINCE OF WALES'S)
(38th, 64th, 80th, 98th)

Formed January 1959 by amalgamation of The South Staffordshire Regiment with The North Staffordshire Regiment (The Prince of Wales's).

Battle honours Guadaloupe 1759, Martinique 1762, Martinique 1794, Egypt (with the Sphinx), St. Lucia 1803, Surinam, Monte Video, Rolica, Vimiera, Corunna, Busaco, Badajoz, Salamanca, Vittoria, St. Sebastian, Nive, Peninsula, China (with the Dragon), Ava, Moodkee, Ferozeshah, Sobraon, Punjaub, Pegu, Alma, Inkerman, Sevastopol, Reshire, Bushire, Koosh-Ab, Persia, Lucknow, Central India, South Africa 1878–79, Egypt 1882, Kirbekan, Nile 1884–85, Hafir, South Africa 1900–02.

The Great War—Mons, Retreat from Mons, Marne 1914, Aisne 1914, 18, Armentieres 1914, Ypres 1914, 17, 18, Langemarck 1914, 17, Gheluvelt, Nonne Bosschen, Neuve Chapelle, Aubers, Festubert 1915, Loos, Somme 1916, 18, Albert 1916, 18, Bazentin, Delville Wood, Pozieres, Guillemont, Flers-Courcelette, Morval, Thiepval, Ancre Heights, Ancre 1916, Bapaume 1917, 18, Arras 1917, 18, Scarpe 1917, 18, Arleux, Bullecourt, Hill 70, Messines 1917, 18, Pilckem, Menin Road, Polygon Wood, Broodseinde, Poelcappelle, Passchendaele, Cambrai 1917, 18, St. Quentin, Rosieres, Avre, Lys, Bailleul, Kemmel, Scherpenberg, Drocourt-Queant, Hindenburg Line, Havrincourt, Canal du Nord, St. Quentin Canal, Beaurevoir, Courtrai, Selle, Valenciennes, Sambre, France and Flanders 1914–18, Piave, Vittorio Veneto, Italy 1917–18, Suvla, Sari Bair, Landing at Suvla, Scimitar Hill, Gallipoli 1915–16, Egypt 1916, Tigris 1916, Kut al Amara 1917, Baghdad, Mesopotamia 1916–18, Baku, Persia 1918, N.W. Frontier, India 1915.

Afghanistan 1919.

The Second World War—Dyle, Defence of Escaut,
Ypres-Comines Canal, Caen, Orne, Noyers, Mont
Pincon, Brieux Bridgehead, Falaise, Arnhem 1944,
North-West Europe 1940, 44, Sidi Barrani, Djebel
Kesskiss, Medjez Plain, Gueriat et Atach Ridge, Gab Gab
Gap, North Africa 1940, 43, Landing in Sicily, Sicily
1943, Anzio, Carroceto, Rome, Advance to Tiber,
Gothic Line, Marradi, Italy 1943–45, Chindits 1944,
Burma 1943, 44.

Uniform Scarlet, piping and facings yellow

Regimental marches [Quick] *The Staffordshire Regiment* (amalgam of *Come Lasses and
Lads* and *The Days we went A-Gypsying*)
[Slow] *God Bless The Prince of Wales* (Richards)

Regimental journal *The Stafford Knot*

Regimental headquarters Whittington Barracks, Lichfield, Staffordshire
WS14 9PY

Regimental museum As above

THE SOUTH STAFFORDSHIRE REGIMENT

(38th and 80th)

Formed 1881 by amalgamation of 38th (1st Staffordshire)
Regiment of Foot with 80th (Staffordshire Volunteers)
Regiment of Foot.

Battle honours Guadaloupe 1759, Martinique 1762, Monte Video,
Egypt (with the Sphinx), Rolica, Vimiera, Corunna,
Busaco, Badajoz, Salamanca, Vittoria, St. Sebastian,
Nive, Peninsula, Ava, Moodkee, Ferozeshah, Sobraon,
Pegu, Alma, Inkerman, Sevastopol, Lucknow, Central
India, South Africa 1878–79, Egypt 1882, Kirbekan, Nile
1884–85, South Africa 1900–02.

The Great War—18 *Battalions*—Mons, Retreat from
Mons, Marne 1914, Aisne 1914, 18, Ypres 1914, 17,
Langemarck 1914, 17, Gheluvelt, Nonne Bosschen,
Neuve Chapelle, Aubers, Festubert 1915, Loos, Somme
1916, 18, Albert 1916, 18, Bazentin, Delville Wood,
Pozieres, Flers-Courcelette, Morval, Thiepval, Ancre
1916, Bapaume 1917, 18, Arras 1917, 18, Scarpe 1917,

18, Arleux, Bullecourt, Hill 70, Messines 1917, 18, Menin Road, Polygon Wood, Broodseinde, Poelcappelle, Passchendaele, Cambrai 1917, 18, St. Quentin, Lys, Bailleul, Kemmel, Scherpenberg, Drocourt-Queant, Hindenburg Line, Havrincourt, Canal du Nord, St. Quentin Canal, Beaurevoir, Selle, Sambre, France and Flanders 1914–18, Piave, Vittorio Veneto, Italy 1917–18, Suvla, Landing at Suvla, Scimitar Hill, Gallipoli 1915, Egypt 1916.

The Second World War—Caen, Noyers, Falaise, Arnhem 1944, North-West Europe 1940, 44, Sidi Barrani, North Africa 1940, Landing in Sicily, Sicily 1943, Italy 1943, Chindits 1944, Burma 1944.

Uniform Scarlet, piping and facings white until 1935, when changed to yellow

Regimental marches [Quick] *Come Lasses and Lads* (Tradit.)
[Slow] *The 80th*

Regimental journal *The Knot*

38th (1st STAFFORDSHIRE) REGIMENT OF FOOT

Raised at Lichfield, Staffordshire, March 1705, by Colonel Luke Lillingston.

Titles 1705 Colonel Lillingston's Regiment of Foot *Title subsequently changed with Colonels' names*
1751 38th Regiment of Foot
1782 38th (or 1st Staffordshire) Regiment of Foot
1881 Amalgamated with 80th (Staffordshire Volunteers) Regiment of Foot to form The South Staffordshire Regiment

Battle honours Monte Video, Rolica, Vimiera, Corunna, Busaco, Badajoz, Salamanca, Vittoria, St. Sebastian, Nive, Peninsula, Ava, Alma, Inkerman, Sevastopol, Lucknow.

Uniform Scarlet, facings yellow

Regimental march [Quick] *Over the Hills and Far Away*

Remarks The 38th were posted to the West Indies in 1707 and spent the next 57 years in those fever-stricken islands. Neglected by the Home authorities, the men were obliged to make part of their uniform out of sugar-bag sacking—later commemorated by the Holland patches worn as backing to the Regimental Badge of The South Staffordshire Regiment, and that of the present Regiment.

80th REGIMENT OF FOOT
(STAFFORDSHIRE VOLUNTEERS)

Raised at Chatham, September 1793, by Lieut-Colonel Henry Lord Paget (later 1st Marquess of Anglesey). The men were mostly volunteers from the Staffordshire Militia, commanded by Paget's father, the Earl of Uxbridge, and the Regiment was thus known as 'Staffordshire Volunteers'.

Titles 1793 80th Regiment of Foot (or Staffordshire Volunteers)
1881 Amalgamated with 38th (1st Staffordshire) Regiment of Foot to form The South Staffordshire Regiment

Battle honours Egypt (with the Sphinx), Moodkee, Ferozeshah, Sobraon, Pegu, Central India, South Africa 1878–79.

Uniform Scarlet, facings yellow

Regimental marches [Quick] *Come Lasses and Lads* (Tradit.)
[Slow] *The Garb of Old Gaul* (Reid)

Nickname The Staffordshire Knots

THE NORTH STAFFORDSHIRE REGIMENT
(THE PRINCE OF WALES'S)
(64th and 98th)

Formed 1881 by amalgamation of the 64th (2nd Staffordshire) Regiment of Foot with the 98th (Prince of Wales's) Regiment of Foot to form The Prince of Wales's (North Staffordshire Regiment). In 1921 the title was varied to The North Staffordshire Regiment (The Prince of Wales's).

Battle honours Guadaloupe 1759, Martinique 1794, St. Lucia 1803, Surinam, China (with the Dragon), Punjaub, Reshire,

Bushire, Koosh-ab, Persia, Lucknow, Hafir, South Africa 1900–02.

*The Great War—17 Battalions—*Aisne 1914, 18, Armentieres 1914, Loos, Somme 1916, 18, Albert 1916, 18, Bazentin, Delville Wood, Pozieres, Guillemont, Ancre Heights, Ancre 1916, Arras 1917, Scarpe 1917, Arleux, Messines 1917, 18, Ypres 1917, 18, Pilckem, Langemarck 1917, Menin Road, Polygon Wood, Broodseinde, Poelcappelle, Passchendaele, Cambrai 1917, 18, St. Quentin, Bapaume 1918, Rosieres, Avre, Lys, Bailleul, Kemmel, Hindenburg Line, Havrincourt, Canal du Nord, St. Quentin Canal, Beaurevoir, Courtrai, Selle, Valenciennes, Sambre, France and Flanders 1914–18, Suvla, Sari Bair, Gallipoli 1915–16, Egypt 1916, Tigris 1916, Kut al Amara 1917, Baghdad, Mesopotamia 1916–18, Baku, Persia 1918, N.W. Frontier India 1915.

Afghanistan 1919.

*The Second World War—*Dyle, Defence of Escaut, Ypres-Comines Canal, Caen, Orne, Noyers, Mont Pincon, Brieux Bridgehead, North-West Europe 1940, 44, Djebel Kesskiss, Medjez Plain, Gueriat el Atach Ridge, Gab Gab Gap, North Africa 1943, Anzio, Carroceto, Rome, Advance to Tiber, Gothic Line, Marradi, Italy 1944–45, Burma 1943.

Uniform Scarlet, piping and facings white until 1937, when changed to black

Regimental marches [Quick] *The Days We Went A-Gypsying*
[Slow] *God Bless The Prince of Wales* (Richards)

Regimental journal *China Dragon*

64th (2nd STAFFORDSHIRE) REGIMENT OF FOOT

Originated in 1756 as 2nd Battalion, 11th Foot. Augmented as separate Regiment in April 1758, commanded by Colonel the Hon. John Barrington, and ranked as 64th Foot.

Titles 1758 64th Regiment of Foot
1782 64th (or 2nd Staffordshire) Regiment of Foot

1881 Amalgamated with 98th (Prince of Wales's) Regiment of Foot to form The Prince of Wales's (North Staffordshire Regiment)

Battle honours St. Lucia 1803, Surinam, Reshire, Bushire, Koosh-Ab, Persia, Lucknow.

Uniform Scarlet, facings black

Regimental march [Quick] *Romaika*

Nickname The Black Knots

98th (PRINCE OF WALES'S) REGIMENT OF FOOT

Raised March 1824, at Chichester, with Lieut-General Henry Conran as Colonel.

Titles 1824 98th Regiment of Foot
1876 98th (Prince of Wales's) Regiment of Foot
1881 Amalgamated with 64th (2nd Staffordshire) Regiment of Foot to form The Prince of Wales's (North Staffordshire Regiment)

Battle honours China (with the Dragon), Punjaub.

Uniform Scarlet, facings white

Regimental march [Quick] *God Bless The Prince of Wales* (Richards)

THE BLACK WATCH
(ROYAL HIGHLAND REGIMENT)
(42nd and 73rd)

Formed 1881 by amalgamation of the 42nd Royal Highland Regiment of Foot (The Black Watch) with the 73rd (Perthshire) Regiment of Foot.

Titles 1881 The Black Watch (Royal Highlanders)
1936 The Black Watch (Royal Highland Regiment)

Battle honours Guadaloupe, 1759, Martinique 1762, Havannah, North America, 1763–64, Mangalore, Mysore, Seringapatam,

Egypt (with the Sphinx), Corunna, Busaco, Fuentes d'Onor, Salamanca, Pyrenees, Nivelle, Nive, Orthes, Toulouse, Peninsula, Waterloo, South Africa 1846–47, 1851–52–53, Alma, Sevastopol, Lucknow, Ashantee 1873–74, Tel-el-Kebir, Egypt 1882, 1884, Kirbekan, Nile 1884–85, Paardeberg, South Africa 1899–1902.

The Great War—Retreat from Mons, Marne 1914, 18, Aisne 1914, La Bassee 1914, Ypres 1914, 17, 18, Langemarck 1914, Gheluvelt, Nonne Bosschen, Givenchy 1914, Neuve Chapelle, Aubers, Festubert 1915, Loos, Somme 1916, 18, Albert 1916, Bazentin Delville Wood, Pozieres, Flers-Courcelette, Morval, Thiepval, Le Transloy, Ancre Heights, Ancre 1916, Arras 1917, 18, Vimy 1917, Scarpe 1917, 18, Arleux, Pilckem, Menin Road, Polygon Wood, Poelcappelle, Passchendaele, Cambrai 1917, 18, St. Quentin, Bapaume 1918, Rosieres, Lys, Estaires, Messines 1918, Hazebrouck, Kemmel, Bethune, Scherpenberg, Soissonnais-Ourcq, Tardenois, Drocourt-Queant, Hindenburg Line, Epehy, St. Quentin Canal, Beaurevoir, Courtrai, Selle, Sambre, France and Flanders 1914–18, Doiran 1917, Macedonia 1915–18, Egypt 1916, Gaza, Jerusalem, Tell 'Asur, Megiddo, Sharon, Damascus, Palestine 1917–18, Tigris 1916, Kut al Amara 1917, Baghdad, Mesopotamia 1915–17.

The Second World War—Defence of Arras, Ypres-Comines Canal, Dunkirk 1940, Somme 1940, St. Valery-en-Caux, Saar, Breville, Odon, Fontenay le Pesnil, Defence of Rauray, Caen, Falaise, Falaise Road, La Vie Crossing, Le Havre, Lower Maas, Venlo Pocket, Ourthe, Rhineland, Reichswald, Goch, Rhine, North-West Europe 1940, 44–45, Barkasan, British Somaliland 1940, Tobruk 1941, Tobruk Sortie, El Alamein, Advance on Tripoli, Medenine, Zemlet el Lebene, Mareth, Akarit, Wadi Akarit East, Djebel Roumana, Medjez Plain, Si Mediene, Tunis, North Africa 1941–43, Landing in Sicily, Vizzini, Sferro, Gerbini, Adrano, Sferro Hills, Sicily 1943, Cassino II, Liri Valley, Advance to Florence, Monte Scalari, Casa Fortis, Rimini Line, Casa Fabbri Ridge, Savio Bridgehead, Italy 1944–45, Athens, Greece 1944–45, Crete, Heraklion, Middle East 1941, Chindits 1944, Burma 1944.

The Hook 1952, Korea 1952–53.

Motto   *Nemo Me Impune Lacessit* (No one provokes me with impunity)

Uniform   Doublet, piper green; kilt, Black Watch tartan; facings blue

Regimental marches [Quick]   *The Highland Laddie* (Tradit.)
[Slow]   *In the Garb of Old Gaul* (Reid)

Regimental journal   *The Red Hackle*

Regimental headquarters   Balhousie Castle, Perth, Scotland

Regimental museum   As above

Nickname   The Watch

Remarks   Originating from independent Companies of loyal Highlanders raised in 1725 to police or 'watch' the doubtful Highland clans, The Black Watch is the senior Highland Regiment. The sombre Black Watch tartan was adopted by the Regiment soon after its formation from the independent Companies, and being the first authorised military tartan was known as 'Government Tartan'. The title of the Regiment is derived from the Gaelic *Am Freiceadan Dubh* ('The Black Watch'), applied to the original Regiment by the Clansmen to distinguish it from the English Redcoats or *Saighdearan Dearg*.

Following an Army Order of 1822 The Black Watch have the unique distinction of wearing a red hackle in their bonnets, and no badge.

42nd ROYAL HIGHLAND REGIMENT OF FOOT
(THE BLACK WATCH)

Raised near Aberfeldy, Perthshire, October 1739, from independent Companies of loyal Highlanders. Command given to Colonel John Lindsay, Earl of Crawford. Ranked as 43rd Foot. Renumbered 42nd in 1749.

Titles   1739 The Earl of Crawford's Regiment of Foot (Also known as 'The Highland Regiment') *Title subsequently changed with Colonels' names*
1751 42nd Regiment of Foot
1758 42nd (The Royal Highland) Regiment of Foot

1861 42nd Royal Highland Regiment of Foot (The Black Watch)

1881 Amalgamated with the 73rd (Perthshire) Regiment of Foot to form The Black Watch (Royal Highlanders)

Battle honours Guadaloupe 1759, Martinique 1762, Havannah, North America 1763–64, Egypt (with the Sphinx), Corunna, Busaco, Fuentes d'Onor, Salamanca, Pyrenees, Nivelle, Nive, Orthes, Toulouse, Peninsula, Waterloo, Alma, Sevastopol, Lucknow, Ashantee 1873–74.

Motto *Nemo Me Impune Lacessit* (No one provokes me with impunity)

Uniform Doublet, scarlet; kilt, Black Watch tartan; facings blue

Regimental marches [Quick] *The Highland Laddie* (Tradit.)
[Slow] *In the Garb of Old Gaul* (Reid)

Nicknames The Watch. The Forty-Twa

73rd (PERTHSHIRE) REGIMENT OF FOOT

Originally raised in 1779 as 2nd Battalion of the 42nd (The Royal Highland) Regiment of Foot, but constituted a separate Regiment in April 1786, with the title 73rd (Highland) Regiment of Foot, the Colonel being Major-General Sir George Osborn.

Titles 1779 2nd Battalion 42nd (The Royal Highland) Regiment of Foot

1786 73rd (Highland) Regiment of Foot

1809 73rd Regiment of Foot

1862 73rd (Perthshire) Regiment of Foot

1881 Amalgamated with the 42nd Royal Highland Regiment of Foot (The Black Watch) to form The Black Watch (Royal Highlanders)

Battle honours Mangalore, Mysore, Seringapatam, Waterloo, South Africa 1846–47, 1851, 52, 53.

Uniform Scarlet, facings dark green

Regimental march [Quick] *My Love is like a Red Red Rose*

THE DUKE OF EDINBURGH'S ROYAL REGIMENT
(BERKSHIRE AND WILTSHIRE)
(49th, 62nd, 66th, 99th)

Formed June 1959 by amalgamation of The Royal Berkshire Regiment (Princess Charlotte of Wales's) and The Wiltshire Regiment (Duke of Edinburgh's).

Battle honours Louisburg, St. Lucia 1778, Egmont-op-Zee, Copenhagen, Douro, Talavera, Albuhera, Queenstown, Vittoria, Pyrenees, Nivelle, Nive, Orthes, Peninsula, China (with the Dragon), New Zealand, Ferozeshah, Sobraon, Alma, Inkerman, Sevastopol, Pekin 1860, Kandahar 1880, Afghanistan 1879–80, Egypt 1882, Tofrek, Suakin 1885, South Africa 1879, 1899–1902.

The Great War—Mons, Le Cateau, Retreat from Mons, Marne 1914, Aisne 1914, 18, La Bassee 1914, Messines 1914, 17, 18, Armentieres 1914, Ypres 1914, 17, Langemarck 1914, 17, Gheluvelt, Nonne Bosschen, Neuve Chappelle, Aubers, Festubert 1915, Loos, Somme 1916, 18, Albert 1916, 18, Bazentin, Delville Wood, Pozieres, Flers-Courcelette, Morval, Thiepval, Le Transloy, Ancre Heights, Ancre 1916, 18, Arras 1917, 18, Scarpe 1917, 18, Arleux, Pilckem, Menin Road, Polygon Wood, Broodseinde, Poelcappelle, Passchendaele, Cambrai 1917, 18, St. Quentin, Bapaume 1918, Rosieres, Avre, Villers Bretonneux, Lys, Hazebrouck, Bailleul, Kemmel, Bethune, Scherpenberg Amiens, Hindenburg Line, Havrincourt, Epehy, Canal du Nord, St. Quentin Canal, Beaurevoir, Selle, Valenciennes, Sambre, France and Flanders 1914–18, Piave, Vittorio Veneto, Italy 1917–18, Doiran 1917, 18, Macedonia 1915–18, Suvla, Sari Bair, Gallipoli 1915–16, Gaza, Nebi Samwil, Jerusalem, Megiddo, Sharon, Palestine 1917–18, Tigris 1916, Kut al Amara 1917, Baghdad, Mesopotamia 1916–18.

The Second World War—Dyle, Defence of Arras, St. Omer-La Bassee, Ypres-Comines Canal, Dunkirk 1940,

Normandy Landing, Odon, Caen, Hill 112, Bourguebus
Ridge, Maltot, Mont Pincon, La Variniere, Seine 1944,
Nederrijn, Roer, Rhineland, Cleve, Goch, Xanten,
Rhine, Bremen, North-West Europe 1940, 44–45,
Solarino, Simeto Bridgehead, Pursuit to Messina, Sicily
1943, Monte Camino, Calabritto, Garigliano Crossing,
Minturno, Damiano, Anzio, Carroceto, Rome, Advance
to Tiber, Italy 1943–45, Middle East 1942, Donbaik,
North Arakan, Point 551, Mayu Tunnels, Ngakyedauk
Pass, Kohima, Mao Songsang, Shwebo, Kyaukmyaung
Bridgehead, Mandalay, Fort Dufferin, Rangoon Road,
Toungoo, Burma 1942–45.

Uniform	Scarlet, piping white, facings blue
Regimental marches [Quick]	*The Farmer's Boy*
[Slow]	*Auld Robin Grey*
Regimental journal	*The Journal of The Duke of Edinburgh's Royal Regiment*
Regimental headquarters	The Wardrobe, 58 The Close, Salisbury, Wiltshire SP1 2EX
Regimental museum	As above

THE ROYAL BERKSHIRE REGIMENT
(PRINCESS CHARLOTTE OF WALES'S)
(49th and 66th)

Formed 1881 by amalgamation of the 49th (Princess
Charlotte of Wales's or Hertfordshire) Regiment of Foot
with the 66th (Berkshire) Regiment of Foot.

Titles 1881 Princess Charlotte of Wales's (Berkshire Regiment)
1885 Princess Charlotte of Wales's (Royal Berkshire Regiment)
1921 The Royal Berkshire Regiment (Princess Charlotte of Wales's)

Battle honours St. Lucia 1778, Egmont-op-Zee, Copenhagen, Douro,
Talavera, Albuhera, Queenstown, Vittoria, Pyrenees,
Nivelle, Nive, Orthes, Peninsula, Alma, Inkerman,
Sevastopol, Kandahar 1880, Afghanistan 1879–80, Egypt
1882, Tofrek, Suakin 1885, China (with the Dragon),
South Africa 1899–1902.

The Great War—16 *Battalions*—Mons, Retreat from Mons, Marne 1914, Aisne 1914, 18, Ypres 1914, 17, Langemarck 1914, 17, Gheluvelt, Nonne Bosschen, Neuve Chapelle, Aubers, Festubert 1915, Loos, Somme 1916, 18, Albert 1916, 18, Bazentin, Delville Wood, Pozieres, Flers-Courcelette, Morval, Thiepval, Le Transloy, Ancre Heights, Ancre 1916, 18, Arras 1917, 18, Scarpe 1917, 18, Arleux, Pilckem, Polygon Wood, Broodseinde, Poelcappelle, Passchendaele, Cambrai 1917, 18, St. Quentin, Bapaume 1918, Rosieres, Avre, Villers Bretonneux, Lys, Hazebrouck, Bethune, Amiens, Hindenburg Line, Havrincourt, Epehy, Canal du Nord, St. Quentin Canal, Selle, Valenciennes, Sambre, France and Flanders 1914–18, Piave, Vittorio Veneto, Italy 1917–18, Doiran 1917–18, Macedonia 1915–18.

The Second World War—Dyle, St. Omer-La Bassee, Dunkirk 1940, Normandy Landing, Rhine, North-West Europe 1940, 44–45, Pursuit to Messina, Sicily 1943, Monte Camino, Calabritto, Garigliano Crossing, Damiano, Anzio, Carroceto, Italy 1943–45, Donbaik, Kohima, Mao Songsang, Shwebo, Kyaukmyaung Bridgehead, Mandalay, Fort Dufferin, Rangoon Road, Toungoo, Burma 1942–45.

Uniform Scarlet, piping white, facings blue

Regimental marches [Quick] *The Dashing White Sergeant* and *The Farmer's Boy*

Regimental journal *The China Dragon*

Nickname The Biscuit Boys

Remarks The 'Royal' title was granted by Queen Victoria in recognition of the 1st Battalion's valour at the battle of Tofrek (Sudan), 22nd March 1885.

49th (PRINCESS CHARLOTTE OF WALES'S OR HERTFORDSHIRE) REGIMENT OF FOOT

Raised in Jamaica, December 1743, by Colonel Edward Trelawny, the Governor, who amalgamated the eight independent companies garrisoning the island.

Titles   1743 Colonel Trelawny's Regiment of Foot (63rd Foot)
1748 49th Regiment of Foot
1782 49th (or Hertfordshire) Regiment of Foot
1816 49th (Princess Charlotte of Wales's or Hertfordshire) Regiment of Foot
1881 Amalgamated with the 66th (Berkshire) Regiment of Foot to form Princess Charlotte of Wales's (Berkshire Regiment)

Battle honours   St. Lucia 1778, Egmont-op-Zee, Copenhagen, China (with the Dragon), Queenstown, Alma, Inkerman, Sevastopol.

Uniform   Scarlet, facings full green

Regimental march [Quick]   *The Dashing White Sergeant*

66th (BERKSHIRE) REGIMENT OF FOOT

Originated in 1755 as 2nd Battalion, 19th Regiment of Foot (Green Howards). Augmented as separate Regiment in April 1758 under Colonel Edward Sandford, and ranked as 66th Foot.

Titles   1755 2nd Battalion, 19th Regiment of Foot
1758 66th Regiment of Foot
1782 66th (Berkshire) Regiment of Foot
1881 Amalgamated with the 49th (Princess Charlotte of Wales's or Hertfordshire) Regiment of Foot to form Princess Charlotte of Wales's (Berkshire Regiment)

Battle honours   Douro, Talavera, Albuhera, Vittoria, Pyrenees, Nivelle, Nive, Orthes, Peninsula, Kandahar 1880, Afghanistan 1879–80.

Uniform   Scarlet, piping white, facings gosling green

Regimental marches [Quick]   *The Farmer's Boy* and *Young May Moon*

Remarks   The heroic stand of the 66th at Maiwand, Afghanistan (1880), when they defended their Colours to the last man, is commemorated by an impressive memorial in Reading, the Regiment's depot before amalgamation with the Wiltshire.

THE WILTSHIRE REGIMENT
(DUKE OF EDINBURGH'S)

Formed 1881 by amalgamation of 62nd (Wiltshire) Regiment of Foot with 99th (Duke of Edinburgh's) Regiment of Foot.

Titles 1881 The Duke of Edinburgh's (Wiltshire Regiment)
1920 The Wiltshire Regiment (Duke of Edinburgh's)

Battle honours Louisburg, Nive, Peninsula, New Zealand, Ferozeshah, Sobraon, Sevastopol, Pekin 1860, South Africa 1879, 1900–02.

The Great War—12 *Battalions*—Mons, Le Cateau, Retreat from Mons, Marne 1914, Aisne 1914, 18, La Bassee 1914, Messines 1914, 17, 18, Armentieres 1914, Ypres 1914, 17, Langemarck 1914, Nonne Bosschen, Neuve Chapelle, Aubers, Festubert 1915, Loos, Somme 1916, 18, Albert 1916, 18, Bazentin, Pozieres, Le Transloy, Ancre Heights, Ancre 1916, Arras 1917, Scarpe 1917, Pilckem, Menin Road, Polygon Wood, Broodseinde, Poelcappelle, Passchendaele, St. Quentin, Lys, Bailleul, Kemmel, Scherpenberg, Bapaume 1918, Hindenburg Line, Epehy, Canal du Nord, St. Quentin Canal, Beaurevoir, Cambrai 1918, Selle, Sambre, France and Flanders 1914–18, Doiran 1917, Macedonia 1915–18, Suvla, Sari Bair, Gallipoli 1915–16, Gaza, Nebi Samwil, Jerusalem, Megiddo, Sharon, Palestine 1917–18, Tigris 1916, Kut al Amara 1917, Baghdad, Mesopotamia 1916–18.

The Second World War—Defence of Arras, Ypres-Comines Canal, Odon, Caen, Hill 112, Bourguebus Ridge, Maltot, Mont Pincon, La Variniere, Seine 1944, Nederrijn, Roer, Rhineland, Cleve, Goch, Xanten, Rhine, Bremen, North-West Europe 1940, 44–45, Solarino, Simeto Bridgehead, Sicily 1943, Garigliano Crossing, Minturno, Anzio, Rome, Advance to Tiber, Italy 1943–44, Middle East 1942, North Arakan, Point 551, Mayu Tunnels, Ngakyedauk Pass, Burma 1943–44.

Uniform Scarlet, piping and facings buff

Regimental marches [Quick] *The Wiltshire*
[Slow] *Auld Robin Grey*

Regimental journal *The Journal of the Wiltshire Regiment*

Nicknames The Moonrakers. The Springers

62nd (WILTSHIRE) REGIMENT OF FOOT

Originated in 1756 as 2nd Battalion, 4th (King's Own) Regiment. Augmented as separate Regiment, April 1758, under Colonel William Strode, and ranked as 62nd Foot.

Titles 1756 2nd Battalion 4th (King's Own) Regiment of Foot
1758 62nd Regiment of Foot
1782 62nd (Wiltshire) Regiment of Foot
1881 Amalgamated with the 99th (Duke of Edinburgh's) Regiment of Foot to form The Duke of Edinburgh's (Wiltshire Regiment)

Battle honours Louisburg, Nive, Peninsula, Ferozeshah, Sobraon, Sevastopol.

Uniform Scarlet, facings buff

Regimental marches [Quick] *The Vly be on The Turmit*
[Slow] *May Blossoms*

Nicknames The Moonrakers. The Springers

Remarks During their stubborn defence of Carrickfergus Castle against French invaders in 1758 the 62nd, out of ammunition, resorted to firing their tunic buttons, and in commemoration were accorded the distinction of wearing a dent or 'splash' on their buttons.

99th (DUKE OF EDINBURGH'S) REGIMENT OF FOOT

Raised March 1824 as 99th (Lanarkshire) Regiment of Foot with Major-General Gage John Hall as Colonel.

Titles 1824 99th (or Lanarkshire) Regiment of Foot
1874 99th (Duke of Edinburgh's) Regiment of Foot

1881 Amalgamated with the 62nd (Wiltshire) Regiment of Foot to form The Duke of Edinburgh's (Wiltshire Regiment)

Battle honours New Zealand, Pekin 1860, South Africa 1879.

Uniform Scarlet, facings yellow

Regimental marches [Quick] *Blue Bonnets over the Border*
[Slow] *Auld Robin Grey*

Nicknames The Queen's Pets. The Nines

THE ROYAL MARINES

Numerous regiments of Marines had been raised and disbanded before the permanent establishment of what became the present Corps in 1755. The earliest of these was the Duke of York and Albany's Maritime Regiment of Foot, raised in 1664 and later known as The Lord High Admiral's Regiment. Other regiments of Foot for 'sea service' came into being during the wars of the 18th century, only to be disbanded at the conclusion of hostilities.

With the growth of British overseas possessions and the Royal Navy increasingly committed to world-wide operations, the need for a permanent body of soldiers to support the Fleet became pressing, and in 1755 such a body was established with the title 'The Marine Corps'. It comprised 5000 regular officers and soldiers and was distributed in three 'Grand Divisions' based at Chatham, Portsmouth and Plymouth. This was the true origin of the present Corps, the title 'Royal Marines' being conferred by King George III in 1802.

In 1804 the Corps was augmented by the formation of artillery companies, later to become the Royal Marine Artillery, and in 1855 the remainder of the Corps were designated Light Infantry, the title Royal Marine Light Infantry being adopted in 1862. In 1923 the RMA and the RMLI were amalgamated under the earlier title, The Royal Marines.

The first Royal Marine Commando units were formed in 1942. The Army Commandos were disbanded in 1946 and thenceforth the Commando role passed exclusively to The Royal Marines.

Since the Corps comes under Admiralty, not Army control, it will not be found in the *Army List*, although its officers are listed therein.

Motto *Per Mare per Terram* (By sea by land)

Uniform Blue, facings scarlet

Corps marches [Quick] *A Life on the Ocean Wave* (Russell)
[Slow] *The Preobrajensky March* (Donajowsky)

This was the March of the Preobrajensky Guards, senior regiment of the Imperial Russian Foot Guards. It was presented to The Royal Marines in 1964 by Earl Mountbatten of Burma, whose Uncle the Grand Duke Serge Alexandrovitch was one of the last Colonels of the Preobrajensky Guards.

In addition to the above, the Royal Marine Commandos have their own March, entitled *Sarie Marais*. This was a Boer trekking song and it commemorates both the term 'commando' adopted by the Boers, and the services of many South African officers in The Royal Marines during the Second World War.

Corps journal *The Globe and Laurel*

Corps headquarters Department of the Commandant General Royal Marines, Ministry of Defence (Navy), Whitehall, London SW1

Corps museum Eastney Barracks, Southsea, Hampshire PO4 9PX

Nicknames The Jollies (not generally used since World War II). Bootnecks

Remarks It will be seen that no Battle Honours are listed for The Royal Marines. In 1827 King George IV was asked to select Honours for display on the Colours from a list of 106 actions placed before him. The reply was:

> The greatness of their number and the difficulty of selecting from amidst so many glorious deeds, such a portion as could be inserted in this space, determined His Majesty in lieu of the usual badges and mottoes on the Colours . . . to direct that the Globe encircled with the Laurel should be the distinguishing Badge as the most appropriate emblem of a Corps, whose duties carried them to all parts of the Globe, in every quarter of which they had earned laurels by their valour and good conduct.

THE YORK AND LANCASTER REGIMENT

(65th and 84th)

Formed 1881 by amalgamation of the 65th (2nd Yorkshire, North Riding) Regiment of Foot with the 84th (York and Lancaster) Regiment of Foot.

Rather than accept amalgamation, this Regiment was disbanded on 14th December 1968, and its Colours were laid up in the Regimental Chapel, Sheffield Cathedral. However, its title and Battle Honours continue to be shown in the Army Lists.

Battle honours Guadaloupe 1759, Martinique 1794, India 1796–1819, Nive, Peninsula, Arabia, New Zealand, Lucknow, Tel-el-Kebir, Egypt 1882–1884, Relief of Ladysmith, South Africa 1899–1902.

The Great War—Aisne 1914, Armentieres 1914, Ypres 1915, 17, 18, Gravenstafel, St. Julien, Frezenberg, Bellewaarde, Hooge 1915, Loos, Somme 1916, 18, Albert 1916, Pozieres, Flers-Courcelette, Morval, Thiepval, Le Transloy, Ancre Heights, Ancre 1916, Arras 1917, 18, Scarpe 1917, 18, Arleux, Oppy, Messines 1917, 18, Langemarck 1917, Menin Road, Polygon Wood, Broodseinde, Poelcappelle, Passchendaele, Cambrai 1917, 18, St. Quentin, Bapaume 1918, Lys, Hazebrouck, Bailleul, Kemmel, Scherpenberg, Marne 1918, Tardenois, Drocourt-Queant, Hindenburg Line, Havrincourt, Epehy, Canal du Nord, Selle, Valenciennes, Sambre, France and Flanders 1914–18, Piave, Vittorio Veneto, Italy 1917–18, Struma, Doiran 1917, Macedonia 1915–18, Suvla, Landing at Suvla, Scimitar Hill, Gallipoli 1915, Egypt 1916.

The Second World War—Norway 1940, Odon, Fontenay Le Pesnil, Caen, La Vie Crossing, La Touques Crossing, Foret de Bretonne, Le Havre, Antwerp-Turnhout Canal, Scheldt, Lower Maas, Arnhem 1945, North-West Europe 1940, 44–45, Tobruk 1941, Tobruk Sortie 1941, Mine de Sedjenane, Djebel Kournine, North Africa 1941, 43, Landing in Sicily, Simeto Bridgehead, Pursuit to

Messina, Sicily 1943, Salerno, Vietri Pass, Capture of
Naples, Cava di Terreni, Volturno Crossing, Monte
Camino, Calabritto, Colle Cedro, Gargliano Crossing,
Minturno, Monte Tuga, Anzio, Advance to Tiber,
Gothic Line, Coriano, San Clemente, Gemmano Ridge,
Carpineta, Lamone Crossing, Defence of Lamone
Bridgehead, Rimini Line, San Marino, Italy 1943–45,
Crete, Heraklion, Middle East 1941, North Arakan,
Maungdaw, Rangoon Road, Toungoo, Arakan Beaches,
Chindits 1944, Burma 1943–45.

Uniform Scarlet, facings white

Regimental marches [Quick] *The York and Lancaster* (Winterbottom)
The Jockey of York (Tradit.)
[Slow] *The Regimental Slow March of The York and Lancaster Regiment*

Regimental journal *The Tiger and Rose*

Regimental headquarters Endcliffe Hall, Endcliffe Vale Road, Sheffield S10 3EU

Regimental museum As above

Nicknames The Young and Lovelies. The Royal Tigers. The Twin Roses

Remarks The York and Lancaster was the only Regiment of the British Army to bear the Battle Honour *Arabia*, gained by the 65th Foot for distinguished services in the Gulf in 1809 and 1821.

65th (2nd YORKSHIRE, NORTH RIDING) REGIMENT OF FOOT

Originated in 1756 as 2nd Battalion 12th Foot (The Suffolk Regiment). In April 1758 the Battalion was augmented as a separate Regiment, ranking as 65th Foot, with Major-General Robert Armiger as Colonel.

Titles 1756 2nd Battalion 12th Regiment of Foot
1758 65th Regiment of Foot
1782 65th (2nd Yorkshire, North Riding) Regiment of Foot
1881 Amalgamated with 84th (York and Lancaster) Regiment of Foot to form The York and Lancaster Regiment

Battle honours Guadaloupe 1759, Martinique 1794, India, Arabia, New Zealand.

Uniform Scarlet, facings white

Regimental marches [Quick] *The York and Lancaster* (Winterbottom)
[Slow] *War March of the Priests* (Mendelssohn)

Nickname The Royal Tigers

84th (YORK AND LANCASTER) REGIMENT OF FOOT

Raised March 1794 by Lieutenant-Colonel George Bernard and ranked as 84th Foot.

Titles 1794 84th Regiment of Foot
1809 84th (York and Lancaster) Regiment of Foot
1881 Amalgamated with the 65th (2nd Yorkshire, North Riding) Regiment of Foot to form The York and Lancaster Regiment

Battle honours Nive, Peninsula, India (with the Royal Tiger), Lucknow.

Uniform Scarlet, facings yellow

Regimental marches [Quick] *The Jockey of York* (Tradit.)
[Slow] (Untitled)

QUEEN'S OWN HIGHLANDERS
(SEAFORTH AND CAMERONS)
(72nd, 78th, 79th)

Formed 7th February 1961 by amalgamation of the Seaforth Highlanders (Ross-Shire Buffs, The Duke of Albany's) with The Queen's Own Cameron Highlanders.

Battle honours Carnatic, Hindoostan, Mysore, Egmont-op-Zee, Egypt (with the Sphinx), Assaye, Cape of Good Hope 1806, Maida, Corunna, Busaco, Fuentes d'Onor, Java, Salamanca, Pyrenees, Nivelle, Nive, Toulouse,

Peninsula, Waterloo, South Africa 1835, Alma,
Sevastopol, Koosh-ab, Persia, Lucknow, Central India,
Peiwar Kotal, Charasiah, Kabul 1879, Kandahar 1880,
Afghanistan 1878–80, Tel-el-Kebir, Egypt 1882, Nile
1884–85, Chitral, Atbara, Khartoum, Paardeberg, South
Africa 1899–1902.

The Great War—Le Cateau, Retreat from Mons, Marne
1914, 18, Aisne 1914, La Bassee 1914, Armentieres
1914, Ypres 1914, 15, 17, 18, Langemarck 1914,
Gheluvelt, Nonne Bosschen, Festubert 1914, 15,
Givenchy 1914, Neuve Chapelle, Hill 60, Gravenstafel,
St. Julien, Frezenberg, Bellewaarde, Aubers, Loos,
Somme 1916, 18, Albert 1916, Bazentin, Delville Wood,
Pozieres, Flers-Courcelette, Morval, Le Transloy, Ancre
Heights, Ancre 1916, Arras 1917, 18, Vimy 1917, Scarpe
1917, 18, Arleux, Pilckem, Menin Road, Polygon Wood,
Broodseinde, Poelcappelle, Passchendaele, Cambrai
1917, 18, St. Quentin, Bapaume 1918, Lys, Estaires,
Messines 1918, Hazebrouck, Bailleul, Kemmel, Bethune,
Soissonais-Ourcq, Tardenois, Drocourt-Queant,
Hindenburg Line, Epehy, St. Quentin Canal, Courtrai,
Selle, Valenciennes, Sambre, France and Flanders 1914–
18, Struma, Macedonia 1915–18, Megiddo, Sharon,
Palestine 1918, Tigris 1916, Kut al Amara 1917,
Baghdad, Mesopotamia 1915–18.

The Second World War—Defence of Escaut, St. Omer-
La Bassee, Ypres-Comines Canal, Somme 1940,
Withdrawal to Seine, St. Valery-en-Caux, Odon, Cheux,
Caen, Troarn, Mont Pincon, Quarry Hill, Falaise,
Falaise Road, Dives Crossing, La Vie Crossing, Lisieux,
Nederrijn, Best, Le Havre, Lower Maas, Meijel, Venlo
Pocket, Ourthe, Rhineland, Reichswald, Goch,
Moyland, Rhine, Uelzen, Artlenberg, North-West
Europe 1940, 44–45, Agordat, Keren, Abyssinia 1941,
Sidi Barrani, Tobruk 1941, 42, Gubi II, Carmusa,
Gazala, El Alamein, Advance on Tripoli, Mareth, Wadi
Zigzaou, Akarit, Djebel Roumana, North Africa 1940–
43, Landing in Sicily, Augusta, Francofonte, Adrano,
Sferro Hills, Sicily 1943, Garigliano Crossing, Anzio,
Cassino I, Poggio del Grillo, Gothic Line, Tavoleto,
Coriano, Pian di Castello, Monte Reggiano, Rimini
Line, San Marino, Italy 1943–44, Madagascar, Middle
East 1942, Imphal, Shenam Pass, Litan, Kohima, Relief
of Kohima, Naga Village, Aradura, Tengnoupal,
Shwebo, Mandalay, Ava, Irrawaddy, Mt. Popa, Burma
1942–45.

Motto   *Cuidich 'n Righ* (Help to the King)

Uniform   Doublet, piper green; Tartans, Mackenzie tartan (Seaforth sett), and 79th or Cameron of Erracht tartan; facings buff and blue

Regimental marches [Quick]   Arrangement of *Scotland for Ever* and *The March of the Cameron Men* (Tradit.)

[Slow]   *The Garb of Old Gaul* (Reid)

Regimental journal   *The Queen's Own Highlander*

Regimental headquarters   Cameron Barracks, Inverness, Scotland IV2 3XD

Regimental museum   Fort George, Ardersier, By Inverness, Scotland

Remarks   The Queen's Own Highlanders are the only Regiment to bear a Gaelic Motto (*Cuidich 'n Righ*) on Colours and appointments. This was inherited from the 78th Highlanders (qv).

SEAFORTH HIGHLANDERS
(ROSS-SHIRE BUFFS, THE DUKE OF ALBANY'S)

Formed 1881 by amalgamation of the 72nd (or the Duke of Albany's Own Highlanders) Regiment of Foot with the 78th (Highland) Regiment of Foot (or the Ross-Shire Buffs).

Battle honours   Carnatic, Hindoostan, Mysore, Assaye, Cape of Good Hope 1806, Maida, Java, South Africa 1835, Sevastopol, Koosh-ab, Persia, Lucknow, Central India, Peiwar Kotal, Charasiah, Kabul 1879, Kandahar 1880, Afghanistan 1878–80, Tel-el-Kebir, Egypt 1882, Chitral, Atbara, Khartoum, Paardeberg, South Africa 1899–1902.

The Great War—19 *Battalions*—Le Cateau, Retreat from Mons, Marne 1914, 18, Aisne 1914, La Bassee 1914, Armentieres 1914, Festubert 1914, 15, Givenchy 1914, Neuve Chapelle, Ypres 1915, 17, 18, St. Julien, Frezenberg, Bellewaarde, Aubers, Loos, Somme 1916, 18, Albert 1916, Bazentin, Delville Wood, Pozieres, Flers-Courcelette, Le Transloy, Ancre Heights, Ancre 1916, Arras 1917, 18, Vimy 1917, Scarpe 1917, 18, Arleux, Pilckem, Menin Road, Polygon Wood, Broodseinde, Poelcappelle, Passchendaele, Cambrai 1917, 18, St. Quentin, Bapaume 1918, Lys, Estaires,

Messines 1918, Hazebrouck, Bailleul, Kemmel, Bethune, Soissonais-Ourcq, Tardenois, Drocourt-Queant, Hindenburg Line, Courtrai, Selle, Valenciennes, France and Flanders 1914–18, Macedonia 1917–18, Megiddo, Sharon, Palestine 1918, Tigris 1916, Kut al Amara 1917, Baghdad, Mesopotamia 1915–18.

The Second World War—Ypres-Comines Canal, Somme 1940, Withdrawal to Seine, St. Valery-en-Caux, Odon, Cheux, Caen, Troarn, Mont Pincon, Quarry Hill, Falaise, Falaise Road, Dives Crossing, La Vie Crossing, Lisieux, Nederrijn, Best, Le Havre, Lower Maas, Meijel, Venlo Pocket, Ourthe, Rhineland, Reichswald, Goch, Moyland, Rhine, Uelzen, Artlenberg, North-West Europe 1940, 44–45, El Alamein, Advance on Tripoli, Mareth, Wadi Zigzaou, Akarit, Djebel Roumana, North Africa 1942–43, Landing in Sicily, Augusta, Francofonte, Adrano, Sferro Hills, Sicily 1943, Garigliano Crossing, Anzio, Italy 1943–44, Madagascar, Middle East 1942, Imphal, Shenam Pass, Litan, Tengnoupal, Burma 1942–44.

Motto *Cuidich 'n Righ* (Help to the King)

Uniform Coatee, piper green; kilt, Mackenzie tartan (Seaforth sett); facings buff

Regimental march [Quick] *Blue Bonnets over the Border*

Regimental journal *Cabar Feidh*

Nicknames The Macraes. The King's Men

72nd (OR THE DUKE OF ALBANY'S OWN HIGHLANDERS) REGIMENT OF FOOT

Raised mainly in Ross-shire and Lewis, first mustered at Elgin, May 1778 by Lieutenant-Colonel Kenneth MacKenzie, Earl of Seaforth, and known as Seaforth's Highlanders. In the same year officially designated the 78th Regiment of (Highland) Foot. Renumbered 72nd in 1786.

Titles 1778 Seaforth's Highlanders, 78th Regiment of (Highland) Foot

1786 72nd (Highland) Regiment of Foot
1809 72nd Regiment of Foot
1823 72nd (or The Duke of Albany's Own Highlanders) Regiment of Foot
1881 Amalgamated with 78th (Highland) Regiment of Foot (or the Ross-Shire Buffs) to form Seaforth Highlanders (Ross-Shire Buffs, The Duke of Albany's)

Battle honours Carnatic, Hindoostan, Mysore, Cape of Good Hope 1806, South Africa 1835, Sevastopol, Central India, Peiwar Kotal, Charasiah, Kabul 1879, Kandahar 1880, Afghanistan 1878–80.

Motto *Cabar Feidh* (The Deer's Horns)

Uniform Scarlet, facings yellow; trews Royal Stuart tartan (Prince Charles Edward sett)

Regimental march [Quick] *Blue Bonnets over the Border*

Nickname The Macraes

78th (HIGHLAND) REGIMENT OF FOOT
(OR THE ROSS-SHIRE BUFFS)

Raised mainly in Ross-shire and Lewis, first mustered at Fort George, July 1793, by Lieutenant-Colonel Francis Humbertson Mackenzie (later Lord Seaforth, Baron Mackenzie of Kintail), and titled 78th (Highland) Regiment of Foot. The same officer raised a 2nd Battalion in 1794, with the title The Ross-Shire Buffs. Both Battalions were amalgamated in 1796.

Titles 1793 (1st Battalion) 78th (Highland) Regiment of Foot
1794 (2nd Battalion) 78th (Highland) Regiment of Foot, The Ross-Shire Buffs
1796 Battalions amalgamated with title 78th (Highland) Regiment of Foot (or the Ross-Shire Buffs)
1881 Amalgamated with 72nd (or The Duke of Albany's Own Highlanders) Regiment of Foot to form Seaforth Highlanders (Ross-Shire Buffs, The Duke of Albany's)

Battle honours Assaye (with the Elephant), Maida, Java, Kooshab, Persia, Lucknow, Afghanistan 1879–80.

Motto *Cuidich 'n Righ* (Help to the King)

Uniform Scarlet, facings buff; kilt Mackenzie of Seaforth tartan

Regimental march [Quick] *Pibroch of Donuil Dubh* (Pipes and Drums)

Remarks For gallantry at the Battle of Assaye (1803) the 78th were awarded an honorary third, or 'Assaye Colour', by the East India Company.

THE QUEEN'S OWN CAMERON HIGHLANDERS

Raised mainly in Lochaber and North Argyll in 1793, first mustered at Stirling in January 1794 by Major (afterwards Lieutenant-General Sir) Alan Cameron of Erracht. Designated 79th Foot.

Titles 1793 79th Regiment of Foot (or Cameronian Volunteers)
1804 79th Regiment of Foot (or Cameronian Highlanders)
1806 79th Regiment of Foot (or Cameron Highlanders)
1873 79th Queen's Own Cameron Highlanders
1881 The Queen's Own Cameron Highlanders

Battle honours Egmont-op-Zee, Egypt (with the Sphinx), Corunna, Busaco, Fuentes d'Onor, Salamanca, Pyrenees, Nivelle, Nive, Toulouse, Peninsula, Waterloo, Alma, Sevastopol, Lucknow, Tel-el-Kebir, Egypt 1882, Nile 1884–85, Atbara, Khartoum, South Africa 1900–02.

The Great War— 13 *Battalions*—Retreat from Mons, Marne 1914, 18, Aisne 1914, Ypres 1914, 15, 17, 18, Langemarck 1914, Gheluvelt, Nonne Bosschen, Givenchy 1914, Neuve Chapelle, Hill 60, Gravenstafel, St. Julien, Frezenberg, Bellewaarde, Aubers, Festubert 1915, Loos, Somme 1916, 18, Albert 1916, Bazentin, Delville Wood, Pozieres, Flers-Courcelette, Morval, Le Transloy, Ancre Heights, Arras 1917, 18, Scarpe 1917, Arleux, Pilckem, Menin Road, Polygon Wood, Poelcappelle, Passchendaele, St. Quentin, Bapaume 1918, Lys, Estaires, Messines 1918, Kemmel, Bethune, Soissonnais-Ourcq, Drocourt-Queant, Hindenburg Line, Epehy, St. Quentin Canal, Courtrai, Selle, Sambre, France and Flanders 1914–18, Struma, Macedonia 1915–18.

The Second World War—Defence of Escaut, St. Omer-La Bassee, Somme 1940, St. Valery-en-Caux, Falaise, Falaise Road, La Vie Crossing, Le Havre, Lower Maas, Venlo Pocket, Rhineland, Reichswald, Goch, Rhine, North-West Europe 1940, 44–45, Agordat, Keren, Abyssinia, 1941, Sidi Barrani, Tobruk 1941, 42, Gubi II, Carmusa, Gazala, El Alamein, Mareth, Wadi Zigzaou, Akarit, Djebel Roumana, North Africa 1940–43, Francofonte, Adrano, Sferro Hills, Sicily 1943, Cassino I, Poggio del Grillo, Gothic Line, Tavoleto, Coriano, Pian di Castello, Monte Reggiano, Rimini Line, San Marino, Italy 1944, Kohima, Relief of Kohima, Naga Village, Aradura, Shwebo, Mandalay, Ava, Irrawaddy, Mt. Popa, Burma 1944–45.

Uniform Coatee, piper green; kilt, 79th or Cameron of Erracht tartan; facings blue

Regimental marches [Quick] *Highland Laddie*
[Slow] *Logie of Buchan*

Regimental journal *The 79th News*

Nickname The Camerons

Remarks The 79th or Cameron of Erracht tartan is the only surviving military tartan not based on The Black Watch (or Government) tartan.

THE GORDON HIGHLANDERS
(75th and 92nd)

Formed 1881 by amalgamation of the 75th (Stirlingshire) Regiment of Foot with the 92nd (Gordon Highlanders) Regiment of Foot.

Battle honours Mysore, Seringapatam, Egmont-op-Zee, Mandora, India (with the Tiger), Egypt (with the Sphinx), Corunna, Fuentes d'Onor, Almaraz, Vittoria, Pyrenees, Nive, Orthes, Peninsula, Waterloo, South Africa 1835, Delhi 1857, Lucknow, Charasiah, Kabul 1879, Kandahar 1880, Afghanistan 1878–80, Tel-el-Kebir, Egypt 1882, 1884,

Nile 1884–85, Chitral, Tirah, Defence of Ladysmith, Paardeberg, South Africa 1899–1902.

The Great War—21 *Battalions*—Mons, Le Cateau, Retreat from Mons, Marne 1914, 18, Aisne 1914, La Bassee 1914, Messines 1914, Armentieres 1914, Ypres 1914, 15, 17, Langemarck 1914, Gheluvelt, Nonne Bosschen, Neuve Chapelle, Frezenberg, Bellewaarde, Aubers, Festubert 1915, Hooge 1915, Loos, Somme 1916, 18, Albert 1916, 18, Bazentin, Delville Wood, Pozieres, Guillemont, Flers-Courcelette, Le Transloy, Ancre 1916, Arras 1917, 18, Vimy 1917, Scarpe 1917, 18, Arleux, Bullecourt, Pilckem, Menin Road, Polygon Wood, Broodseinde, Poelcappelle, Passchendaele, Cambrai 1917, 18, St. Quentin, Bapaume 1918, Rosieres, Lys, Estaires, Hazebrouck, Bethune, Soissonnais-Ourcq, Tardenois, Hindenburg Line, Canal du Nord, Selle, Sambre, France and Flanders 1914–18, Piave, Vittorio Veneto, Italy 1917–18.

The Second World War—Withdrawal to Escaut, Ypres-Comines Canal, Dunkirk 1940, Somme 1940, St. Valery-en-Caux, Odon, La Vie Crossing, Lower Maas, Venlo Pocket, Rhineland, Reichswald, Cleve, Goch, Rhine, North-West Europe 1940, 44–45, El Alamein, Advance on Tripoli, Mareth, Medjez Plain, North Africa 1942–43, Landing in Sicily, Sferro, Sicily 1943, Anzio, Rome, Italy 1944–45.

Motto	*Bydand* (Stand Fast)
Uniform	Doublet, piper green; kilt, Gordon tartan; facings yellow
Regimental marches [Quick]	*Cock o' the North* (Tradit.)
[Slow]	*The Garb of Old Gaul* (Reid) and *St. Andrew's Cross*
Regimental journal	*The Tiger and Sphinx*
Regimental headquarters	Viewfield Road, Aberdeen, Scotland AB1 7XH
Regimental museum	As above

75th (STIRLINGSHIRE) REGIMENT OF FOOT

Raised at Stirling, October 1787, by Colonel Robert Abercromby, for service with the East India Company's forces.

Titles 1787 75th (Highland) Regiment of Foot (Also known as
Abercromby's Highlanders)
1807 75th Regiment of Foot
1862 75th (Stirlingshire) Regiment of Foot
1881 Amalgamated with 92nd (Gordon Highlanders)
Regiment of Foot to form The Gordon Highlanders

Battle honours Mysore, Seringapatam, India (with the Tiger), South
Africa 1835, Delhi 1857, Lucknow.

Uniform Scarlet, facings yellow

92nd (GORDON HIGHLANDERS) REGIMENT OF FOOT

Raised February 1794 by the 4th Duke of Gordon,
command being given to his son, George, Marquis of
Huntly, (later 5th, and last, Duke of Gordon). Ranked as
100th Regiment of Foot; renumbered 92nd in 1798.

Titles 1794 100th Regiment of Foot (Also known as 'Gordon
Highlanders')
1798 92nd Regiment of Foot (or 'Gordon Highlanders')
1861 92nd (Gordon Highlanders) Regiment of Foot
1881 Amalgamated with 75th (Stirlingshire) Regiment of
Foot to form The Gordon Highlanders

Battle honours Egmont-op-Zee, Mandora, Egypt (with the Sphinx),
Corunna, Fuentes d'Onor, Almaraz, Vittoria, Pyrenees,
Nive, Orthes, Peninsula, Waterloo, Charasiah, Kabul
1879, Kandahar 1880, Afghanistan 1879–80

Motto *Bydand* (Stand Fast)

Uniform Scarlet, facings yellow

Regimental march [Quick] *Cock o' the North*

THE ARGYLL AND SUTHERLAND HIGHLANDERS
(PRINCESS LOUISE'S)
(91st and 93rd)

Formed 1881 by amalgamation of 91st (Princess Louise's Argyllshire Highlanders) Regiment of Foot with 93rd (Sutherland Highlanders) Regiment of Foot.

Titles 1881 Princess Louise's (Sutherland and Argyll Highlanders)
1882 Princess Louise's (Argyll and Sutherland Highlanders)
1920 Argyll and Sutherland Highlanders (Princess Louise's)

Battle honours Cape of Good Hope 1806, Rolica, Vimiera, Corunna, Pyrenees, Nivelle, Nive, Orthes, Toulouse, Peninsula, South Africa 1846–47, 1851–52–53, Alma, Balaklava, Sevastopol, Lucknow, South Africa 1879, Modder River, Paardeberg, South Africa, 1899–1902.

The Great War— 27 *Battalions*—Mons, Le Cateau, Retreat from Mons, Marne 1914, 18, Aisne 1914, La Bassee 1914, Messines 1914, 18, Armentieres 1914, Ypres 1915, 17, 18, Gravenstafel, St. Julien, Frezenberg, Bellewaarde, Festubert 1915, Loos, Somme 1916, 18, Albert 1916, 18, Bazentin, Delville Wood, Pozieres, Flers-Courcelette, Morval, Le Transloy, Ancre Heights, Ancre 1916, Arras 1917, 18, Scarpe 1917, 18, Arleux, Pilckem, Menin Road, Polygon Wood, Broodseinde, Poelcappelle, Passchendaele, Cambrai 1917, 18, St. Quentin, Bapaume 1918, Rosieres, Lys, Estaires, Hazebrouck, Bailleul, Kemmel, Bethune, Soissonnais-Ourcq, Tardenois, Amiens, Hindenburg Line, Epehy, Canal du Nord, St. Quentin Canal, Beaurevoir, Courtrai, Selle, Sambre, France and Flanders 1914–18, Italy 1917–18, Struma, Doiran 1917, 18, Macedonia 1915–18, Gallipoli 1915–16, Rumani, Egypt 1916, Gaza, El Mughar, Nebi Samwil, Jaffa, Palestine 1917–18.

The Second World War—Somme 1940, Odon,
Tourmauville Bridge, Caen, Esquay, Mont Pincon,
Quarry Hill, Estry, Falaise, Dives Crossing, Aart, Lower
Maas, Meijel, Venlo Pocket, Ourthe, Rhineland,
Reichswald, Rhine, Uelzen, Artlenberg, North-West
Europe 1940, 44–45, Abyssinia 1941, Sidi Barrani, El
Alamein, Medenine, Akarit, Djebel Azzag 1942, Kef
Ouiba Pass, Mine de Sedjenane, Medjez Plain, Longstop
Hill 1943, North Africa 1940–43, Landing in Sicily,
Gerbini, Adrano, Centuripe, Sicily 1943, Termoli,
Sangro, Cassino II, Liri Valley, Aquino, Monte
Casalino, Monte Spaduro, Monte Grande, Senio,
Santerno Crossing, Argenta Gap, Italy 1943–45, Crete,
Heraklion, Middle East 1941, North Malaya, Grik Road,
Central Malaya, Ipoh, Slim River, Singapore Island,
Malaya 1941–42.

Pakchon, Korea, 1950–51.

Mottoes *Ne Obliviscaris* (Do not forget)
Sans Peur (Fearless)

Uniform Doublet, piper green; kilt, Black Watch tartan; facings
yellow

Regimental marches [Quick] *The Thin Red Line* (Alford) and *The Garb of
Old Gaul* (Reid)
[Slow] *The Skye Boat Song* (Kennedy-Fraser)

Regimental journal *The Thin Red Line*

Regimental headquarters The Castle, Stirling, Scotland FK8 1EH

Regimental museum As above

Nickname The Thin Red Line

Remarks The Argyll and Sutherland Highlanders are the only
infantry Regiment to bear the Battle Honour *Balaklava*,
in which action the 93rd stood firm to repel a large force
of Russian cavalry, thus also earning their nickname 'The
Thin Red Line'. During the relief of Lucknow in 1857
the same Regiment gained six VCs.

In 1970 the Regiment was threatened with
disbandment, but public outcry was such that it was
permitted to survive in the attenuated form of one
company, aptly named the 'Balaklava Company'. In April
1972 the Regiment was reformed with one Regular
Battalion as before.

91st (PRINCESS LOUISE'S ARGYLLSHIRE HIGHLANDERS) REGIMENT OF FOOT

Raised February 1794 by Colonel Duncan Campbell of Lochnell, and ranked as 98th Foot. Renumbered 91st in 1798.

Titles 1794 98th (Argyllshire) Regiment of Foot (Highlanders)
1798 91st (Argyllshire) Regiment of Foot (Highlanders)
1809 91st Regiment of Foot
1820 91st (Argyllshire) Regiment of Foot
1864 91st (Argyllshire Highlanders) Regiment of Foot
1872 91st (Princess Louise's Argyllshire Highlanders) Regiment of Foot
1881 Amalgamated with 93rd (Sutherland Highlanders) Regiment of Foot to form Princess Louise's (Sutherland and Argyll Highlanders)

Battle honours Rolica, Vimiera, Corunna, Pyrenees, Nivelle, Nive, Orthes, Toulouse, Peninsula, South Africa 1846–47, 1851–52–53, 1879.

Motto *Ne Obliviscaris* (Do not forget)

Uniform Scarlet, facings yellow

Regimental march [Quick] *The Campbells are Coming* (Tradit.)

93rd (SUTHERLAND HIGHLANDERS) REGIMENT OF FOOT

Raised April 1799 by General William Wemyss of Wemyss.

Titles 1799 93rd (Highland) Regiment of Foot
1861 93rd (Sutherland Highlanders) Regiment of Foot
1881 Amalgamated with 91st (Princess Louise's Argyllshire Highlanders) to form Princess Louise's (Sutherland and Argyll Highlanders)

Battle honours Cape of Good Hope 1806, Alma, Balaklava, Sevastopol, Lucknow.

Motto *Sans Peur* (Fearless)

Uniform Doublet, scarlet; kilt, Government tartan; facings yellow

Regimental march [Quick] *Highland Laddie* (Tradit.)

Nickname The Thin Red Line

THE PARACHUTE REGIMENT

The Regiment was officially formed on 1st August 1942, but its personnel have always regarded June 1940 as the true birth date, when on Churchill's orders the first battalion of volunteer parachute troops was formed at Ringway Airport, near Manchester. Formed from No 2 Commando, the unit was renamed 11th Special Air Service Battalion in November 1940 and became 1st Parachute Battalion in September 1941. During 1941–42 three more battalions were formed, and the four were regimented on 1st August 1942 as The Parachute Regiment.

For administrative purposes The Parachute Regiment was attached to the Army Air Corps (qv), but in 1949 this connection was severed; the Regiment became a corps in its own right as part of the Infantry of the Line, and now takes precedence after the Argyll and Sutherland Highlanders.

Until 1953 the Regiment was manned by volunteers seconded from other units, but in that year direct enlistment for Other Ranks was authorised. In 1958 a Regular cadre of Officers was approved, and since then officers have been commissioned direct from the RMA Sandhurst.

Battle honours *The Second World War*—Bruneval, Normandy Landing, Pegasus Bridge, Merville Battery, Breville, Dives Crossing, La Touques Crossing, Arnhem 1944, Ourthe, Rhine, Southern France, North-West Europe 1942, 44–45, Soudia, Oudna, Djebel Azzag 1943, Djebel Alliliga, El Hadjeba, Tamera, Djebel Dahra, Kef el Debna,

North Africa 1942–43, Primosole Bridge, Sicily 1943, Taranto, Orsogna, Italy 1943–44, Athens, Greece 1944–45.

Falkland Islands 1982, Goose Green, Mount Longdon, Wireless Ridge.

Motto	*Utrinque Paratus* (Ready for anything)
Uniform	Cambridge blue piping with maroon facings
Regimental march [Quick]	*Ride of the Valkyrie* (Wagner)
Regimental journal	*Pegasus*
Regimental headquarters	Browning Barracks, Aldershot, Hampshire GU11 2BU
Regimental museum	Airborne Forces Museum, as above
Nicknames	Red Devils. The Paras
Remarks	The two most recent awards of the Victoria Cross were gazetted posthumously to Lieutenant-Colonel Herbert Jones OBE of 2 Para and Sergeant Ian John McKay of 3 Para for their gallantry with the Falklands Task Force, May/June 1982.

THE BRIGADE OF GURKHAS

After the Treaty of Friendship which concluded the Nepalese Wars of 1814–16, it was agreed that Gurkha hillmen from Nepal should be voluntarily enlisted to serve in the armies of the Hon. East India Company. On the abolition of that Company and transfer of government to the Crown in 1858, the Gurkha regiments were absorbed in the (British) Indian Army.

With the granting of Independence to India in 1947, a tripartite agreement between Britain, India and Nepal decreed that four of the ten regiments of Gurkha Rifles should be transferred to the British Army, the remaining six continuing in the new Indian Army.

In January 1948 the following four regiments were constituted as the Brigade of Gurkhas and incorporated in the British Army:

2nd King Edward VII's Own Gurkha Rifles (The

Sirmoor Rifles)
6th Gurkha Rifles
7th Gurkha Rifles
10th Gurkha Rifles

Subsequently the Brigade was augmented with its own supporting units: The Queen's Gurkha Engineers, Queen's Gurkha Signals and Gurkha Transport Regiment.

Recruiting for the Brigade, on a voluntary basis, continues to be organised by Gurkha officers in Nepal. Suitably qualified Gurkha candidates can now be admitted to the RMA Sandhurst as officer cadets and receive Regular commissions in the normal way. But such officers can serve only in Gurkha regiments.

Another class of officer in the Gurkhas is the Queen's Gurkha Officer (QGO) who, despite the title, does not hold the Queen's commission, but is midway between Warrant and full commission rank, and is equivalent to the former VCO or Viceroy's Commissioned Officer of the (British) Indian Army.

The splendid fighting qualities of the Gurkha soldiers and their unswerving loyalty are exemplified by their Motto.

Motto *Kaphar Hunnu Bhanda Marnu Ramro* (It is better to die than to live a coward)

Brigade headquarters Hong Kong (BFPO 1)

Brigade museum Queen Elizabeth Barracks, Church Crookham, Aldershot, Hampshire GU13 ORJ

Brigade journal *The Kukri*

2nd KING EDWARD VII's OWN GURKHA RIFLES
(THE SIRMOOR RIFLES)

Raised April 1815 at Nahan in Sirmoor, from Nepalese recruits.

Titles 1815 The Sirmoor Battalion
1823 8th or Sirmoor Local Battalion
1858 The Sirmoor Rifle Regiment
1861 2nd Goorkha Regiment

1864 2nd Goorkha (The Sirmoor Rifles) Regiment

1876 2nd (The Prince of Wales's Own) Gurkha Regiment (The Sirmoor Rifles)

1906 2nd King Edward's Own Gurkha Rifles (The Sirmoor Regiment)

1922 2nd King Edward VII's Own Gurkha Rifles (The Sirmoor Rifles)

Battle honours Bhurtpore, Aliwal, Sobraon, Delhi 1857, Kabul 1879, Kandahar 1880, Afghanistan 1878–80, Tirah, Punjaub Frontier.

The Great War—La Bassee 1914, Festubert 1914–15, Givenchy 1914, Neuve Chapelle, Aubers, Loos, France and Flanders 1914–15, Egypt 1915, Tigris 1916, Kut al Amara 1917, Baghdad 1915, Mesopotamia 1916, 18, Persia 1918, Baluchistan 1918.

Afghanistan 1919.

The Second World War—El Alamein, Mareth, Akarit, Djebel el Meida, Enfidaville, Tunis, North Africa 1942–43, Cassino I, Monastery Hill, Pian di Maggio, Gothic Line, Coriano, Poggio San Giovanni, Monte Reggiano, Italy 1944–45, Greece 1944–45, North Malaya, Jitra, Central Malaya, Kampar, Slim River, Johore, Singapore Island, Malaya 1941–42, North Arakan, Irrawaddy, Magwe, Sittang 1945, Point 1433, Arakan Beaches, Myebon, Tamandu, Chindits 1943, Burma 1943–45.

Uniform Rifle green, piping and facings scarlet

Regimental marches [Quick] *Lutzow's Wild Hunt* and *Wha's the Steer Kimmer*

Remarks When the Sirmoor Battalion was honoured by being made a Rifle Regiment after the Indian Mutiny it was obliged to relinquish its Colours (never carried by Rifles). In recognition of its gallant services during the siege of Delhi, Queen Victoria directed that the laid-up Colours should be replaced by a 6-ft bronze 'Truncheon', to be carried and honoured in the same manner as Colours. Still carried, this emblem is unique in the Armed Forces of the Commonwealth.

In 1901 while serving in Waziristan, the Regiment adopted a felt slouch hat for wear in the field. This was the origin of the familiar service headdress of all Gurkha Regiments down to the present day.

6th QUEEN ELIZABETH'S OWN GURKHA RIFLES

Raised in Cuttack, 1817, as irregular military police and known as the Cuttack Legion.

Titles 1817 Cuttack Legion
1823 Rangpur Light Infantry Battalion
1826 8th Rangpur Local Light Infantry
1827 8th Assam Light Infantry
1850 1st Assam Light Infantry
1861 46th Bengal Native Infantry
42nd (Assam) Regiment of Bengal Native Infantry (Light Infantry)
1865 42nd (Assam) Regiment of Bengal Native (Light Infantry)
1886 42nd Goorkha Light Infantry
1889 42nd (Goorkha) Regiment of Bengal (Light) Infantry
1891 42nd Gurkha (Rifle) Regiment Bengal Infantry
1901 42nd Gurkha Rifles
1903 6th Gurkha Rifles
1959 6th Queen Elizabeth's Own Gurkha Rifles

Battle honours Burma 1885–87.

The Great War—Helles, Krithia, Suvla, Sari Bair, Gallipoli 1915, Suez Canal, Egypt 1915–16, Khan Baghdadi, Mesopotamia 1916–18, Persia 1918, N.W. Frontier, India 1915.

Afghanistan 1919.

The Second World War—Coriano, Santarcangelo, Monte Chicco, Lamone Crossing, Senio Floodbank, Medicina, Gaiana Crossing, Italy 1944–45, Shwebo, Kyaukmyaung Bridgehead, Mandalay, Fort Duffiren, Maymyo, Rangoon Road, Toungoo, Sittang 1945, Chindits 1944, Burma 1944–45.

Uniform Rifle green, piping and facings black

Regimental march [Quick] *Queen Elizabeth's Own*

7th DUKE OF EDINBURGH'S OWN GURKHA RIFLES

Raised at Thayetmo (Burma), 1902, as regiment of Gurkha Rifles.

Titles 1902 8th Gurkha Rifles
1903 2nd Battalion 10th Gurkha Rifles
1907 7th Gurkha Rifles
1959 7th Duke of Edinburgh's Own Gurkha Rifles

Battle honours *The Great War*—Suez Canal, Egypt 1915, Meggido, Sharon, Palestine 1918, Shaiba, Kut al Amara 1915, 17, Ctesiphon, Defence of Kut al Amara, Baghdad, Sharqat, Mesopotamia 1915–18.

Afghanistan 1919.

The Second World War—Tobruk 1942, North Africa 1942, Cassino I, Campriano, Poggio del Grillo, Tavoleto, Montebello-Scorticata Ridge, Italy 1944, Sittang 1942, 45, Pegu 1942, Kyaukse 1942, Shwegyin, Imphal, Bishenpur, Meiktila, Capture of Meiktila, Defence of Meiktila, Rangoon Road, Pyawbwe, Burma 1942–45.

Falkland Islands 1982.

Uniform Rifle green, piping and facings black

Regimental march [Quick] *Old Monmouthshire*

Remarks In 1948 it was ordered that the newly-formed Gurkha Division should have its own Gurkha supporting arms, and the 7th Gurkha Rifles were ordered to convert to field artillery with the title '101st Field Regiment RA (7th Gurkha Rifles)'. The Regiment accordingly began training as Gunners—though not without some dismay at the relinquishment of their traditional 'Rifles' role. However, with eruption of Communist guerrilla activities in Malaya and the demand for jungle-fighting infantry, gunner training was halted and the Regiment served as infantry in the Malayan Emergency. The plan to create 'Gurkha Gunners' was abandoned.

10th PRINCESS MARY'S OWN GURKHA RIFLES

Raised in the Kubo Valley, Burma, 1887, as Battalion of military police.

Titles 1887 Kubo Valley Police Battalion
1890 10th (Burma) Regiment Madras Infantry
1892 10th Regiment (1st Burma Rifles) Madras Infantry
1896 10th Regiment (1st Burma Gurkha Rifles) Madras Infantry
1901 10th Gurkha Rifles
1949 10th Princess Mary's Own Gurkha Rifles

Battle honours *The Great War*—Helles, Krithia, Suvla, Sari Bair, Gallipoli 1915, Suez Canal, Egypt 1915, Sharqat, Mesopotamia 1916–18.

Afghanistan 1919.

The Second World War—Iraq 1941, Deir ez Zor, Syria 1941, Coriano, Santarcangelo, Senio Floodbank, Bologna, Sillaro Crossing, Gaiana Crossing, Italy 1944–45, Monywa 1942, Imphal, Tultum, Tamu Road, Shenam Pass, Litan, Bishenpur, Tengnoupal, Mandalay, Myinmu Bridgehead, Kyaukse 1945, Meiktila, Capture of Meiktila, Defence of Meiktila, Irrawaddy, Rangoon Road, Pegu 1945, Sittang 1945, Burma 1942–45.

Uniform Rifle green, piping and facings black

Regimental march [Quick] *Hundred Pipers*

THE QUEEN'S GURKHA ENGINEERS

Formed September 1955 as The Gurkha Engineers. The unit was affiliated to the Corps of Royal Engineers in 1958. Prefix 'The Queen's' granted in 1977.

QUEEN'S GURKHA SIGNALS

Formed September 1955. In 1958 the unit was affiliated to the Royal Corps of Signals. Prefix 'Queen's' granted in 1977.

GURKHA TRANSPORT REGIMENT

Formed July 1958 as the Gurkha Army Service Corps. Redesignated Gurkha Transport Regiment in July 1965. Affiliated to the Royal Corps of Transport.

THE ROYAL GREEN JACKETS
(43rd, 52nd, KING'S ROYAL RIFLE CORPS, RIFLE BRIGADE)

Formed January 1966 by amalgamation of
1st Green Jackets, 43rd and 52nd
2nd Green Jackets, The King's Royal Rifle Corps
3rd Green Jackets, The Rifle Brigade

Battle honours   Louisburg, Quebec 1759, Martinique 1762, Havannah, North America 1763–64, Mysore, Hindoostan, Martinique 1794, Copenhagen, Monte Video, Rolica, Vimiera, Corunna, Martinique 1809, Talavera, Busaco, Barrosa, Fuentes d'Onor, Albuhera, Ciudad Rodrigo, Badajoz, Salamanca, Vittoria, Pyrenees, Nivelle, Nive, Orthes, Toulouse, Peninsula, Waterloo, South Africa 1846–47, Mooltan, Goojerat, Punjaub, South Africa 1851–53, Alma, Inkerman, Sevastopol, Delhi 1857, Lucknow, Taku Forts, Pekin 1860, New Zealand, Ashantee 1873–74, Ali Masjid, South Africa 1879, Ahmad Khel, Kandahar 1880, Afghanistan 1878–80,

Tel-el-Kebir, Egypt 1882–84, Burma 1885–87, Chitral, Khartoum, Defence of Ladysmith, Relief of Kimberley, Paardeberg, Relief of Ladysmith, South Africa 1899–1902.

The Great War—Mons, Le Cateau, Retreat from Mons, Marne 1914, Aisne 1914, 18, Armentieres 1914, Ypres 1914, 15, 17, 18, Langemarck 1914, 17, Gheluvelt, Nonne Bosschen, Givenchy 1914, Neuve Chapelle, Gravenstafel, St. Julien, Frezenberg, Bellewaarde, Aubers, Festubert 1915, Hooge 1915, Loos, Mount Sorrel, Somme 1916, 18, Albert 1916, 18, Bazentin, Deville Wood, Pozieres, Guillemont, Flers-Courcelette, Morval, Le Transloy, Ancre Heights, Ancre 1916, 18, Baupaume 1917, 18, Arras 1917, 18, Vimy 1917, Scarpe 1917, 18, Arleux, Messines 1917, 18, Pilckem, Menin Road, Polygon Wood, Broodseinde, Poelcappelle, Passchendaele, Cambrai 1917, 18, St. Quentin, Rosieres, Avre, Villers-Bretonneux, Lys, Hazebrouck, Bailleul, Kemmel, Bethune, Drocourt-Queant, Hindenburg Line, Havrincourt, Epehy, Canal du Nord, St. Quentin Canal, Beaurevoir, Courtrai, Selle, Valenciennes, Sambre, France and Flanders 1914–18, Piave, Vittorio Veneto, Italy 1917–18, Doiran 1917, 18, Macedonia 1915–18, Kut al Amara 1915, Ctesiphon, Defence of Kut al Amara, Tigris 1916, Khan Baghdadi, Mesopotamia 1914–18, Archangel 1919.

The Second World War—Defence of Escaut, Calais 1940, Cassel, Ypres-Comines Canal, Normandy Landing, Pegasus Bridge, Villers Bocage, Odon, Caen, Esquay, Bourguebus Ridge, Mont Pincon, Le Perier Ridge, Falaise, Antwerp, Hechtel, Nederrijn, Lower Maas, Roer, Ourthe, Rhineland, Reichswald, Cleve, Goch, Hochwald, Rhine, Ibbenburen, Dreirwalde, Leese, Aller, North-West Europe 1940, 44–45, Egyptian Frontier 1940, Sidi Barrani, Beda Fomm, Mersa el Brega, Agedabia, Derna Aerodrome, Tobruk 1941, Sidi Rezegh 1941, Chor es Sufan, Saunnu, Gazala, Bir Hacheim, Knightsbridge, Defence of Alamein Line, Ruweisat, Fuka Airfield, Alam el Halfa, El Alamein, Capture of Halfaya Pass, Nofilia, Tebaga Gap, Enfidaville, Medjez el Bab, Kasserine, Thala, Fondouk, Fondouk Pass, El Kourzia, Djebel Kournine, Argoub el Megas, Tunis, Hamman Lif, North Africa 1940–43, Sangro, Salerno, Santa Lucia, Salerno Hills, Cardito, Teano, Monte Camino, Garigliano Crossing, Damiano,

Anzio, Cassino II, Liri Valley, Melfa Crossing, Monte Rotondo, Capture of Perugia, Monte Malbe, Arezzo, Advance to Florence, Gothic Line, Coriano Gemmano Ridge, Lamone Crossing, Orsara, Tossignano, Argenta Gap, Fossa Cembalina, Italy 1943–45, Veve, Greece 1941, 44, 45, Crete, Middle East 1941, Arakan Beaches, Tamandu, Burma 1943–44.

Uniform Rifle green, facings black

Regimental marches [Quick] Arrangement of *Huntsmen's Chorus* (Weber) and *The Italian Song* (Anon.)

[Double Past] *The Road to the Isles*

Regimental journal *The Royal Green Jackets Chronicle*

Regimental headquarters Peninsula Barracks, Winchester, Hampshire SO23 8TS

Regimental museum As above

1st GREEN JACKETS
(43rd and 52nd)

Formed November 1958 by redesignation of The Oxfordshire and Buckinghamshire Light Infantry (43rd and 52nd).

THE OXFORDSHIRE AND BUCKINGHAMSHIRE LIGHT INFANTRY
(43rd and 52nd)

Formed 1881 by amalgamation of the 43rd (Monmouthshire Light Infantry) Regiment of Foot with the 52nd (Oxfordshire Light Infantry) Regiment of Foot to form The Oxfordshire Light Infantry.

1908 Title changed to The Oxfordshire and Buckinghamshire Light Infantry.

Battle honours Quebec 1759, Martinique 1762, Havannah, Mysore, Hindoostan, Martinique 1794, Vimiera, Corunna, Busaco, Fuentes d'Onor, Ciudad Rodrigo, Badajoz, Salamanca, Vittoria, Pyrenees, Nivelle, Nive, Orthes, Toulouse, Peninsula, Waterloo, South Africa 1851, 52,

53, Delhi 1857, New Zealand, Relief of Kimberley, Paardeberg, South Africa 1900–02.

The Great War—17 *Battalions*—Mons, Retreat from Mons, Marne 1914, Aisne 1914, Ypres 1914, 17, Langemarck 1914, 17, Gheluvelt, Nonne Bosschen, Aubers, Festubert 1915, Hooge 1915, Loos, Mount Sorrel, Somme 1916, 18, Albert 1916, 18, Bazentin, Delville Wood, Pozieres, Guillemont, Flers-Courcelette, Morval, Le Transloy, Ancre Heights, Ancre 1916, Bapaume 1917, 18, Arras 1917, Vimy 1917, Scarpe 1917, Arleux, Menin Road, Polygon Wood, Broodseinde, Poelcappelle, Passchendaele, Cambrai 1917, 18, St. Quentin, Rosieres, Avre, Lys, Hazebrouck, Bethune, Hindenburg Line, Havrincourt, Canal du Nord, Selle, Valenciennes, France and Flanders 1914–18, Piave, Vittorio Veneto, Italy 1917–18, Doiran 1917, 18, Macedonia 1915–18, Kut al Amara 1915, Ctesiphon, Defence of Kut al Amara, Tigris 1916, Khan Baghdadi, Mesopotamia 1914–18, Archangel 1919.

The Second World War—Defence of Escaut, Cassel, Ypres-Comines Canal, Normandy Landing, Pegasus Bridge, Caen, Esquay, Lower Maas, Ourthe, Rhineland, Reichswald, Rhine, Ibbenburen, North-West Europe 1940, 44–45, Enfidaville, North Africa 1943, Salerno, St. Lucia, Salerno Hills, Teano, Monte Camino, Garigliano Crossing, Damiano, Anzio, Coriano, Gemmano Ridge, Italy 1943–45, Arakan Beaches, Tamandu, Burma 1943–45.

Uniform Jacket, dark green; trousers, blue; piping and facings, white

Regimental marches [Quick] *Ein Schütze bin ich* (Tradit. German)
The Lower Castle Yard (Anon.)

Regimental journal *The Oxfordshire and Buckinghamshire Light Infantry Journal*

Nickname The Light Bobs

43rd (MONMOUTHSHIRE LIGHT INFANTRY) REGIMENT OF FOOT

Raised January 1741 by Colonel Thomas Fowke and ranked as 54th Foot. Re-ranked as 43rd in 1748.

Titles 1741 Colonel Fowke's Regiment of Foot *Title subsequently changed with Colonels' names*
(1748 Renumbered 43rd Foot)
1751 43rd Regiment of Foot
1782 43rd (or the Monmouthshire) Regiment of Foot
1803 43rd (or Monmouthshire) Regiment of Foot (Light Infantry) (later known as 43rd (Monmouthshire Light Infantry) Regiment of Foot)
1881 Amalgamated with 52nd (Oxfordshire Light Infantry) Regiment of Foot to form The Oxfordshire Light Infantry

Battle honours Quebec 1759, Martinique 1762, Havannah, North America 1763–64, Vimiera, Corunna, Busaco, Fuentes d'Onor, Ciudad Rodrigo, Badajoz, Salamanca, Vittoria, Nivelle, Nive, Toulouse, Peninsula, South Africa 1851, 52, 53, New Zealand.

Uniform Scarlet, facings white

Nickname The Light Bobs

52nd (OXFORDSHIRE LIGHT INFANTRY) REGIMENT OF FOOT

Raised December 1755 by Colonel Hedworth Lambton and ranked as 54th Foot. Re-ranked 52nd in 1757.

Titles 1755 54th Regiment of Foot
1757 52nd Regiment of Foot
1782 52nd (or the Oxfordshire) Regiment of Foot
1803 52nd (or the Oxfordshire) Regiment of Foot (Light Infantry)

1881 Amalgamated with 43rd (Monmouthshire Light
Infantry) Regiment of Foot to form The Oxfordshire
Light Infantry

Battle honours Mysore, Hindoostan, Vimiera, Corunna, Busaco,
Fuentes d'Onor, Ciudad Rodrigo, Badajoz Salamanca,
Vittoria, Nivelle, Nive, Orthes, Toulouse, Peninsula,
Waterloo, Delhi 1857.

Uniform Scarlet, facings buff

2nd GREEN JACKETS
(THE KING'S ROYAL RIFLE CORPS)

Formed November 1958 by redesignation of The King's
Royal Rifle Corps.

THE KING'S ROYAL RIFLE CORPS
(60th)

Raised in Pennsylvania, Virginia and Maryland,
December 1755, by John Campbell, Earl of Loudon, and
styled 62nd or The Royal American Regiment of Foot.
Re-ranked 60th in 1756.

Titles 1755 62nd, or The Royal American Regiment of Foot
1756 60th, or The Royal American Regiment of Foot
1824 60th, or The Duke of York's Rifle Corps
1830 60th, or The King's Royal Rifle Corps Regiment of
Foot
1881 The King's Royal Rifle Corps
1958 2nd Green Jackets (The King's Royal Rifle Corps)

Battle honours Louisburg, Quebec 1759, Martinique 1762, Havannah,
North America 1763–64, Rolica, Vimiera, Martinique
1809, Talavera, Busaco, Fuentes d'Onor, Albuhera,
Ciudad Rodrigo, Badajoz, Salamanca, Vittoria, Pyrenees,
Nivelle, Nive, Orthes, Toulouse, Peninsula, Mooltan,
Goojerat, Punjaub, South Africa 1851, 52, 53, Delhi
1857, Taku Forts, Pekin 1860, South Africa 1879,
Ahmad Khel, Kandahar, 1880, Afghanistan 1878–80,
Tel-el-Kebir, Egypt 1882, 1884, Chitral, Defence of

Ladysmith, Relief of Ladysmith, South Africa 1899–1902.

The Great War—26 *Battalions*—Mons, Retreat from Mons, Marne 1914, Aisne 1914, Ypres, 1914, 15, 17, 18, Langemarck 1914, 17, Gheluvelt, Nonne Bosschen, Givenchy 1914, Gravenstafel, St. Julien, Frezenberg, Bellewaarde, Aubers, Festubert 1915, Hooge 1915, Loos, Somme 1916, 18, Albert 1916, 18, Bazentin, Delville Wood, Pozieres, Guillemont, Flers-Courcelette, Morval, Le Transloy, Ancre Heights, Ancre 1916, 18, Arras 1917, 18, Scarpe 1917, Arleux, Messines 1917, 18, Pilckem, Menin Road, Polygon Wood, Broodseinde, Poelcappelle, Passchendaele, Cambrai 1917, 18, St. Quentin, Rosieres, Avre, Lys, Bailleul, Kemmel, Bethune, Bapaume 1918, Drocourt-Queant, Hindenburg Line, Havrincourt, Epehy, Canal du Nord, St. Quentin Canal, Beaurevoir, Courtrai, Selle, Sambre, France and Flanders 1914–18, Macedonia 1915–18, Italy 1917–18.

The Second World War—Calais 1940, Mont Pincon, Falaise, Roer, Rhineland, Cleve, Goch, Hochwald, Rhine, Dreirwalde, Aller, North-West Europe 1940, 44–45, Egyptian Frontier 1940, Sidi Barrani, Derna Aerodrome, Tobruk 1941, Sidi Rezegh 1941, Gazala, Bir Hacheim, Knightsbridge, Defence of Alamein Line, Ruweisat, Fuka Airfield, Alam el Halfa, El Alamein, Capture of Halfaya Pass, Nofilia, Tebaga Gap, Argoub el Megas, Tunis, North Africa, 1940–43, Sangro, Arezzo, Coriano, Lamone Crossing, Argenta Gap, Italy 1943–45, Veve, Greece 1941, 44–45, Crete, Middle East 1941.

Motto *Celer et Audax* (Swift and bold)

Uniform Rifle green, piping and facings scarlet

Regimental march [Quick] *Lutzow's Wild Hunt*

Regimental journal *The King's Royal Rifle Corps Regimental Chronicle*

Nickname The Green Jackets

3rd GREEN JACKETS
(THE RIFLE BRIGADE)

Formed November 1958 by redesignation of The Rifle Brigade (Prince Consort's Own).

THE RIFLE BRIGADE
(PRINCE CONSORT'S OWN)

Raised August 1800 from selected detachments of other regiments, as Experimental Corps of Riflemen, commanded by Colonel Coote Manningham. Ranked as 95th Foot in 1803.

Titles 1800 Experimental Corps of Riflemen *or* Rifle Corps
1803 95th or Rifle Regiment
1816 Rifle Brigade
1862 The Prince Consort's Own Rifle Brigade
1868 Rifle Brigade (Prince Consort's Own)
1881 The Prince Consort's Own (Rifle Brigade)
1882 The Rifle Brigade (The Prince Consort's Own)
1920 The Rifle Brigade (Prince Consort's Own)
1958 3rd Green Jackets (The Rifle Brigade)

Battle honours Copenhagen, Monte Video, Rolica, Vimiera, Corunna, Busaco, Barrosa, Fuentes d'Onor, Ciudad Rodrigo, Badajoz, Salamanca, Vittoria, Pyrenees, Nivelle, Nive, Orthes, Toulouse, Peninsula, Waterloo, South Africa 1846–47, 1851, 52, 53, Alma, Inkerman, Sevastopol, Lucknow, Ashantee 1873–74, Ali Masjid, Afghanistan 1878–79, Burma 1885–87, Khartoum, Defence of Ladysmith, Relief of Ladysmith, South Africa 1899–1902.

The Great War—21 Battalions—Le Cateau, Retreat from Mons, Marne 1914, Aisne 1914, 18, Armentieres 1914, Neuve Chapelle, Ypres 1915, 17, Gravenstafel, St. Julien, Frezenberg, Bellewaarde, Aubers, Hooge 1915, Somme 1916, 18, Albert 1916, 18, Bazentin, Delville Wood, Guillemont, Flers-Courcelette, Morval, Le Transloy, Ancre Heights, Ancre 1916, 18, Arras 1917, 18, Vimy 1917, Scarpe 1917, 18, Arleux, Messines 1917, Pilckem, Langemarck 1917, Menin Road, Polygon Wood, Broodseinde, Poelcappelle, Passchendaele, Cambrai 1917, 18, St. Quentin, Rosieres, Avre, Villers Bretonneux, Lys, Hazebrouck, Bethune, Drocourt-Queant, Hindenburg Line, Havrincourt, Canal du Nord, Selle, Valenciennes, Sambre, France and Flanders 1914–18, Macedonia 1915–18.

The Second World War—Calais 1940, Villers Bocage, Odon, Bourguebus Ridge, Mont Pincon, Le Perier Ridge, Falaise, Antwerp, Hechtel, Nederrijn, Lower Maas, Roer, Leese, Aller, North-West Europe 1940, 44–45, Egyptian Frontier 1940, Beda Fomm, Mersa el Brega, Agedabia, Derna Aerodrome, Tobruk 1941, Sidi Rezegh 1941, Chor es Sufan, Saunnu, Gazala, Knightsbridge, Defence of Alamein Line, Ruweisat, Alam el Halfa, El Alamein, Tebaga Gap, Medjez el Bab, Kasserine, Thala, Fondouk, Fondouk Pass, El Kourzia, Djebel Kournine, Tunis, Hammam Lif, North Africa 1940–43, Cardito, Cassino II, Liri Valley, Melfa Crossing, Monte Rotondo, Capture of Perugia, Monte Malbe, Arezzo, Advance to Florence, Gothic Line, Orsara, Tossignano, Argenta Gap, Fossa Cembalina, Italy 1943–45.

Uniform Rifle green, piping and facings black

Regimental march [Quick] *I'm Ninety-Five*

Regimental journal *The Rifle Brigade Chronicle*

Nicknames Green Jackets. The Sweeps

Remarks In recognition of its distinguished services under Wellington, culminating with the Battle of Waterloo, the Regiment was removed from the numbered regiments of Infantry of the Line in February 1816, and constituted a separate corps as the Rifle Brigade. After that date it bore no official number and was proud to rank as 'Left of the Line', a distinction inherited by The Royal Green Jackets of today.

SPECIAL AIR SERVICE REGIMENT

Although British commando units had been created by Churchill in 1940, the Special Air Service Regiment owes its inception to Colonel David Stirling who, as a Scots Guards subaltern attached to No 8 Commando in North Africa, was responsible for the formation of small independent raiding parties to be dropped behind enemy lines. The first force of picked men was authorised in

July 1941, with the deliberately deceptive title 'L' Detachment Special Air Service Brigade. The 'Brigade' consisted only of 66 all ranks.

By January 1943 the term 'L' Detachment had been discarded and the greatly expanded force was formally recognised as the 1st SAS Regiment. At the same time, a second Regiment was raised by the founder's brother, Lieut-Colonel William Stirling, while a Special Boat Section was formed from the 1st Regiment. This Section was later divorced from the SAS and eventually became Special Boat Service of the Royal Marines.

In 1944 the two SAS Regiments were expanded into a Brigade with the addition of two French regiments and one Belgian. At the conclusion of hostilities in 1945 the British 1st and 2nd SAS Regiments were disbanded, the two French regiments were absorbed in the French Army and the Belgian regiment went to its own Army.

In 1947 the familiar winged dagger Badge reappeared in Britain, but this time in the Territorial Army, with the formation in London of the 21st SAS (Artists) Regiment—'Artists' inherited from the old Territorial unit, the Artists' Rifles. Meanwhile, the Communist guerrilla 'Emergency' in Malaya had seen the creation of the Malayan Scouts from Volunteers from 21st SAS and other units. In 1952 the Malayan Scouts were absorbed into the Regular Army as the 22nd Special Air Service Regiment, which thus became, and remains, the only post-War Regular unit of the SAS.

A second Territorial regiment, 23rd SAS (TA) was formed in London in 1959, and was later based in Birmingham.

From 1944 to 1950 the SAS were officially regarded as part of the Army Air Corps together with the Glider Pilot Regiment and the Parachute Regiment, but on the latter date, when the Army Air Corps was (temporarily) disbanded, the SAS became a corps in their own right.

Battle honours *The Second World War*—North-West Europe 1944–45, Tobruk 1941, Benghazi Raid, North Africa 1940–43, Landing in Sicily, Sicily 1943, Termoli, Valli di Comacchio, Italy 1943–45, Greece 1944–45, Adriatic, Middle East 1943–44.

Falkland Islands 1982.

Motto Who Dares Wins

Regimental march [Quick] *Marche du Régiment Parachutiste Belge*

Regimental headquarters Centre Block, Duke of York's Headquarters, Chelsea, London SW3

Remarks Although the SAS have long been one of the best-known Regiments in the British Army, the nature of their duties necessitates the highest security measures, to the extent that the names of their serving officers are never published in the *Army List*, or elsewhere, nor are the names of other ranks ever made public. A unique exception to this policy was the Gazetting of the names of five NCOs of the Regiment who won awards with the Falklands Task Force, April–June 1982.

The numbering of the SAS Regiments came about in a curiously tortuous way. When the 21st (TA) Regiment was raised, the authorities proposed to style it the 12th SAS, perpetuating the '1' and '2' of the war-time 1st and 2nd Regiments. However, it was pointed out that confusion might arise with the then existing 12th Airborne TA unit, and so the figures were reversed to give 21.

ARMY AIR CORPS

Although the present Corps dates only from 1957, its origins can be traced to the early days of World War II. In 1942 demands for battlefield air reconnaissance and direction of artillery fire led to the formation of Air OP (Observation Post) squadrons of light observation aircraft, piloted by Royal Artillery officers. The same year saw the raising of an Army Air Corps comprising the Glider Pilot Regiment and the Parachute Regiment (Army Order 21/42). In 1944 the recently formed Special Air Service Regiment was also incorporated in the Corps.

In 1945 the SAS was (temporarily) disbanded; the Parachute Regiment was divorced from the Corps in 1949 to join the Infantry of the Line, and in 1950 the original Army Air Corps was disbanded. The remaining glider pilots were retrained to fly powered aircraft and were formed into Light Liaison Flights operating alongside or as part of the Air OP squadrons.

It soon became clear that the Army had an increasing need of light aircraft and helicopter support for a variety of tasks, and under Army Order 82 of 1957 the existing

Army Air Corps was formed from the Air OP and Light Liaison units. Its depot and training centre were located, as today, at Middle Wallop, Hampshire, a former RAF station.

From 1957 until 1973 the new Army Air Corps consisted of a small cadre of Officer and NCO pilots supplemented by volunteers attached from other Arms. Ground crew duties were also performed by attached soldiers, mainly from the Royal Armoured Corps and Royal Artillery. However in 1973 the Army Air Corps began to recruit its own ground crew soldiers. Private soldiers in the Corps are known as Air Troopers.

Since 1957 all field maintenance, recovery and repair of the Corps' aircraft have been carried out by attached personnel of the Royal Electrical and Mechanical Engineers.

Corps march [Quick] *Recce Flight*

Corps headquarters Army Air Corps Centre, Middle Wallop, Nr. Stockbridge, Hampshire SO20 8DY

Corps museum Museum of Army Flying, Address as above

ROYAL ARMY CHAPLAINS' DEPARTMENT

Although clerics had ministered to the troops in peace and war since mediaeval times, it was only in September 1796 that a centralised Army Chaplains' Department was formed under a Chaplain-General.

Until 1827 the Department could accept only Church of England priests as Chaplains, but in that year Presbyterians were authorised, followed by Roman Catholics in 1836. In 1881 Wesleyans were admitted, and the first Jewish Chaplain was appointed in 1892.

Chaplains were given military seniority in 1816, although they did not wear military uniforms until 1860.

In recognition of the devoted services of some 4,500 Army Chaplains in all theatres of World War I, the

'Royal' title was conferred by King George V in February 1919.

Motto	*In This Sign Conquer*
Departmental march	*Trumpet Tune* (Jeremiah Clark) (Often mistitled '—Voluntary' and wrongly attributed to Purcell)
Departmental journal	*Journal of The Royal Army Chaplains' Department* (Half-Yearly)
Departmental headquarters	Royal Army Chaplains' Department Centre, Bagshot Park, Bagshot, Surrey GU19 5PL
Nickname	The Padres

ROYAL CORPS OF TRANSPORT

Under its present title the Corps dates from July 1965, when the Royal Army Service Corps was thus redesignated and was joined by the transportation elements and movement control service of the Corps of Royal Engineers. The new Corps became responsible for all forms of transport, movement control, driver-training, and road safety in the Army. At the same time the responsibilities for providing rations, forage and fuel, together with barracks and fire-service elements, and military staff clerks, were transferred to the Royal Army Ordnance Corps.

Prior to 1794 supply and transport services were under the control of the Commissary General, who was directly responsible to the Treasury and not to Horse Guards (War Office), but in that year a Corps of Waggoners was formed to serve on the Continent under the Commander-in-Chief, the Duke of York. This corps was reformed as the Royal Waggon Corps in 1799 and became the Royal Waggon Train in 1802. It was disbanded in 1833. In 1855 a Land Transport Corps was raised, becoming The Military Train in 1856.

The Army Service Corps was formed from The Military Train in 1869 and consisted of non-commissioned ranks only; officers were provided by the Control Department, which was an officer-corps formed to control a Supply and Transport sub-department. A further change took place in 1875 when the Control Department was split up and a Commissariat and Transport Department was formed, which in 1880 was redesignated the Commissariat and Transport Staff, officers from which commanded the ASC companies until 1881, when they became the Commissariat and Transport Corps.

In 1888 General Sir Redvers Buller, then Quartermaster-General, effected the formation of the fully combatant Army Service Corps consisting of supply and transport units under their own specially trained officers.

In November 1918 King George V conferred the Royal prefix for outstanding services in the 1914–18 War.

Motto	*Nil sine Labore* (Nothing without work)
Uniform	Blue, stripes and facings white
Corps march	Arrangement of *Wait for the Wagon* and *Boer Trek song*
Corps journals	*The Waggoner, Royal Corps of Transport Review*
Corps headquarters	Buller Barracks, Aldershot, Hampshire
Corps museums	Buller Barracks, Aldershot, Hampshire Museum of Army Transport (contains the RCT vehicle collection), Beverley, North Humberside

ROYAL ARMY MEDICAL CORPS

Although doctors, or Surgeons as they were termed, had served with regiments since the earliest days of the Standing Army, there was no organised medical branch until the formation of a Medical Staff Corps in 1855, consisting of soldier medical orderlies. This was renamed Army Hospital Corps in 1857. In 1873 medical officers were organised as the Army Medical Staff, and in 1884 officers and other ranks joined in a single Corps, again styled the Medical Staff Corps. Finally by Royal Warrant of June 1898 the Royal Army Medical Corps was formed.

Motto	*In Arduis Fidelis* (Faithful in adversity)
Uniform	Blue, piping and facings dull cherry
Corps march	*Here's a Health unto Her Majesty*
Corps journals	*Journal of the Royal Army Medical Corps, Army Medical Services Magazine*
Corps headquarters	Royal Army Medical College, Millbank, London SW1P 4RJ
Corps museum	Keogh Barracks, Ash Vale, Aldershot, Hampshire GU12 5RQ

THE ROYAL ARMY ORDNANCE CORPS

Traditionally the roles of this Corps and its forbears have always been the procurement, storage and issue of armaments, ammunition and other warlike *matériel*. When in 1965 the Royal Corps of Transport was formed from the Royal Army Service Corps, the latter's supply functions were taken over by the RAOC, and since then the Corps has been responsible for supplying the Army with everything needed to fight, move and subsist.

Under its present title the Corps dates only from 1918, but its extremely complex origins can be traced to the establishment of an Office of Ordnance in 1414, which developed into the Board of Ordnance in 1683. Until its abolition in 1855 the Board supplied weapons and ammunition to the whole Army and was entirely responsible for the Royal Artillery and the Royal Engineers. The ramifications of the Board and its successors, which include the RAOC, can only be briefly outlined as under.

Titles 1414 Office of Ordnance (civilians)
1683 Board of Ordnance (civilians)
1792 Field Train Department formed under the Board
1855 Board of Ordnance abolished
1857 Military Store Department formed (commissioned officers)
1859 Field Train disbanded

1865 Military Store Staff Corps (soldiers under officers of
Military Store Department)

1870 Army Service Corps formed (soldiers)
Control Department superseded Military Store
Department

1875 Ordnance Store Department formed (officers)

1877 Ordnance Store Branch formed (soldiers)

1881 Ordnance Store Corps supersedes above

1896 Army Ordnance Department (officers) supersedes
Ordnance Store Department
Army Ordnance Corps (soldiers) supersedes
Ordnance Store Corps

1918 Merger of Army Ordnance Department with Army
Ordnance Corps to form Royal Army Ordnance Corps

Motto *Sua Tela Tonanti* (Literally 'His missiles thundering' (of
Jupiter). But within the Corps historical usage is 'To the
warrior his arms')

Uniform Blue, piping and facings scarlet

Corps march *The Village Blacksmith*

Corps journal *The Royal Army Ordnance Corps Gazette*

Corps headquarters Director-General of Ordnance Services, Logistic
Executive (Army), Portway, Monxton Road, Andover,
Hampshire

Corps museum Blackdown Barracks, Deepcut, Camberley, Surrey
GU16 6RW

CORPS OF ROYAL ELECTRICAL AND MECHANICAL ENGINEERS

Prior to the Second World War, units were normally
capable of dealing with the repair and maintenance of
their own weapons, equipment and vehicles, aided when
necessary by specialists from such technical Corps as the
RAOC, Royal Signals and the RASC. With the advent of
mechanisation and the vast diversity of new weapons and

equipment, the tasks of prompt recovery, repair and maintenance in the field posed problems beyond the skills of non-technical unit personnel, and it became clear that a new specialist Corps was needed to perform these tasks.

Army Order 70 of May 1942 directed the formation of The Royal Electrical and Mechanical Engineers. The majority of its personnel were transferred from the RAOC, others from the RE and RASC. Wartime duties included the provision of Light Aid Detachments to front line units and the operating of field and base workshops.

In 1949 the designation was altered to its present form, Corps of Royal Electrical and Mechanical Engineers.

As its title implies, the Corps is responsible for the extra-unit capacity inspection, modification, repair and recovery of all the highly complex armament and equipment of the modern Army, ranging from fighting vehicles to electronic and optical instruments and medical and dental equipment. It also advises on design and user parameters of projected new equipment, and provides general technical advice to all levels of command.

Uniform	Blue, piping scarlet, facings blue
Corps marches [Quick]	*Lilliburlero* and *Auprès de ma Blonde*
[Slow]	*Duchess of Kent*
Corps journals	*The Craftsman, Journal of the Royal Electrical and Mechanical Engineers*
Corps headquarters	Corps Secretariat REME, Isaac Newton Road, Arborfield, Reading, Berkshire RG2 9LN
Corps museum	As above
Nickname	The REME

CORPS OF ROYAL MILITARY POLICE

Formed at Aldershot, 1926. Although one of the younger units of the British Army, the Corps' origins go back to mediaeval times when a Provost-Marshal was appointed, as at Agincourt and Crécy, to supervise the general discipline of the King's forces when they took the field.

The Provost Service, forerunner of the Corps, was established with the creation of Britain's first Standing Army by Charles II in 1661, but it functioned only in time of war. There were also, as now, the regimental police of individual units, but these had no authority outside their own units.

In 1855 the nucleus of the present Corps came into being at Aldershot with the formation of a troop of mounted police drawn from selected cavalry NCOs. It was not, however, until 1877 that this unit, now greatly expanded, became officially designated the Corps of Military Mounted Police.

In 1885 a Corps of Military Foot Police was raised, and in 1926 the two were amalgamated to form the Corps of Military Police.

In recognition of the Corps' services in two World Wars, King George VI granted the 'Royal' prefix in 1946.

Until 1953 officers were seconded from other units on a two-year posting, but in fact few of them returned to their own units, preferring to continue serving with the Corps. Since 1953 all officers have been permanently posted on a full-career basis.

Motto	*Exemplo Ducemus* (We lead by example)
Uniform	Blue, with scarlet piping and facings. In service dress a crimson top is worn on the khaki cap: hence the familiar nickname.
Corps march	*The Watchtower*
Corps journal	*Royal Military Police Journal*
Corps headquarters	Roussillon Barracks, Chichester, West Sussex
Corps museum	As above
Nickname	The Redcaps

ROYAL ARMY PAY CORPS

This Corps as such was not formed until 1920, but its origins can be traced to the earliest days of the 17th century Standing Army, when the Regimental Colonels engaged civilian clerks known as Agents to handle their units' pay and financial affairs. In due course these Agents developed into professional companies, such as the well-known Cox's and King's, who provided civilian paymasters to regiments. In 1797 commissioned Paymasters were introduced in the rank of Captain.

In 1878 War Office assumed direct control of financial matters and the Army Pay Department was formed, consisting of suitably qualified officers. These officers were assisted by soldier-clerks, who in 1893 were organised in a separate corps styled the Army Pay Corps. With the enormous expansion of the Services during the First World War and the increased burden of accountancy, a third Corps, known as the Corps of Military Accountants, was formed in 1919.

Army Order 146 of 1920 conferred the title 'Royal' on both the Army Pay Department and the Army Pay Corps, and finally under Army Order 498/1920 the two Corps were merged into one with the present title. The Corps of Military Accountants was disbanded in 1925, a number of its officers and soldiers being absorbed in the Royal Army Pay Corps.

Motto *Fide et Fiducia* (In faith and trust)

Corps march *Imperial Echoes* (Safroni-Middleton)

Corps journal *The Royal Army Pay Corps Journal*

Corps headquarters Worthy Down, Winchester, Hampshire SO21 2RG

ROYAL ARMY VETERINARY CORPS

The RAVC as a Corps in its own right dates from a Royal Warrant of October 1903, authorising the formation of the Army Veterinary Corps, consisting of commissioned veterinary surgeons assisted by non-commissioned ranks.

The 'Royal' prefix was conferred by King George V in 1918, in recognition of the Corps' devoted services during World War I.

However, the true origins date back to the 18th century. Prior to the 1790's there were no qualified veterinary surgeons, either military or civilian. Mounted units of the Army were dependent on the very limited skills of their own farriers. Formal veterinary training began in 1791 with the foundation of a School of Veterinary Medicine in London, and in 1796 the Head of the Veterinary School was appointed Principal Veterinary Surgeon to the Cavalry and Veterinary Surgeon to the Board of Ordnance (responsible for Artillery and Engineers). He was also charged with the formation of the Army Veterinary Service, through which a qualified veterinary surgeon was appointed to each cavalry regiment.

In 1858 the Veterinary Medical Department was formed, with commissioned veterinary surgeons who were borne on the strength of individual units. In April 1881 the officers gained corporate identity as members of the Army Veterinary Department, and finally in October 1903 the formation of the Army Veterinary Corps united officers and soldiers under a common cap badge.

Until 1941 the procurement and supply of horses to the Army was the responsibility of the Army Remount Department, but in that year the Department was reorganised as the Army Veterinary and Remount Services, staffed by RAVC personnel.

Mechanisation banished the horse from the Army except for ceremonial purposes, and today the equine responsibilities of the Corps are limited to the procurement and veterinary care of the few hundred mounts for the Household Cavalry, The King's Troop RHA and the Royal Military Police. But as horses have declined in importance, so dogs have increased, and the number in the Service has never been greater than at present. Besides the procurement of dogs, the RAVC is responsible for training them and their handlers for all military tasks.

Uniform	Blue, piping and facings maroon
Corps march	Arrangement of *Drink Puppy Drink* and *A-Hunting We Will Go*
Corps journals	*The Royal Army Veterinary Corps Journal* (1929–1971), *Chiron Calling* (1975–)
Corps headquarters	Ministry of Defence (AVR), Government Buildings, Worcester Road, Droitwich, Worcestershire WR9 8AU
Corps museum	RAVC Laboratory and Stores, Gallwey Road, Aldershot, Hampshire GU11 2OQ

ROYAL MILITARY ACADEMY SANDHURST BAND CORPS

The exact foundation date for this unique body of soldier-musicians is conjectural. The earliest official record of the Band's existence dates only from 1815, when The Royal Military College records showed an establishment of one Bandmaster and fourteen musicians.

The present Royal Military Academy Sandhurst is the descendant of The Royal Military College, Sandhurst, which was amalgamated with The Royal Military Academy, Woolwich in January 1947. The RMC originated in 1799 with the foundation by Lieut-Colonel (later Major-General) Gaspard Le Marchant of a College for the training of cavalry and infantry officers. This was shortly augmented in two Departments, the Senior becoming The Staff College Camberley, the Junior The Royal Military College, Sandhurst. The latter was first (1802) located at Great Marlow, Buckinghamshire, but in 1812 it moved to its permanent location at Sandhurst. At that date there is no record of any 'Band of Musick' on the strength, and all that can be said is, the RMC Band came into being some time between 1813 and 1815.

Unlike Regimental Bands which were then tolerated rather than authorised by Horse Guards (War Office), and were funded entirely by units' own officers, the RMC Band was from the first under Horse Guards control and paid out of Government funds. The only other equivalent in the Army was the Royal Artillery Band which was administered by the Board of Ordnance.

One of the early Bandmasters of the RMC Band was Thomas Sullivan (appointed 1845), father of Sir Arthur of the Gilbert and Sullivan partnership.

In 1923 the Band officially became a Corps with the designation 'The Royal Military College Band Corps', but the title had already been in unofficial use since well before the First World War. Needless to say, with an establishment never exceeding 39 all ranks, the Band boasted of being the smallest Corps in the British Army.

Following the merger of The Royal Military Academy Woolwich with The Royal Military College Sandhurst, in 1947 the title of the Band conformed with that of the new establishment, becoming The Royal Military Academy Sandhurst Band Corps.

Classed as a Staff Band rather than Regimental, it is headed by a Director of Music, not Bandmaster, and its bandsmen rank as Musicians. The present establishment is one Director of Music (Major), eight senior NCOs and 30 junior NCOs and Musicians. In addition to musical duties, the latter are trained as Medical Assistants and as a Light Rescue team for the Academy in the event of war or major emergency.

Motto   *Serve to Lead* (Motto of The RMA Sandhurst)

Uniform (Until 1904)   Royal blue, facings red
(To date)   Scarlet, facings blue

Corps marches [Quick]   *The British Grenadiers* (Tradit.)
[Slow]   *Scipio* (Handel)
(The above are the Marches of the RMA Sandhurst)

Headquarters   Royal Military Academy, Sandhurst, Surrey GU15

Note   It is sad to record that as this work went to press orders were issued for the abolition of The Royal Military Academy Sandhurst Band Corp, in the name of Government defence cuts.

SMALL ARMS SCHOOL CORPS

The origins of this Corps are traced to the School of Musketry established at Hythe (Kent) in 1854, at the instigation of FM Visct. Hardinge, C-in-C. In 1919 the School was redesignated Small Arms School. In the same year a Machine Gun School was formed at Seaford (Sussex), shortly afterwards moving to Netheravon, (Wiltshire). In 1923 the two Schools were given Corps status with the title Corps of Small Arms and Machine Gun Schools, though they each retained their separate identities and locations. The final amalgamation came in 1929 when the Machine Gun School was absorbed in the Small Arms School at Hythe, and the present title came into use.

The Small Arms School Corps is represented at virtually every infantry training establishment at home and overseas, being manned and deployed by HQ Director of Infantry. There are no private soldiers in the Corps, the lowest rank being Sergeant.

Uniform Blue, piping and facings Cambridge blue

Corps march *The March of the Bowmen* (Curzon)

Corps journal *The SASC Journal* (Annual)

Corps headquarters Depot SASC, Small Arms Wing, The School of Infantry, Warminster, Wiltshire

Corps museum The Weapons Museum, The School of Infantry, as above

MILITARY PROVOST STAFF CORPS

Formed under Army Order 241 of 1901 as The Military Prison Staff Corps. Redesignated with present title in 1906. Since its establishment the Corps has staffed military prisons, now known as Military Corrective Training Centres.

Uniform Blue, piping and facings scarlet

Corps march *The Metropolitan*

Corps journal *The Journal of The Military Provost Staff Corps*

Corps headquarters Berechurch Hall Camp, Colchester, Essex CO2 9NU

ROYAL ARMY EDUCATIONAL CORPS

Although individual regimental schools had been introduced by 1812, it was not until 1846 that Army education was put on an organised basis with the formation of a Corps of Army Schoolmasters, staffed by Warrant Officers and senior NCOs, together with civilian teachers.

In 1920 this Corps was disbanded and in its place was formed the Army Educational Corps (Army Order 231/1920), which comprised commissioned as well as non-commissioned personnel. The 'Royal' prefix was conferred by Army Order 167 of 1946.

Since 1962 the Corps has been staffed exclusively by commissioned officers.

Uniform Blue, piping and facings Cambridge blue

Corps journal *The Torch*

Corps headquarters Eltham Palace, Eltham, London SE9 5QE

ROYAL ARMY DENTAL CORPS

Dental officers had served with the RAMC during the War of 1914–18, but it was only in 1921 that the authorities recognised the need for a separate dental service, and the Army Dental Corps was accordingly formed in January of that year.

The Corps was granted the 'Royal' prefix in 1946.

Motto   *Ex Dentibus Ensis* (From the teeth a sword)

Uniform   Blue, piping and facings emerald green

Corps march   *Green Facings*

Corps headquarters   Headquarters and Training Centre RADC, Evelyn Woods Road, Aldershot, Hampshire GU11 2LS

Corps museum   As above

ROYAL PIONEER CORPS

Formed October 1939 as the Auxiliary Military Pioneer Corps. Unlike the Labour Corps of the 1st World War, from which its role is said to have derived, the Royal Pioneer Corps was, and is, composed entirely of combatant soldiers.

Titles   1939 Auxiliary Military Pioneer Corps
1940 Pioneer Corps
1946 Royal Pioneer Corps

Motto   *Labor Omnia Vincit* (Work conquers all things)

Uniform   Blue, piping and facings scarlet

Corps march   *Pioneer Corps* (Demuth)

Corps journal   *The Royal Pioneer*

Corps headquarters   Simpson Barracks, Northampton NN4 0HX

INTELLIGENCE CORPS

Having existed throughout World War I the Corps was disbanded in 1929, but was reactivated on an emergency basis in September 1939 to accompany the British Expeditionary Force to France.

On 15th July 1940 the Corps was officially re-raised when King George VI approved its establishment and insignia. Officers and other ranks were transferred from other units to supplement the nucleus of personnel remaining from 1939. Since 1957 officers have been commissioned directly into the Corps.

Motto *Manui Dat Cognitio Vires* (Knowledge gives strength to the arm)

Uniform Blue, piping and facings green

Corps march *The Rose and the Laurel*

Corps journal *The Rose and the Laurel*

Corps headquarters Templer Barracks, Ashford, Kent TN23 3HH

Corps museum As above

ARMY PHYSICAL TRAINING CORPS

Formed originally as the Army Gymnastic Staff in 1860. In 1918 the title changed to Army Physical Training Staff, and in 1940 Corps status was conferred and the present title assumed.

Uniform Black, piping and facings scarlet

Corps journal *Mind Body and Spirit*

Corps headquarters HQ and Depot APTC, Army School of Physical Training, Queen's Avenue, Aldershot, Hants GU11 2LB

ARMY CATERING CORPS

Formed at Aldershot, March 1941, its nucleus being the Army School of Cookery which had been established at Aldershot before the First World War.

Motto   We Sustain

Uniform   Scarlet, piping and facings Grebe grey

Corps journals   *Sustainer. The House Journal of the Army Catering Corps*

Corps headquarters   St. Omer Barracks, Aldershot, Hampshire GU11 2BN

ARMY LEGAL CORPS

The Army Legal Corps was formed on 1st November 1978 as the successor to the Army Legal Services Staff List. That organisation in turn was created in 1948 as the successor to the uniformed section of the Judge Advocate-General's office.

The Corps consists of legally qualified male and female advocates, barristers and solicitors, and is responsible for providing legal advice, prosecuting at certain courts-martial, and on occasion defending at such trials. Other work undertaken by the Corps consists of advising personnel on their personal legal problems, lecturing on Service Law and Law of Armed Conflict. Officers of the Corps also edit and publish military publications, including the Manual of Military Law. There are currently 53 officers in the Corps.

Motto   *Justitia in Armis* (Justice in Arms)

Corps headquarters   ALS1 Ministry of Defence, Empress State Building, Lillie Road, London SW6 1TR

QUEEN ALEXANDRA'S ROYAL ARMY NURSING CORPS

It was not until after the devoted services of Florence Nightingale and her *ad hoc* band of nurses in the Crimea that the authorities were persuaded to give serious thought to the nursing of sick and wounded soldiers. The first purpose-built military hospital was opened at Netley, Southampton, by Queen Victoria in 1856, and ten years later the Queen authorised the appointment of trained civilian nurses in military hospitals.

In 1881 the nurses gained corporate identity with the formation of the Army Nursing Service.

In March 1902, under the patronage of Queen Alexandra the Service was augmented and redesignated Queen Alexandra's Imperial Military Nursing Service. The Badge was designed by the Queen herself, to incorporate the *Dannebrog* or Cross of her native Denmark.

In 1949 the QAIMNS was amalgamated with the Territorial Army Nursing Service (dating from 1907) to form a regular Corps of the British Army with the present title Queen Alexandra's Royal Army Nursing Corps. At the same date the Sisters were for the first time granted regular commissions with Army rank (although they had been accorded officer status in 1904). In 1950 Other Ranks, or Servicewomen, were admitted for training.

Motto   *Sub Cruce Candida* (Under the White Cross)

Uniform   Dark grey, facings scarlet
(*Ward uniform* Officers: grey dress, scarlet tippet, white veil. Servicewomen: grey dress, white caps.)

Corps march   *Grey and Scarlet*

Corps headquarters   The Royal Pavilion, Farnborough Road, Aldershot, Hampshire GU11 1PZ

Corps museum   As above

WOMEN'S ROYAL ARMY CORPS

The ancestor of the present Corps was the Women's Army Auxiliary Corps, formed in 1917 to perform non-combatant duties behind the lines in France. Renamed Queen Mary's Army Auxiliary Corps in 1918, it was disbanded the following year. In 1938 a women's service was again raised with the title Auxiliary Territorial Service, which gave valuable service in most theatres of the Second World War.

The present Corps was formed 1st February 1949 and incorporated the remaining cadre of the ATS.

Motto *Suaviter in Modo, Fortiter in Re* (Gentle in manner, resolute in deed)

Uniform Bottle green and beech brown

Corps journal *The Lioness*

Corps headquarters Queen Elizabeth Park, Guildford, Surrey GU2 6QH

INDEX TO REGIMENTS AND CORPS

Named regiments and corps are given in alphabetical order, not in order of seniority.